CONCEDING COMPOSITION

CONCEDING COMPOSITION

*A Crooked History of Composition's
Institutional Fortunes*

RYAN SKINNELL

UTAH STATE UNIVERSITY PRESS
Logan

Published by Utah State University Press
An imprint of University Press of Colorado
5589 Arapahoe Avenue, Suite 206C
Boulder, Colorado 80303

 The University Press of Colorado is a proud member of
The Association of American University Presses.

The University Press of Colorado is a cooperative publishing enterprise supported,
in part, by Adams State University, Colorado State University, Fort Lewis College,
Metropolitan State University of Denver, Regis University, University of Colorado,
University of Northern Colorado, Utah State University, and Western State Colorado
University.

The paper used in this publication meets the minimum requirements of the American
National Standard for Information Sciences—Permanence of Paper for Printed Library
Materials. ANSI Z39.48-1992

ISBN: 978-1-60732-504-8 (paperback)
ISBN: 978-1-60732-505-5 (ebook)

Library of Congress Cataloging-in-Publication Data

Names: Skinnell, Ryan, 1978– author.
Title: Conceding composition : a crooked history of composition's institutional fortunes
/ Ryan Skinnell.
Description: Logan : Utah State University Press, [2016] | Includes bibliographical refer-
ences.
Identifiers: LCCN 2015044250| ISBN 9781607325048 (pbk.) | ISBN 9781607325055
(ebook)
Subjects: LCSH: Composition (Language arts)—Study and teaching (Higher)—History. |
Rhetoric—Study and teaching—History.
Classification: LCC LB1631 .S517 2016 | DDC 808/.0420711—dc23
LC record available at http://lccn.loc.gov/2015044250

Cover photograph: Emry Kopta's "Kachina Fountain," 1934, courtesy Arizona State
University Archives.

for
Mom and Dad

[One] does what one can with the materials at one's disposal. Or, to put it another way, work in composition is inevitably pragmatic and thus, like all good teaching, the administration and dissemination of writing instruction necessarily involves a series of compromises and concessions.
—Richard E. Miller, "From Intellectual
Wasteland to Resource-Rich Colony"

CONTENTS

PREFACE

It is an auspicious time to be writing about institutions of higher education. Even as I write this, university funding models, faculty governance, and college admissions criteria are being hotly debated (I am tempted to write "mercilessly attacked") in the highest levels of all three branches of American government. In recent years, President Barack Obama has proposed tying federal higher education funding to institutions' "value" as assessed by the federal "college scorecard." In Wisconsin, state legislators recently passed a bill that undermines the University of Wisconsin's once-exemplary tenure statutes and cuts $250 million from the state's higher education budget. And the US Supreme Court has recently agreed to re-hear arguments in *Fisher v. University of Texas* about the validity of affirmative action in college admissions decisions.

These examples barely scratch the surface of arguments circulating about education in America. Controversies are raging around the country about corporate-backed standardized testing, the advisability of teaching internship programs like Teach for America, the widespread implementation of Common Core standards, intensifying efforts to privatize every level of education through vouchers and charter schools, the utility of teacher tenure, innovations and calamities of market-based education "reform," the proper emphasis of teaching objectives and credentialing, the suitability of public funding models, the proper role of ideology in textbooks, and on and on and on.

As the complexities of education become increasingly complex, those of us who work in higher education view many of the effects from the front row. In the decade-plus since I entered my MA program at California State University, Northridge, I've witnessed higher education institutions react to the sorts of external exigencies sketched above by hiring corporate presidents and paying them seven-figure salaries (Erwin and Wood 2014), outsourcing essential services—such as the campus bookstore, facilities and maintenance, and even instructional services—to external vendors (Milstone 2010), deactivating programs once considered indispensable to liberal education (Jaschik 2010), and accepting large private donations attached to strings that appear questionable if not outright unethical (Levinthal 2014). Administrators at

Arizona State University (ASU), one of the central sites of investigation in this book, recently announced that as a cost-saving measure, non–tenure track English instructors will be required to teach five courses per semester, many of which will be first-year composition, for unacceptably low wages (Flaherty 2014). ASU is hardly unique in exploiting non–tenure track educators.

It is probably clear that I am not sanguine about the state of education. At the same time, however, I am not convinced that American education is doomed. In cataloging these crazy times, the sheer volume of assaults on American education is most apparent—they feel different, novel, unusual, and infinite. But they are not. One benefit of studying composition as a function of education history is that you discover again and again that education has always been controversial. Throughout the nineteenth century, there was staunch opposition to publicly funded schooling and repeated attempts to privatize education. At the turn of the twentieth century, teachers, principals, and superintendents were often appointed by local politicians, which meant that every election could result in a whole new slate of (sometimes unqualified) teachers and administrators at the local schoolhouse. And, of course, students of American history know that 1954's *Brown v. Board of Education of Topeka* overturned a half-century of educational precedent established in 1896 by the *Plessy v. Fergusson* white supremacist doctrine of "separate but equal." The point is that since the colonization of America and certainly long before that in Europe and elsewhere, education has been one of the most hotly contested issues in public debate. Often, public deliberation plays an important role in what policies get enacted.

In noting the long, tempestuous history of education debate, I want to emphasize that education is always up for further debate. For those of us who believe that high-quality, publicly funded, universally accessible primary, secondary, and postsecondary education is the gold standard to which America should aspire, this is potentially good news. There is always still time to make persuasive arguments on behalf of education. Of course, even this positive possibility raises its own set of complications. The arguments that paved the way for the twentieth century to be one of the most progressive centuries in education history have, in many cases, lost their luster. For people who value and support what education was in the twentieth century and who want to see it resuscitated, one common course of action has been to reanimate those old arguments, many of which date back at least to the Progressive Era at the end of the nineteenth century. In some cases, this has worked; in many cases, it has not. The real challenge for advocates of American education, at least to my mind, is not to reanimate those old arguments but to invent new ones. I believe this is where rhetoric and composition scholars may be of special service.

In advocating the invention of new arguments, I use invention not in the post-Cartesian sense of "creating something new" but in the ancient rhetorical sense of "discovering available means." If we adopt Aristotle's definition of rhetoric as "an ability, in each [particular] case, to see the available means of persuasion" (Aristotle 2007, I.2.1355a), then an essential function of rhetoric is discovering persuasive possibilities that are already available (if dormant) in language and culture. This process of discovery is rhetorical invention. As Sharon Crowley makes plain, Aristotle's definition of rhetoric

> emphasizes the art of finding or discovering arguments. The definition also ties rhetoric to culture by locating the need for it within disagreements that arise in the course of events and by locating the available arguments themselves within those events. As ancient rhetors such as Gorgias and Cicero argued in theory and personified in practice, any art or practice entitled to be called "rhetoric" must intervene in some way in the beliefs and practices of the community it serves. Hence any rhetorical theory must at minimum formulate an art of invention, as Aristotle did; furthermore, the arguments generated by rhetorical invention must be conceived as produced and circulated within a network of social and civic discourse, practices, images, and events. (Crowley 2006, 27)

Invention helps rhetors and rhetoricians discover possibilities and compose arguments that take advantage of them. Working from Crowley's explication, it is clear that rhetorical invention requires (1) analyzing arguments and beliefs in circulation (2) in specific times and places (3) to determine what arguments have been persuasive (4) in order to determine what available means still exist. It is worth mentioning that this is the special training of rhetoricians.

As stated, many of the old arguments about education are no longer persuasive. What we need, then, is reinvention. In *Conceding Composition*, I undertake a small inventive step by rereading the history of composition as an institutional, rather than an intellectual, entity. Contrary to popular belief, I contend that composition is, and has long been, a boon for postsecondary institutions. Beginning in the late nineteenth century, composition has routinely been used to evince postsecondary institutions' credentials as providers of mass education, with the goal of maintaining political and economic support for higher education. In other words, at one point composition was itself an available mean, and it has served postsecondary institutions well. I am confident that surveying and analyzing the historical arguments that circulated in this vein may alert us to institutional aspects of composition that have been broadly persuasive but which may nevertheless have escaped our attention. I am hopeful, therefore, that this book will shed light on argumentative possibilities—newly available means—that may bolster composition in particular, and American education more generally, in our particular time and place.

ACKNOWLEDGMENTS

The writing of this book has stretched over the better part of a decade—across three jobs (including graduate school), three states, and the births of two of my three daughters. It is impossible to account for all the people who have contributed to its development in that time. What I can say is that *Conceding Composition* has only come into being because of the support, kindness, insight, care, and love of an untold number of people, including, in some cases, total strangers. For all of them, I am thankful. Anything that is good in the book is to their credit. (Of course, any blunders are mine alone.)

Alongside this blanket acknowledgment, I need also to thank some specific individuals. First, special credit belongs to Matt Heard (University of North Texas), who read and responded to every chapter in this book with generosity, insight, and patience. This would be a far inferior book without his input. Judy Holiday, Maureen Daly Goggin, Andrea Alden, David Grant, and Rebecca Hohn each read all or parts of chapters and offered constructive feedback. Duane Roen, Risa Applegarth, Michael Bernard-Donals, David Gold, Davis Houck, Susan Jarratt, Kyle Jensen, Stephanie Kirschbaum, Mark McBeth, Kelly Ritter, Susan Romano, Robert Upchurch, and several fellow participants in the 2013 Rhetoric Society of America Summer Institute also responded to my materials with critical insight and shared materials of their own. Their generosity has been invaluable. Other people who have (sometimes unknowingly) mentored me in this process include Ian Barnard, Irene L. Clark, Sharon Crowley, Paul Kei Matsuda, and Shirley Rose. Michael Spooner, the staff at Utah State University Press, and two anonymous reviewers deserve immense credit for their professionalism and care. It is a constant source of amazement and inspiration to me that I work in a profession and field in which such generosity is so prevalent.

I am grateful to my outstanding colleagues at Arizona State University, the University of North Texas, the National University of Modern Languages in Islamabad, and San José State University. In particular, at ASU, Kendall Gerdes, Elizabeth Lowry, Karen Engler, Adrienne Leavy, Michelle Martinez, Shillana Sanchez, and Beth Tobin were amazing soundboards, readers, and critics. At UNT, Gabriel Cervantes, Kevin

Curran, Dahlia Porter, and Kelly Wisecup spent the better part of two years supporting my writing and thinking through a shared love of bureaucracy. Kelly and Nora Gilbert, most especially, drank me through numerous writing obstacles at Cool Beans, Oak St., and Eastside. Masood Raja took me to Pakistan and listened to me prattle on about some of these issues while we strolled. The wonderful people I have worked with at NUML and SJSU have also been tremendously supportive. Thanks are also due to UNT's English Department, College of Arts and Sciences, Office of the Provost, and Office of Research and Economic Development for funding and support.

I am proud to be writing this book in a disciplinary moment in which unsung heroes—specifically, archivists and librarians—are being sung. Thanks to Barbara Hoddy, Katherine Krzys, Michael Lotstein, and Christine Marin at ASU; Courtney Jacobs, Perri Hamilton, Sam Ivie, Robert Lay, and Marta Hoffman Wodnicka at UNT; Christine H. Guyonneau at the University of Indianapolis; and Michelle Gachette at Harvard. Several other Harvard archivists whose names I do not know heroically shuttled materials back and forth across the length of the library to get them to me after the elevator broke. Archivists and librarians at Berkeley and Kansas also did exceptional work on my behalf.

Finally and most important, I want to thank my family and friends. Mom, Dad, Heidi, Matt, Madeline, Travis, Christopher, Kerri, Anya, Geoffrey, Katrina, and Gabrielle—thank you for almost two centuries (you have to do the math creatively) of cumulative love and support. To Ed, Consorcia, Kris, Melissa, and Kensington—thank you for supporting me and for supporting everyone else who was supporting me. To Xochilt Almendarez, Justin Collier-Banks, Kevin Collier-Banks, Keith Bonnici, Monique Bonnici, Howard Wittenburg, Shereen Wittenburg, and Michael Vosti—I hope you all know what you mean to me. Sophia, Sydney, and Shane: I love you and I'm so proud of each of you. And Charie: I love you and "scraps from the kitchen."

CONCEDING COMPOSITION

Introduction

UNRAVELING AN ALIEN SYSTEM OF MEANING
Composition as Concession

> When we cannot get a proverb, or a joke, or a ritual, or a poem, we
> know we are on to something. By picking at the document where it is
> most opaque, we may be able to unravel an alien system of meaning.
> The thread might even lead us into a strange and wonderful world view.
> —Robert Darnton, *The Great Cat Massacre and*
> *Other Episodes in French Cultural History*

> What is called for, I think, is "getting the story crooked," looking into
> the various strands of meaning in a text in such a way as to make the
> categories, trends, and reliable identities of history a little less inevita-
> ble . . . What else but rhetoric will make a claim for the "other" sources,
> and show a deeper respect for reality by reading texts in crooked ways?
> —Hans Kellner, "After the Fall: Reflections
> on Histories of Rhetoric"

Conceding Composition is not the book I set out to write. I originally conceived this study as a local history of the writing program at Arizona State
University (ASU), covering an approximately twenty-five-year period from
the mid-1980s through the first decade of the twenty-first century.[1] During
these two and a half decades, ASU's writing program was host to a number
of influential rhetoric and composition scholars[2] and the site of important
advances in the field of rhetoric and composition studies.[3] When I began
this research as a doctoral student at ASU, documenting the contributions of ASU's writing program to the field in the 1980s, 1990s, and 2000s
seemed a worthy goal, especially given the increasing importance of local
histories in rhetoric and composition at the time.[4] *Conceding Composition*,
however, is not the realization of that goal for several reasons, and understanding why can help make sense of what it has become.

For starters, I wanted to know how ASU's writing program became so
prominent. The contemporary writing program I initially had in mind

DOI: 10.7330/9780874219906.c000

may be said to start in the mid-1980s, when David Schwalm took over the position of director of composition. Almost all of ASU's composition directors had been junior faculty members dating back to the late 1950s when the position was created. But in the early 1980s, administrators at ASU, including the English department chair, recognized that the responsibilities for writing programs and writing program administration were increasing substantially, both at the university and across the state (ASU Department of English 1984). In light of the changing realities of the position, Schwalm was hired as a tenured associate professor and director of composition in 1986, and his appointment marked the first time a tenured faculty member was hired at ASU expressly to administer the writing program. It is not too much to claim that Schwalm helped establish ASU's writing program as an exemplary model of what professionalized writing programs could be. Originally, then, this study was to be a history of ASU's writing program beginning with Schwalm and carrying forward to the present day. My research took me in other directions, however.

In the process of trying to contextualize Schwalm's momentous appointment at ASU using archival materials, department histories, and interviews with current and former faculty (including Schwalm), I realized that I needed to begin my history earlier than 1986. I discovered, for instance, that although Schwalm was the first tenured director of composition, one of his predecessors, Dorothy M. Guinn, was the first faculty member hired at ASU specifically to direct the writing program (she was also the first female writing program administrator at ASU). Before Guinn, all the composition directors had been chosen from faculty members in the department—usually a junior faculty member who needed to build a tenure case by demonstrating "publications, research, or other service of special value to the institution," which included writing program administration ("Faculty Personnel Policy" 1956, 3).[5] Guinn was the first external hire brought in to run the writing program. And while she was not the first rhetoric and composition specialist to do so, she was the first person hired to run the program specifically because of her disciplinary affiliation.

Guinn had an impressive résumé at the time of her hire—she earned her PhD from the famed rhetoric program at the University of Southern California in 1978, she was an early participant at Rhetoric Society of America meetings in the 1970s and at the first Wyoming Conference in 1976, and she came to ASU after directing the University of Tulsa's writing program for two years (D'Angelo 1999c, 272; ASU Department of English 1984). Guinn was hired at ASU in 1981 as an assistant professor with the expectation that she would assume writing program administration duties in 1982, which she did. She ended up leaving ASU in 1984, however, which precipitated Schwalm's hiring two years later.[6] Although Guinn's departure set the stage for Schwalm's appointment, her entry at ASU also invited questions that pointed backward in history—for instance, what circumstances occasioned her hire? Guinn, as it turns out, was recruited to ASU by Frank D'Angelo.

Frank D'Angelo is an icon in rhetoric and composition for his efforts to recuperate the classical rhetorical tradition and to advance the study of rhetoric in popular culture. At ASU, he was likewise an influential figure. D'Angelo first came to ASU in 1970 and took over as director of composition in 1971. He served in that capacity for eight years, during which time he also spearheaded ASU's graduate concentration in rhetoric and composition (along with John Gage). He relinquished the composition director position when he was elected to chair the Conference on College Composition and Communication (CCCC) in 1979 (see D'Angelo 1999b, 1999c), which ultimately led to Guinn's recruitment. I quickly realized that I needed to start my history well before Schwalm's hiring in 1986 or even Guinn's hiring in 1981 in recognition of D'Angelo's formative contributions to ASU's writing program and to the field of rhetoric and composition. The discovery process that took me from Schwalm to Guinn to D'Angelo turned out to be symptomatic of my early research process.

I learned that D'Angelo was hired by former ASU English department chair Jerome W. Archer. Archer came to ASU from Marquette University in 1963, and he was primarily known as a medieval literature and Chaucer scholar. Frankly, I had no particular interest in Archer, given his literature credentials, so I figured he would be a natural bulwark in my backward research trajectory. As it happens, however, I discovered that Archer played a formative role in rhetoric and composition's early professionalization efforts. Prior to moving to ASU, he was a charter member of CCCC. He was also elected to the CCCC Executive Committee in the early 1950s and was elected to preside over the sixth annual CCCC convention in Chicago in 1955. In addition, Archer organized a major conference at ASU in 1965 that was jointly sponsored by the CCCC, the National Council of Teachers of English, and the US Office of Education to consider the place of English instruction in junior colleges (Archer and Ferrell 1965).[7] In short, Archer was instrumental in rhetoric and composition history.

The same can be said for the man Archer replaced as ASU's English department chair, Louis M. Myers. Myers was a well-regarded linguist, textbook author, composition teacher, and CCCC Executive Board member, and he chaired ASU's English department in the 1930s, 1940s, and 1950s.[8] Myers studied the ways linguistic knowledge could be used to improve the teaching of writing in high schools and colleges, and he helped pioneer the use of descriptive grammar in composition instruction years before there was even a field to speak of (see Myers 1940, 1948, 1954, 1959). He advised the state of Arizona on education policy and was a consultant for the State Board of Education on teaching English in elementary and secondary schools. As chair of ASU's English department, Myers administered the first-year composition program for nearly two decades; and in the late 1950s he played an integral role in establishing the director of composition position, which was for the first time distinct from the department chair. Myers plays a relatively minor role in *Conceding Composition* for reasons that will become clearer below, but a strong case could be made that he was the most influential person in composition's 130+ year history at ASU. As ASU's university archives make abundantly clear, however, he was not the first influential faculty member in composition at the school.

The process of discovery I have been describing is both the signature blessing and the preponderant curse of archival research. As I followed successive research leads in the archives, each step back required additional steps back—an infinite regress any historian will surely recognize. In fact, rhetoric and composition teacher-scholars have a long history at ASU, dating at least as far back as 1911 when second-year English faculty member and department chair James Lee Felton published "Difficulties in English Composition" in the *Arizona Journal of Education*.

Felton is an interesting character in his own right. He chaired the English department at ASU (called Tempe Normal School when he was hired in 1910 and then Tempe State Teachers' College after 1925) for approximately twenty years. In 1926, Felton took a two-year leave of absence from the faculty to serve as mayor of Tempe, Arizona. He returned to chair the English department in 1928, and two years later he was relieved of his chairmanship because he had only earned a masters degree and new accreditation standards required that department chairs hold doctorates. In 1932, purportedly as a result of stress related to Depression-era layoffs, Felton died of a massive heart attack. But during his time on the faculty, Felton taught the introductory composition course nearly every semester. In fact, he taught composition far more than any other course, and he may well have taught more composition courses than anyone else on the faculty between 1910 and 1932. Noteworthy though Felton was in the history of composition at ASU, it should come as no surprise that the materials in ASU's archives dragged me ever further backward. By the time I was looking closely at Felton's materials, it was readily apparent to me that composition had existed in various forms at the institution since it was founded as a normal school in the 1880s.

The extension of my time frame by approximately a century, while not insignificant, was not necessarily an insurmountable obstacle to constructing a local history of ASU's writing program. In fact, it seemed at first to allow me to add substantial scholarly heft to a history that might otherwise have been deemed too laudatory or insufficiently "objective," given my position as a graduate student at ASU. What also became increasingly clear as I researched, however, was that the existence of composition at ASU far exceeded the familiar scope of rhetoric and composition history. Or, more precisely, the further back I researched ASU's "writing program," such as it was, the less sense I could make of it by reference to (1) commonly recognized historical developments related to the field of rhetoric and composition or (2) influential people who were connected in some instructive way to rhetoric and composition's history.

To give one example of this investigative obstacle, while researching Felton, I discovered in ASU's early course catalogs that there was an abrupt shift in English course titles in the mid-1920s, from "English 1–6" to "English 101/102: First Year English." This shift marked the establishment of first-year composition[9] as a requirement at ASU, but I could not determine why the change happened or why it took ASU's administrators so long to adopt a first-year composition requirement that, according to most composition historians, "by 1900 had taken hold almost everywhere" (Brereton 1995, 13).[10] It was especially perplexing because prior to 1927, when the name change officially happened, composition at ASU seemed to reflect the intellectual conditions composition historians have described in the period more generally. For all the reading and research I was doing about composition at ASU and for all I was learning about the important people affiliated with the writing program, I struggled to find a satisfying answer to explain the name change. In short, there was no disciplinary frame—historical, pedagogical, theoretical, professional, or ideological—that helped me explain why ASU suddenly replaced "English 1: Rhetoric and Composition" with "English 101: First Year English," seemingly out of the blue.[11]

INSTITUTING FIRST-YEAR COMPOSITION

My effort to comprehend the reasons for renaming ASU's first-year composition course(s) in the mid-1920s literally kept me awake nights. I spent hours in the archives trying to make sense of the change. It was, to borrow Robert Darnton's provocative phrase, "an alien system of meaning" (1999, 5); and the only way I was eventually able to unravel it was by temporarily exchanging my disciplinary frame of reference for an institutional one.[12] That is, rather than trying to understand the composition curriculum at ASU as it related to rhetoric and composition theories, pedagogies, histories, or people or even as it related to ASU's writing program or English department, I ultimately came to consider the shift from English 1 to English 101 in reference to contemporaneous institution-level changes taking place at ASU that were all but wholly detached from the intellectual considerations that constituted the majority of my early research.

Less abstractly, when I couldn't make intellectual sense of ASU's introduction of first-year composition, I started rereading Ernest Hopkins and Alfred Thomas Jr.'s *The Arizona State University Story* (1960). What was impressed upon me on this second reading of ASU's early history was that the institution transformed from a normal school to a teachers' college in 1925 to meet new accreditation standards. I discuss the important distinctions between normal schools and teachers' colleges and their relationship to accreditation at more length in chapters 2 and 3, but for now the thing worth knowing is that normal schools primarily offered a split curriculum, which included high school curricula plus teacher-training courses—essentially, a two-year high school course and a two-year pedagogical methods course. In contrast, teachers' colleges confined their curricula to a four-year collegiate course of study, which included teacher education but, more important, deliberately excluded high school coursework. The upshot is that the transformation in Tempe from normal school to teachers' college required a redesigned ("collegiate") curriculum. "English 101/102: First Year English" came into being soon thereafter. In effect, the institution transformed and composition transformed with it.

This may seem like an obvious realization, but it was not obvious to me at the time I was conducting research in ASU's archives. Nor was it explicitly spelled out in the materials I was examining for evidence of more identifiable intellectual/disciplinary connections—materials consisting largely of course listings, course descriptions, pedagogical materials, textbook adoptions, teaching assignments, teaching reflections, and student writing (consisting of exactly one theme from 1938 titled "What America Means to Me" [Manulat 1938]). These are precisely the kinds of materials rhetoric and composition historians have enumerated as the most valuable sources for disciplinary histories.[13] But despite the general abundance of such archival materials, there was almost no reference, much less explicit deliberation, in them about the change from English 1 to English 101. There was certainly no indication in the archival materials I was reading that there might be some connection between the course's name change and the institution's change from normal school to teachers' college. In fact, I routinely glossed over other evidence concerning the institution's transformation because it did not register as an important change in composition course materials, textbook adoptions, teaching assignments, and so on.

Even after I recognized the chronological correlation between changes to the institution and changes to the composition course names, it still required significant investigation in the archives to track down any evidence of causation, but I did. And when I did, what I discovered again did not match my expectations. I mentioned that ASU transformed in the mid-1920s and the composition curriculum transformed with it. It is more precise to say that the institution transformed *by virtue of* transformations to composition.

The newly constituted "English 101/102" was related to an extensive campaign beginning in the early 1920s to turn the normal school into a teachers' college. According to ASU historian Alfred Thomas Jr.:

> By the year 1922 it had become evident that the tendency to elevate the qualifications required of public school teachers must be met by advancement and improvement in the opportunities for preparation to be offered to Arizona Youth by the Normal School. The Tempe Normal School Alumni Association began by publicizing the issue and bringing the advantages of such a move into the open. The Board of Education encouraged the employment of such better trained instructors and encouraged long time members of the faculty to secure advanced degrees. The alumni association had the issue discussed before civic groups, education meetings, the press, and after three years of extensive publicity, in January 1925, the question was presented to the Legislature. (Thomas 1960b, 315–16)

I initially discovered this campaign because English department chair and perennial composition instructor James Lee Felton was traveling throughout the region, arguing for liberal re-conceptions of English instruction in 1925 to drum up support for the change from normal school to teachers' college (Thomas 1960b, 348). The campaign to convert the normal school into a teachers' college was predicated on changes to the entire curriculum, which in most cases meant removing secondary-level courses and adding postsecondary-level courses in each department. This is precisely what happened in the English department—dozens of new courses, almost all literature courses, were added to the books in 1926.

As I describe in chapters 2 and 3, however, English 101/102 played a unique role in the change from normal school to teachers' college. In fact, English 101/102 was not part of the curriculum in the teachers' college's first year in existence. There was still required composition instruction, "English 1–6," but it was not explicitly in the form of first-year composition. Almost immediately, however, the absence of first-year composition became a sticking point in transfer agreements with other colleges and universities. To make a long story short, the teachers' college was not recognized as such without the proper "collegiate" curriculum, which by that point conventionally included required first-year composition. In addition, first-year composition requirements—or the lack thereof—were tied to larger discussions about regional accreditation taking place around the country, including whether normal schools or teachers' colleges could even qualify for accreditation. As a result of these and other complicating factors, in 1926 some schools (notably, the University of Arizona in Tucson) refused to accept transfer students from the newly constituted teachers' college in Tempe (Thomas 1960b, 415–30). In 1927, therefore, administrators at Tempe State Teachers' College readjusted the curriculum and brought "English 101/102: First Year English" into existence.

It will seem counterintuitive to most rhetoric and composition specialists, but "English 101/102: First Year English" helped legitimize the newly established teachers' college as properly "collegiate." In other words, the change from "English 1" to "English 101" was not simply a matter of updating course names or redistributing pedagogical offerings or inaugurating new requirements. Nor was it related to research advances in the teaching of writing or new pedagogical goals or even evolving student writing objectives. In fact, from what I can tell, despite all the other changes to the English curriculum—which turned out to be far more extensive than I initially realized—not much changed with regard to composition *instruction* except for its institutional conditions. The intellectual (i.e., theoretical and pedagogical) foundations seem to have been relatively untouched. Nevertheless, installing "English 101/102: First Year English" was a necessary aspect of the normal school's institutional transformation into a teachers' college.

The introduction of English 101/102 proved an important point of insight for me about how ASU officials had historically used composition to address pressing institutional exigencies. Rather than speculate about why the connection between institutional exigencies and composition curricula perplexed me for so long, I am content to say that the consequent shift in perspective enabled me to recognize that shifts in composition at ASU *often* correlated closely with attempts to address institutional exigencies, generally irrespective of disciplinary developments in rhetoric and writing theories and/or pedagogies. English 101/102 turned out to be just one obvious example among many. I ultimately came to realize that an important history of composition is the history of composition's relationship to ASU's non-disciplinary institutional exigencies. Broadly conceived, that is what this book has become.

It may seem strange for a history of first-year composition to focus primarily on non-disciplinary institutional exigencies, especially when such institution-level concerns often seem distant from the specific demands of composition classrooms. But as Mary Soliday (2002) and Jane Stanley (2010) demonstrate in their groundbreaking studies, writing instruction is often closely tied to broader institutional concerns. Soliday points out that "faculty and administrators in every segment of private and public higher education have skirmished over writing curriculums, complained about student writing, and lamented the decline of standards" for over a century (2002, 3). For Soliday, composition and literacy education, particularly remedial education, "serves immediate institutional needs to solve crises in growth . . . as much as it does to solve students' needs" (ibid., 2). Stanley makes the further case that "well-published lamentations about students' 'illiteracy' (and later, 'deficiency'; and later, 'need for remediation'; and recently, 'underpreparation') have accomplished important political—that is to say rhetorical—work for the university [University of California, Berkeley], and for California herself" (2010, 6).

Both Stanley and Soliday focus specifically on "remedial" work to assess how it authorizes particular institutional arguments and supports particular institutional needs that are all but independent of the realities of classroom instruction. Remediation as such is a small element in *Conceding Composition*, but institutional—that is to say political, which is to say rhetorical—functions of composition education are central to this study. I consider specifically some of the ways administrators and faculty have over time marshaled composition at Arizona State University to make and support claims about what the institution was doing, as well as what it could and should be doing. In other words, studying composition in relation to non-disciplinary institutional exigencies has the potential to significantly reshape what we know about composition's history.

Some of ASU's most significant institutional exigencies and corresponding changes in composition education provide the core around which this book is constructed. In chapter 2 I argue that composition was necessary to fulfill the institution's mission, first as a normal school beginning in the 1880s and then, as discussed above, as a teachers' college in the 1920s. Composition was an indispensable component of a traditional "normal school" curriculum and therefore an indispensable component of the normal school's institutional mission for forty years. Of course, this was the curriculum (and mission) that was eventually surrendered in the pursuit of teachers' college status, but composition in its various normal school permutations was the cornerstone of the school's existence for four decades, and it eventually played a singular role in proving that the teachers' college was no longer normal.

In chapter 3 I argue that composition was also an important factor in administrators' decade-long struggle to earn regional accreditation, from the mid-1920s to the mid-1930s. As noted, one of the primary reasons for the change from normal school to teachers' college in 1926 was the advancement of regional accreditation as a force in American education. By the 1920s, accreditation was becoming obligatory for all sorts of institutions—secondary, postsecondary, and otherwise. To resist accreditation was to risk obsolescence. The establishment of Tempe State Teachers' College described above was the culmination of efforts that began in 1922, when Tempe Normal School's alumni association, Arizona's Board of Education, and the whole of Tempe Normal's faculty and administration were campaigning to transform the normal school into a teachers' college. But the establishment of the teachers' college was just one early milestone in a much longer campaign to meet the increasing demands of accreditation—a campaign not fully realized for almost ten years after the normal school was little more than a memory.

In chapter 4 I pick up in the aftermath of accreditation and argue that composition played multiple and shifting roles in faculty and administrators' attempts to attract various forms of federal funding beginning in the 1930s and stretching into the 1960s. Throughout the 1930s, 1940s, and 1950s, federal agencies introduced new funding programs, which could be accessed by postsecondary institutions. These programs, including parts of the New Deal, the GI Bill, and the National Defense Education Act (NDEA), had increasingly specific parameters for qualified institutions, which were regularly interconnected with various aspects of composition education. As the federal parameters changed, so too did composition's place in the institution.

In examining composition from an institutional perspective, *Conceding Composition* suggests new possibilities for disciplinary histories. The contributors to Barbara L'Eplattenier and Lisa Mastrangelo's landmark collection, *Historical Studies of Writing Program Administration*, set writing programs and their administrative concerns "within the larger institutional context that so often explains their formation" (2004, xix).

Notwithstanding the invaluable insights these histories provide, most of them cast writing programs and classrooms as the inheritors of institutional decision-making—a sort of institutional trickle-down effect. Institutional contexts undoubtedly shaped writing programs and the instruction they sponsored, but I am claiming that historians can push L'Eplattenier, Mastrangelo, and their contributors' good insights even further to consider how institutions were profoundly entangled with composition *education* as an institutional construct, even if they were simultaneously divided from composition *instruction* as an intellectual, disciplinary endeavor. Put differently, attempts to address Arizona State University's non-disciplinary institutional exigencies certainly shaped the conditions in which ASU's composition instruction existed, and I discuss some ways they did so throughout this book. But, as should be clear by now, I do not believe the institution can be relegated to context—it was not simply the scene in which more obviously disciplinary events played out. Where composition is concerned, the needs of the institution have generally taken precedence, as evidenced in the brief examples above, but they were not inadvertent consequences of oblivious decision-making. To the contrary, this study is predicated on the contention that at different moments in its institutional history, ASU's composition education deliberately reflected, and in some cases actively facilitated, the school's attempts to meet new and pressing institutional exigencies.

CONCEDING COMPOSITION

In *Conceding Composition* I elaborate the institutional perspective sketched above to offer insights into the way ASU changed as an institution over the course of a century *in relation to* the school's composition education and *because of* composition education. I contend that the institution has long been intertwined with, even inextricable from, composition education. Of course, composition was not entirely unique in this regard—other courses and requirements developed in relation to institutional needs (think business majors, gender studies departments, and the recent rise in Massive Open Online Courses [MOOCs]). But composition is distinct in that it has been involved in institutional change at ASU as much as, or more than, any other single course. In other words, the examples introduced above were not anomalies—they are indicative of a regular, even ordinary, relationship between the institution and composition. This contention informs one of *Conceding Composition*'s major claims, which is that the connection of institutional needs to composition education was neither incidental nor accidental.

In contrast to Robert J. Connors's claim in "The Octalog" that composition was "created to solve a social problem and not by the evolution of a body of knowledge" (1988, 6–7), I am arguing that composition education, particularly in the form of first-year composition, has been routinely implemented by ASU administrators and faculty in efforts to solve *institutional* problems—problems that were not coterminous with the kinds of social or intellectual problems Connors and other historians have commonly identified. In fact, the absence of a "body of knowledge" was one characteristic that made composition advantageous for solving institutional problems—it is a truism in rhetoric and composition that everyone thinks they know how to teach writing.[14] Composition was (and is) marketable, negotiable, and fungible, which is not necessarily the case even with other introductory courses like college algebra or Western civilization or intro to chemistry. In other words, composition is generally more open to wildly varying interpretation, and, as such, it has been particularly susceptible to institutional intervention. This, I argue, was generally the case at ASU. At various times and for various reasons, ASU administrators and faculty introduced, reformed, maintained, threatened, or eliminated first-year composition as part of negotiations related to larger, non-disciplinary institutional exigencies. Viewed from this perspective, I contend that composition can be usefully understood as an institutional "concession."

The metaphor of concession is obviously an important one for *Conceding Composition*, and as such it bears some explanation. As I use it here, concession most directly refers to something that is yielded or surrendered, either in deference to a more powerful authority or in exchange for other benefits. For example, a public prosecutor might concede a lower sentence in exchange for a defendant's confession. Likewise, the defendant concedes the right to defend him- or herself in court in exchange for a lighter sentence. This sense of concession needn't be penal. A student-athlete might concede a chance to finish college in exchange for a professional athletic contract. Or one country might concede some amount of territorial rights to a second country to ensure an alliance against a third country. Or under certain circumstances, a senator might concede her seat in the US Congress to run for president. The most important aspect of concession in this sense of the term is that it entails yielding one thing to attain another desirable thing or outcome. It is in this sense that I most frequently use the figure of "concession" in this book. I contend throughout *Conceding Composition* that composition was routinely offered by administrators and faculty at ASU as a concession—a symbolic token manipulated as necessary to curry educational, promotional, or political favor for the institution.

Claiming that ASU administrators and faculty "manipulated" compo- sition and that it was an institutional "token" or "concession" may not seem remarkable given the long history of hostility and abuses relating to composition that has been cataloged by rhetoric and composition his- torians, scholars, teachers, and administrators. In *From Form to Meaning*, David Fleming gives voice to the common belief that first-year composi- tion "seems always and everywhere on the border of things, the margin or threshold" (2011, 205). If composition is stereotypically marginal, so too is anything associated with it—faculty and staff, writing programs, students, curriculum, and so on. Susan Miller's (1991) now-famous "sad women in the basement" provides one of the more striking analogs to the presumed status of composition more generally. The perceived mar- ginality of first-year composition among rhetoric and composition spe- cialists rests on the belief that writing instruction in American higher education has consistently been conceived by non-specialists—that is, administrators and other faculty members—as temporary and dispos- able, what Mike Rose (1985) labels a "transient" need until lower schools finally meet their responsibility for preparing students to do the real work of college.[15] Additional evidence that composition has been histori- cally "sold out" does not seem entirely necessary. And it is certainly possi- ble to read ASU's history as precisely that—one more damning example of composition's unwarranted (intellectual) marginality.

In *Conceding Composition*, however, I argue something like the oppo- site. I contend that composition has been anything but marginal at ASU—in fact, first-year composition in particular has often been cen- tral to ASU's institutional development. The major claim of this book is that composition, specifically first-year composition, endures as the most common requirement in American postsecondary education because of its significant, positive value to institutions and to various stakeholders, which makes it available to concede. At ASU, composition has been, and continues to be, a crucial concession proffered in broader institutional negotiations with upper administrators, legislators, accrediting bodies, federal education officials, private donors, faculty across the disciplines, and other interested parties. Explaining why composition is valuable to stakeholders is part of the task of this book, but in brief, the vast major- ity of people invested in higher education think students should be required to take composition classes.

Describing composition as a concession in this way raises additional meanings that haunt the term but which may be less consistent through- out this book. For instance, a second possible definition of concession is "admission of a point claimed in argument; acknowledgement of the validity or justice of a proposition or idea. In *Rhetoric*, the surrender by a disputant of a controvertible point or position, in order to ground a fresh argument thereon, or to clear the way for one of greater importance" (*Oxford English Dictionary*, "Concession, n." 2015). In other words, concessions open up new argumentative options, and sometimes composition is conceded as the ground on which other arguments may proceed. This sense of the term has had cascading effects for composition throughout its history. Administrators concede the importance of composition instruction to, in turn, concede it in negotiations with other stakeholders. Composition teachers, scholars, and administrators concede universal composition requirements to ensure students received some measure of direct instruction in reading and writing.[16] And most institutions have historically conceded the necessity of such a requirement in accord with conventional (if shifting) notions of liberal education. In other words, conceding composition is, not incidentally, an acknowledgment of its validity, the act of which clears the way for other arguments to be made—about what it entails, who teaches it, how often, to what population, to what effect, and so on. The ubiquity of composition's concession at ASU invites us to consider the degree to which it represents the surrender of a controvertible point to achieve other goals.

Even as I unpack this sense of concession, however, it is not to say, as Susan Miller and others do, that first-year composition was the necessary "Other" against which literary studies was defined as a valuable academic enterprise. Nor, for that matter, is it to say that composition was important at ASU for teaching students to be better writers, better thinkers, or better citizens—the course's ostensible theoretical and pedagogical aims. Whether first-year composition has been central to advancing literary studies' academic credentials or to advancing students' literate development—either of which may or may not be the case, and both of which debates I leave for other people to advance—I contend that first-year composition has been essential to the development of ASU as an institution of higher education, from normal school to teachers' college to regional college to research university and points in between.[17] In other words, it is not my intention to weigh in on debates about whether first-year composition at ASU was intellectually marginalized. It is not necessary to do so to make the case that first-year composition was not institutionally "marginal" in the sense of being temporary or imperiled as a result of administrative or interdisciplinary hostility.

To be sure, there is ample evidence that scores of people at ASU, from teaching assistants to university presidents, aligned against first-year composition and in some cases openly sought its eradication. In 1965, for instance, ASU president G. Homer Durham corresponded with Jerome Archer, then chair of English, and indicated his (Durham's) ambivalence about first-year composition: "Dr. Keast (Wayne State) is prepared to eliminate freshman composition and force all members of every faculty to be in fact teachers of English as well as teachers of their own subject fields . . . I am sure the results would be salutary in the lives of all faculty members who do not now appreciate the work and service preformed by the Department of English" (Durham 1965).

In this letter and elsewhere, Durham seems amenable to the dissolution of first-year composition on intellectual grounds. And we might reasonably conclude, given the utter lack of defensiveness in Durham's message, that Archer was a relatively receptive audience.[18] Nevertheless, first-year composition was not eliminated at ASU (nor, to my knowledge, at Wayne State). Moreover, composition was rarely under serious threat at ASU because it served other crucial institutional interests—by 1965, for instance, teaching assistantships in first-year composition classrooms funded both English and education graduate students. The first-year composition requirement has persisted at ASU without interruption since 1927 because, to put it bluntly, composition education served the institution in numerous ways that were not *necessarily* tied to theoretical or pedagogical best practices (though it was not necessarily impervious to them either). This is also not to suggest that first-year composition was never vulnerable or marginal at ASU but that its vulnerability and marginality were a consequence of its substantial institutional value, not of the sincere belief that intellectual responsibility for composition could eventually be returned to its "proper" place in the lower schools or to anywhere else for that matter.

In *Conceding Composition*, I assert that despite well-documented and broad-ranging criticisms of first-year composition's pedagogical, theoretical, and socio-cultural efficacy, the course's enduring existence in American higher education can be usefully understood by considering its positive value for meeting specific institutional needs irrespective of student needs, demographics, disciplinary knowledge, pedagogical best practices, or even improved student writing. This points up a third common usage of concession that pervades this book. This third sense of concession is most commonly used in reference to concessions at concerts or sporting events and designates the allotment of "a small area or of a portion of premises for some specified purpose, e.g. for the establishment of a refreshment stand" (*Oxford English Dictionary*, "Concession, n." 2015). Business is transacted in these spaces of concession, goods are exchanged, services are rendered; but the business that is transacted does not necessarily bear on or relate to the larger enterprise that supports its existence. That is, the sale of beer and hot dogs has no direct bearing on whether pitches are pitched, outs are recorded, or runs are scored (though it may affect the funding and enjoyment of such events).

Used in this way, the metaphor of concession returns attention to the state of composition in the university, where the business of teaching, learning, and practicing writing is transacted. And here again, we'd do well to recognize that the business of writing instruction does not *necessarily* bear on the larger enterprise of the institution, no matter how much first-year composition may be used to institutional ends. It is allotted, presumably because it can be made to serve the larger institution in some way(s). In this sense of concession, first-year composition might best be characterized as institutionally "flexible" or "malleable" as opposed to marginal or vulnerable. As such, ASU's composition education helped administrators and faculty produce institutional change, if not necessarily intellectual progress.

As noted earlier, first-year composition was introduced at ASU in the mid-1920s and helped save the school from being decommissioned. In the 1930s, the course was stratified into three versions—remedial, regular, and advanced—to mirror course offerings at other colleges and universities. In the 1940s, first-year composition was redefined as part of the general education requirements, the provision of which enabled the school to offer MAs and PhDs. In the 1950s, exemptions were introduced to attract top students who refused to take the required "remedial" classes. In the 1960s, primary teaching responsibilities for first-year composition were transferred from full professors to teaching assistants, part-time faculty, and assistant professors to facilitate the recruitment of research faculty. And so on and so forth. In each case, without exception, composition was conceded—sometimes by faculty but usually by administrators or committees—to address institutional exigencies.

Course descriptions in ASU's general catalogs over this period were virtually unchanged—verbiage was updated with the times, but the core concepts stayed relatively stable. We might reasonably surmise that the intellectual content of the courses changed only inasmuch as writing teachers and writing program administrators changed it. In other words, it seems fairly apparent that course content was generally left to disciplinary specialists. Despite the consistency in course descriptions, however, the institutional place of composition education changed considerably on a number of occasions to address new institutional challenges. The baseline presumption seems always to have been that good teaching and good learning could happen in first-year composition, but ultimately the course persisted at ASU because administrators and faculty could concede it in some sense of the term to meet changing institutional exigencies.

CONCEDING (IN) RHETORIC AND COMPOSITION

In the next section, I argue that recognizing composition's institutional value as a "concession" at Arizona State University can help historians recognize that the practice of conceding composition has vastly exceeded ASU's individual case. Before doing so, however, I return briefly to some disciplinary—that is, pedagogical, theoretical, and professional—considerations. The institutional perspective I have been describing thus far is pointedly not "disciplinary" for reasons I explicate in chapter 1. It is therefore not necessarily intended to illuminate pedagogical and theoretical implications for composition classrooms. Nevertheless, I believe *Conceding Composition* potentially has serious pedagogical, theoretical, and professional implications for composition teachers, scholars, and even administrators. I contemplate some of these implications more specifically in the conclusion of the book, but they deserve a few words here as well. In fact, I believe the radical dissociation of composition-as-institutional-need from rhetoric and writing pedagogy and research has the potential to open productive new avenues for the field.

In the field's conventional historical narrative, composition is marginalized in higher education because institutions are ambivalent at best and hostile at worst to composition as a scholarly and pedagogical object. This institutional hostility, according to historians, proceeds from the belief that composition and its disciplinary consorts (e.g., rhetoric, writing, literacy) are insufficiently intellectual. Sharon Crowley (1998a, 4) makes precisely this point in *Composition in the University*: "The history of composition studies has been written in the fortunes of the required introductory course in composition. Unfortunately, this course enjoys very little status within the university, and so its history and status negatively affect the current status of composition studies."

Implicit in most historical accounts of this belief, and explicit throughout a good deal of composition scholarship, is the assurance that better teaching and better scholarship can eventually enable the field to overcome this form of institutional hostility (e.g., Fleming 2011, 13). The promise of overcoming hostility, in turn, has long linked rhetoric and composition's disciplinary aims to assumptions about what institutions expect from composition education. This belief is probably stated nowhere more succinctly than in the most recent edition of *A Guide to Composition Pedagogies*, in which the authors write, "The field's desire to become a legitimate scholarly field like others in higher education led to the development of serious pedagogical scholarship involving theoretical and qualitative methods and even empirical research" (Tate et al. 2014, 16–17).[19] Crowley (1998b, 112) has characterized this governing desire as "the topos of improvement = appreciation." If institutions are unsatisfied with student writers, writing programs, composition instruction, and/or rhetoric and composition scholarship, then the best way to earn institutional approbation is by demonstrating intellectual excellence—providing irrefutable evidence of better teaching and improved research. Massive efforts to professionalize composition teachers and program administrators have been advanced on these grounds in the past seven decades.

It should be clear, however, that I do not necessarily think better teaching or better scholarship will lead to institutional approval. A central assumption of this book, in fact, is that the notion that inadequate teaching and scholarship are the cause of institutional hostility is fundamentally a misdiagnosis. This notion is based on the very reasonable assumption that everyone involved with composition education, at whatever level, shares the common goal of helping students become better writers—that better student writing is a stasis point. But as I argue, composition has served and continues to serve institutional ends that do not necessarily correspond with the production of better student writers.

Perhaps the most bracing illustration of this reality is described by Chris Anson (2002), who explains the circumstances in which the University of Minnesota's (UM) independent writing program, which he administered, was unceremoniously disbanded in 1996 by an interim dean while Anson was attending a conference in Europe. Despite the fact that the program "boasted a first-rate training and development program; a strong team of teachers; a solid, nationally recognized curriculum informed by current work in the field and keeping pace with university-wide liberal education initiatives; productive faculty; and a consensus-based management system that helped to prepare graduate students in composition for possible roles as writing program administrators" (ibid., 153), it was rolled back into the English department from which it had split a decade and a half earlier. From Anson's description of the program's intellectual contributions plus the program's economic contributions to the College of Liberal Arts, it was patently excellent and should have been a prime candidate for administrative appreciation. Obviously, given the outcome, it wasn't appreciated enough.

Anson weighs the possibility that the dissolution of UM's independent writing program was part of a disciplinary turf war, but he ultimately concludes that it was conceded to support the English department's attempts to prosper within a new funding model. To make the causal chain more explicit, (1) upper administrators changed the funding model to strengthen the institution, (2) lower administrators reconceived smaller units' organization to streamline costs, (3) English needed more full-time enrollment hours (FTEs) to meet the new funding guidelines, and (4) composition was ultimately taken over (conceded) by the interim dean because it was suited to the "larger" cause (ibid., 160). In other words, the program's concession seems to have had nothing to do with intellectual issues—least of all, actual writing instruction. In fact, it seems highly likely, though admittedly speculative, that the interim dean figured the intellectual content of the courses would be wholly unchanged by the institutional reconfiguration. All the more reason, then, to dissolve it.

Although I am skeptical of this particular interim dean's motives, in my broader reading it is clear that the vast majority of administrators and faculty are actually quite interested in what happens in composition classes. Most of them genuinely want students to be better writers and more successful students, and they even regularly trust rhetoric and composition specialists to meet that charge, all evidence to the contrary. But such pedagogical/intellectual interest is regularly (and most administrators would no doubt say unavoidably) subordinated to larger "essential" institutional needs. In other words, for all its important pedagogical/intellectual value, institutions and administrators also appreciate composition for very different reasons than "the topos of improvement = appreciation" suggests. Put even more bluntly, composition's intellectual value as a teaching and research subject often has little, if anything, to do with its value as an institutional concession.

As such, better teaching and scholarship on their own cannot address the non-disciplinary institutional needs composition education is routinely conceded to meet. No doubt, the immediate impulse among writing specialists would be to combat the use of composition for such ends. That certainly seems to be Anson's impulse, and understandably so. But if tertiary education is to continue to exist, such non-disciplinary institutional needs do need to be met, and the institution's keepers are constitutionally pitched toward doing so. Given a choice between better first-year writers and efforts to secure institutional well-being against hazards (real or perceived), it is not hard to guess where most people who make decisions for postsecondary institutions will come down. More often than not, then, the principled actions of composition faculty will probably have little lasting effect on those decision-makers' decision-making. In other words, the prospects for preventing institutions from conceding composition seem to me to be pretty low.

My attempts to separate intellectual objectives from institutional imperatives in *Conceding Composition* may therefore seem cause for cynicism and despair, but I think they actually represent a potentially important opportunity for rhetoric and composition teachers and scholars. My larger point is that a better understanding of the tenor of institutional expectations as analytically separable, if not functionally separate, from intellectual considerations affords rhetoric and composition specialists new, exciting disciplinary opportunities. Redefining composition as a "concession," as opposed to a "service," can function in at least two substantial ways.

First, redefining composition as a "concession" effectually mitigates the pernicious expectation that composition can eventually meet institutional needs by way of intellectual, disciplinary advances. It can't. The dissolution of this psychic link, however, means that rhetoric and writing instruction might be expanded to augment the current disciplinary mission of making better writers. Composition classes could be developed to include ethical, political, and epistemological inquiry (which I know already happens in many places but which might be brought further into the open). For instance, what might a composition class, even a first-year composition class, look like that is designed to help students think, research, and write about "basic" questions like "what is writing" (Nicotra 2009, W260); "how does writing work" (Bazerman 1988, 9); "who owns writing" (Hesse 2005); or even "should writing be taught" (Vitanza 1991, 161). These are questions we pursue in our scholarship, certainly, but they do not seem to me to be questions we often invite students to pursue in our classes, especially first-year classes. Moreover, although my point is not that these are *the* necessary questions to be asked, they are potentially fruitful pedagogical questions among many that are hard to ask and answer within current disciplinary assumptions about the nature of institutional constraints. Reconsidering those disciplinary grounds, therefore, can potentially open spaces for productively rethinking the field's pedagogical limits. This kind of expansion would work well with broad-ranging disciplinary efforts to develop undergraduate majors (see, e.g., Giberson and Moriarty 2010).

Second, redefining composition invites new research questions about why composition exists in the university, how it exists, and how it might be productively reconceived in light of non-disciplinary circumstances with which the field has not previously grappled. *Conceding Composition* is an early foray into raising questions and thinking through some answers from a non-disciplinary institutional perspective. But much work remains to be done in this vein if we are to understand the complicated roles composition is designed to fill in and for postsecondary institutions.

The ultimate goal, of course, is to discover ways to strengthen composition as a teaching and research subject and as a profession in light of deepening understandings about institutional needs. As this work is carried out, rhetoric and composition teachers and scholars may find new, more effective ways to position the field's commitment to composition instruction in relation to composition education's non-disciplinary institutional functions. For if composition education cannot be made to please institutions in such a way as to completely prevent "concession," perhaps it can be made to mollify institutions in the service of good instruction. I have in mind a sort of disciplinary analog to Robert Brooke's "underlife," which Brooke says "refers to those behaviors which undercut the roles expected of participants in a situation" (1987, 141). Mollifying could be, in Brooke's words, "a *contained* form of underlife, a form which . . . attempts to exist within the existing structure without introducing too much friction" (ibid., 151, original emphasis).[20] And mollifying can potentially create the kind of disciplinary space necessary for teachers and scholars to pursue dramatically enhanced opportunities not generally afforded by attempts to please. I do not mean to suggest that the field will suddenly find itself in an "anything goes" environment or that teachers, researchers, or writing program administrators would even want that. But by reducing the cognitive demands of one kind of institutional constraint, the so-called service function, rhetoric and composition specialists might suddenly discover (1) pedagogical and scholarly opportunities that were previously obscured and (2) new lines of argument that can effectively advance the profession, both within institutions and potentially outside of them.

CONCEDING COMPOSITION AS A NATIONAL TREND

One of *Conceding Composition*'s premises is that rhetoric and composition specialists can learn important lessons about the history of postsecondary composition education—and consider possibilities for rethinking our relationship to it in theoretically, pedagogically, and professionally gratifying ways—by considering it more precisely in relation to Arizona State University's institutional exigencies, as opposed to the more conventional pedagogical, intellectual, or socio-cultural ones. However, as Richard E. Miller cogently articulates in his study of education reform, "The 'turn to cases' must be followed by a *return* to generalities, hypotheses, overarching observations, and speculations if this methodological interest in the local is to have any chance of escaping the charge of mere parochialism" (1998, 17, original emphasis).

Although ASU's example provides the initial emphasis for my investigation, *Conceding Composition* is not simply a case study. Rather, ASU provides a point of departure for larger claims I make about how composition as an institutional concession developed in American higher education more generally. Put succinctly, I set my intensive examination of ASU's example against intensive examinations of other institutional examples to argue that first-year composition has had wide-ranging value as a "concession" throughout its existence in American higher education. I contend that first-year composition has been "conceded" by administrators and faculty *around the country* to advance broader, non-disciplinary institutional interests tied to organizational development and daily operations.

This realization dawned on me nearly as slowly as the realization that ASU's writing course numbers and titles were somehow tied to its institutional mission.[21] In examining ASU's history through an institutional perspective, I discovered that the university's institutional exigencies often correlated closely to institutional exigencies at other schools around the country. It is hardly a revelation, I suppose, that attempts to address exigencies related to institutional mission, accreditation, and federal funding, among many others, have been widely consequential across multiple institutions in American education. As it turns out, for instance, the vast majority of normal schools in America transformed into teachers' colleges alongside ASU in the mid-1920s.[22] ASU's shift from normal school to teachers' college was in many ways one datum in a national trend. This is not to say that ASU's local situation was not distinctive. It was in a number of ways, both dramatic and mundane, and I detail some of the more noteworthy idiosyncrasies for rhetoric and composition scholars.[23] Nevertheless, one goal of this book is to demonstrate that ASU's institutional story is not simply a local one.

Beginning with its establishment as a normal school, ASU was closely associated with other institutions. Its curricular, organizational, and bureaucratic structures were consciously modeled on comparable structures at other institutions throughout the country. Decisions about what courses to offer, what majors to emphasize, what degree tracks to support, and many more were made in light of, and sometimes as a response to, other institutions' actions. Not only did ASU not exist in a vacuum, but the exigencies to which it was compelled to respond often originated in other institutions and organizations, educational and otherwise.[24]

In the early 1940s, for instance, ASU was still a teachers' college: Tempe State Teachers' College. For all intents and purposes, this meant the school could only issue teaching degrees, a BA in education and an MA in education. Although there were specializations (students could get a Bachelor of Education degree with a specialization in English or math, for instance), the school was not authorized to offer standard BA and BS degrees. In 1945, however, in view of the needs of returning GIs, the teachers' college became Arizona State College, a regional comprehensive college with the authorization to grant BA and BS degrees in fourteen majors ("New ASU Story" 2001). According to Edward P.J. Corbett, the flood of new students following World War II was a consequence of "newly adopted open admissions policies" that proliferated throughout higher education in the mid-1940s (1993, 63). Although he ties composition and writing program administration directly to this increase in enrollments, Corbett doesn't spend much time discussing these policy changes. But at least at ASU, such policies were hard won based on the conscious decision—and significant administrative and political efforts—to transform the institution from a teachers' college to a regional college. Moreover, as I discuss in chapter 4, this decision was explicitly predicated on decisions made by federal and state governments, administrators at other postsecondary institutions, and extra-institutional organizations (e.g., accreditation associations).

Historians have often characterized these sorts of institutional transformations in romanticized terms—usually in classic bootstraps narratives of individual (if institutional, and therefore also collective) fortitude. ASU's institutional historians, Ernest J. Hopkins and Alfred Thomas Jr., conceive of ASU's evolution from normal school to university as a story of western grit, triumph over adversity, and Manifest Destiny.[25] Narratives of localized, independent gumption serve a variety of purposes, one of which is to reinforce the sense that colleges and universities strive for and achieve continual progress. Evidence of persistent institutional advancement supports rhetorical claims about the educational, promotional, and political importance of tertiary education. This striving is inseparable from the institutional uses to which composition is put in local situations. Such "striving" narratives, however, belie the dynamic relationships among institutions, which affected and were affected by institutional transformations.

Institutional achievement narratives also belie the dynamic relationships among (1) institutions, (2) their institutional affiliations, and (3) their curricula. I argue in this book that certain kinds of composition education evinced ASU's affiliation with other institutions or institution types—"English 101: First Year English" was properly "collegiate," whereas "English 1: Rhetoric and Composition" was not. If course descriptions are any indication, the classroom experience was essentially unchanged; but being demonstrably "collegiate" granted ASU (née Tempe State Teachers' College) the affiliations necessary for its continued existence.

In the introduction to his compendious documentary history of ASU, Alfred Thomas Jr. argues that such matters were characteristic of the "institutional rivalry" between ASU and the University of Arizona and that they served as an "opposing and limiting force" in ASU's development (Thomas 1960a, n.p.). Opposing and limiting though the rivalry may have been, inter-institutional hostility was also profoundly formative. It was, after all, a powerful contributing factor in administrators' decision to adjust ASU's curriculum in 1927 to include first-year composition—the introduction of which helped prove that ASU's course offerings were comparable to the University of Arizona's and resuscitated transfer agreements. Although commonly cast in pedagogical and intellectual terms, it should be clear that such decisions served institutional needs as much as, or more than, any pressing instructional needs. In short, particular kinds of composition education (as well as particular kinds of history education, math education, and so on), as opposed to specific kinds of writing instruction, served as bridges between various institutions and evinced a kind of group membership.[26]

Historian Hans Kellner asserts that "each academic tribe produces and harbors a system of anxieties that, perhaps more than anything else, identifies a scholar as a member of the group" (1989, 129). We might usefully extend Kellner's observation to describe institutions inasmuch as different types of institutions (e.g., normal schools, teachers' colleges, regional colleges, universities) often share anxieties within the group that identify members. The most obvious anxiety among colleges and universities is that students receive at least nominally the same education from one constituent institution to the next. Another prominently shared anxiety is that graduates will register as competently literate and numerate subjects. Given the shared quality of anxieties, I contend in *Conceding Composition* that ASU's individual institutional anxieties direct historians' attention to ways composition education was used in higher education *at large* to address common institutional exigencies.

To paraphrase Kellner, members of particular institutional tribes generally faced comparable anxieties, and sometimes exactly the same anxieties, as in the examples I analyze in this book. The proliferation and subsequent demise of normal schools, the ascendance of regional accreditation associations, and the growth in importance of federal grant funds reverberated widely throughout American education. These are not the only examples that can be discovered. But my goal is not to be comprehensive in this regard; it is, in James A. Berlin's words, to conduct "a search for interpretations that cast the past and present in new conceptual formulations" (1994, 123).

In the following chapters, I offer just such a search for interpretations by directing attention to non-disciplinary institutional exigencies and their simultaneously momentous and mundane consequences for composition in American higher education. In chapter 1, I elaborate a new methodology for undertaking the history I have been describing to this point, and in my concluding chapter I reflect on some implications of this study for the field of rhetoric and composition. I do not intend to repeat that work here, but I do want to point out one additional contribution of *Conceding Composition* as a way of framing the larger study. In offering the notion of composition as a concession, this book is an attempt to provide a more precise explanation for why first-year composition continues to exist in spite of, and maybe because of, the many competing assessments about its functions and value.

In claiming that composition has been a concession, I contend that first-year composition was intended less as a gate-keeping mechanism, as most rhetoric and composition historians have claimed, than as evidence of postsecondary institutions' suitability for educating large numbers of high school graduates. First-year composition might, in fact, be considered a wide-ranging form of curricular public relations inasmuch as it has helped colleges and universities across the country demonstrate their broad appeal following several centuries as cloisters of elite privilege. This is all to say, we may stand to learn valuable lessons about how composition education—particularly in the form of first-year composition—came to exist, how it proliferated, and how it has endured in American higher education from this history because it allows us to consider what kinds of rhetorical, political, organizational, institutional, and promotional options conceding composition, or specific forms of composition, opened up for institutions of higher education. One important challenge in re-describing first-year composition as a concession, then, is to envision what the course and the field might look like if the thing we have long thought of as a barrier—composition's transience—is reimagined as the consummate institutional value.

1

GENITIVE HISTORY
Or, the Exception That Suggests a Rule

[The] theoretical mutuality between what we perceive as impersonal,
even deterministic, structures and personal, even creative, identities is
particularly relevant as we reread the history of composition.
—Susan Miller, "Composition as a Cultural
Artifact: Rethinking History as Theory"

How we understand history depends on the method of writing history.
—Lester Faigley, "Veterans' Stories on the Porch"

French philosopher and polymath Giorgio Agamben begins his methodological treatise, *The Signature of All Things: On Method,* by observing:
"Anyone familiar with research in the human sciences knows that, contrary to common opinion, a reflection on method usually follows practical application, rather than preceding it. It is a matter, then, of ultimate
or penultimate thoughts, to be discussed among friends and colleagues,
which can legitimately be articulated only after extensive research"
(2009, 7).

Agamben's thinking accords well with my experience writing this
book, which, as I described in the introduction, takes a non-disciplinary institutional perspective on the history of composition. While I was
researching and writing *Conceding Composition,* I felt at many points compelled to situate my research in relation to the exceptional histories of
composition that already exist. That effort, however, has been somewhat
more challenging that it might seem for reasons I discuss below—reasons that for now can be characterized generally as methodological.
Given the structure of books, this chapter is necessarily located near the
beginning, as if to suggest that I thoughtfully located a research gap in
composition's history, carefully developed my clever methodology, and
then systematically set it into action—methodological precision informing methodical rigor.[1] To the contrary and in keeping with Agamben's

DOI: 10.7330/9781607325055.c001

observation, it was only after extensive research (and extensive fumbling) that I felt as though I could legitimately articulate how this book makes sense in the context of rhetoric and composition's history and histories. The methodology unfolded from there. I have therefore structured this chapter to reflect in some small way the unfolding process by which I came to the methodology I theorize here.

On the one hand, it should be clear by now that this book is a historical examination of composition education in American higher education during the nineteenth and twentieth centuries. It therefore aligns with and extends a long list of historical work by well-known rhetoric and composition historians. On the other hand, it should also be clear that *Conceding Composition* diverges from other histories in the field inasmuch as it is a history of the discipline that focuses on institutional issues which are not principally, or even recognizably, disciplinary. In this chapter, therefore, I take up recent invitations in the field, particularly Michelle Ballif's in *Theorizing Histories of Rhetoric*, "to envision alternative methodologies" that provoke questions about "what it means, what it should mean, what it could mean to write histories of rhetoric, composition, communication" (2013b, 3–4).

In the introduction I opted not to speculate about why the connection between non-disciplinary institutional changes at ASU and changes in the composition curriculum perplexed me for so long. I also do not intend to speculate about why it took me so long to recognize that my initial inability to shift perspective was a methodological obstacle.[2] Nevertheless, it was. Events such as ASU's transformation from normal school to teachers' college in the 1920s, which brought first-year composition into being in Tempe, raise a number of questions that the field's conventional disciplinary historical methodologies are not well suited to ask or answer—about why the change from normal school to teachers' college occurred, why it occurred when it did, how composition education influenced the change, and how composition education could change dramatically on an institutional level without concomitant changes in intellectual or disciplinary practices. As it turns out, these are questions about how composition education was used positively to shape postsecondary institutions as much as they are questions about how higher education negatively shaped composition. That is, these are questions about how composition opened up institutional possibilities as much as they are questions of how institutions constrained composition.

Following these and other traces can take us far afield of more traditional disciplinary concerns with the goal of developing more complex, situated, historical, *institutional* understandings of composition's role in the academy. *Conceding Composition* might therefore best be character-ized as an attempt to consider composition's concession not just in rela-tion to institutional conditions of possibility but also *as* an institutional condition of possibility—as a mechanism that made certain institutional action(s) possible. Discussing composition as a "concession" in the ways I advanced in the introduction, therefore, requires that I stake my claims on different, if complementary, methodological grounds than other his-tories in the field.

PROBLEMS OF PERSISTENCE AND LONGEVITY

In my introductory chapter, I elaborated a personal justification for developing the non-disciplinary institutional perspective that distin-guishes *Conceding Composition*—as a teacher, researcher, and junior writ-ing program administrator, I wanted to make sense of the historical cir-cumstances at ASU in which "English 1" became "English 101" so I could better understand the contemporary conditions in which I was working. But as I intimated, there are broader questions that derive from this localized dilemma. First and foremost, why does first-year composition still exist in American higher education?

This question is not intended as mere provocation—I ask it in ear-nest given the apparent historical forces aligned against the course. First-year composition is the most common form literacy education takes in postsecondary institutions, and it remains one of the most common requirements in American higher education (Fleming 2011, 1–3; Slevin 1991, 5). John C. Brereton calls it "the largest single enter-prise in American higher education" (1995, x). Remarkably, it has persisted in institutions across the country for nearly 150 years despite open hostility from administrators and faculty for nearly as long. In 1969, Leonard Greenbaum wrote: "If freshman English really began in 1874, the first complaint was probably registered in 1875. But on record, in black print, the assault against freshman English began in 1911, and continued in 1928, 1929, 1931, 19 . . . " (1969, 175).[3] Anyone with even a passing familiarity with composition's history knows that the critiques have not ceased in the nearly 50 years since Greenbaum's article was published, and neither has first-year composition suc-cumbed to them. In many places around the country, the requirement is as strong as it has ever been. I submit that first-year composition's persistence and longevity are rather more curious than historians have considered to this point given the prolonged intensity of "the assault against freshman English."

To offer one instructive example, in 1916 the Modern Language Association (MLA) commissioned a wide-ranging report on first-year composition, and one of the committee's conclusions was that composition teaching was a professional dead end because the "ultimate administrators do not, in effect, regard this course as important" (quoted in Crowley 1998a, 124–25). The MLA is hardly known for its vigorous support of composition teaching, and this report was published just four years after the National Council of Teachers of English (NCTE) was founded to compensate for the MLA's disinterest in pedagogy. The MLA's teaching report was all the more striking, then, because the committee's conclusions were a powerful indictment not of composition's intrinsic worth but of the conditions in which composition teachers labored.

Intra-disciplinary politics aside, there is not, to my mind, a convincing disciplinary explanation as to why "ultimate administrators" at institutions far and wide have continued to require and fund a course they deemed unimportant, especially given the immense resources it requires and the well-known headaches associated with staffing, assessing, and maintaining it. William Riley Parker's provocative assertion that first-year composition "rarely accomplishes any of its announced objectives" makes its longevity even more perplexing (1967, 347).[4] If ASU's president G. Homer Durham wanted to eliminate first-year composition in 1965, for instance, and especially if the English department chair concurred, and if furthermore the course failed to meet its educational charge, why did it remain? The same question can be directed at any number of institutions at virtually any time in the past century and a half, right up to the present moment. It seems worthwhile to consider why first-year composition persists year after year, seemingly against all odds.

Rhetoric and composition historians have not ignored this question, of course. The assessments about why first-year composition developed and persists are wide-ranging. Many relate to what Crowley calls "the discourse of student need" (1998a, 250). First-year composition exists either to bar the "Great Unwashed" from gaining access to higher education, the so-called gate-keeping function;[5] or conversely because students are believed to "need" it for one reason or another, whether because they are negatively considered "underprepared"[6] or positively considered "developing."[7] Other assertions about composition's persistence may be characterized as socio-cultural: the course is a consequence of societal anxieties about correctness and propriety[8] and is an increasing function of business and industry that students suddenly need to be prepared for.[9] Still other scholars' claims might perhaps be best described as "experiential," based on rhetoric and compositionists' professional experiences teaching and administering first-year composition. One such explanation that circulates widely, if apocryphally, is that first-year composition is a "cash cow."[10] As a result of the confluence of cheap labor and minimal material demands, the theory goes, first-year composition brings in more tuition dollars than it expends, unlike courses that require extensive laboratory space, full professors, and costly equipment or materials.[11] The field is rife with different versions of these arguments, which are every bit as reasonable as they are familiar. But ultimately, I maintain that they are extrapolated from distinctly disciplinary observations about how composition, pedagogy, and students are valued in institutions—which is to say, they are apparently not.

I contend, on the other hand, that understanding first-year composition's persistence entails a reconsideration of institutions' decisions to invest in first-year composition (sometimes explicitly in economic terms but oftentimes not). Moreover, I contend that such reconsideration is predicated on developing a more capacious understanding of first-year composition's relationship to institutions than a distinctly disciplinary lens affords. Of course, like first-year composition's persistence, institutions have long received attention from composition historians, most directly in Susan Miller's, Thomas Miller's, and David Russell's influential work. In his *Writing in the Academic Disciplines, 1870–1990*, Russell even designates his investigative lens an "institutional perspective" (2002, 31–32). But Russell's "institutional perspective" is not focused on the institution proper so much as it views writing instruction in places throughout the institution. The same can generally be said of Susan Miller's and Thomas Miller's institutional perspectives, though with slightly different emphases.[12] In other words, "institutional perspective" has commonly designated an attempt to locate the discipline (i.e., writing instruction) in nontraditional spaces within institutions (i.e., outside the English department or first-year writing program). My institutional perspective, in contrast, is a perspective on institutions themselves and how composition education was used to advance institutional goals. Mine is not a history of institutions exploiting composition—it is a history of symbiotic development. As such, it requires investigating nondisciplinary institutional matters that exceed, and sometimes ignore, writing instruction. Examining such matters, I contend, can better illuminate "ultimate administrators'" decision-making about why composition perseveres.

To carry out this analysis, I develop a new historiographical methodology, for which I coin the term *genitive history*. *Genitive* is a term I borrow from linguistics, and, as I explain below, I introduce it as a means for retaining valuable historiographical concepts that circulate in rhetoric and composition while also facilitating the methodological shift necessary for writing a different kind of history. In brief, genitive history allows me to balance the concentrated focus of local history against the broader visions of "universal" histories and to retain disciplinary connections while also exploring non-disciplinary avenues. Before I define "genitive history" more specifically and explain how it informs this book's larger claims, it is first worth the effort to sketch some common historiographical methodologies adopted by rhetoric and composition historians as a way to stake out their affordances and limitations.

SCOPE: ON MACRO AND MICRO

The main purpose of developing a genitive history is to address two methodological concerns implicit in my introduction: one of scope, the other of focus. My goal is to clear theoretical ground for the non-disciplinary institutional investigation I have been describing. But one consequence of this particular aim is that I need to proceed *via negativa*—that is, defining a genitive history by what it is not—before offering a more affirmative definition of what it is. In the next two sections of this chapter, I put *Conceding Composition*'s investigation in tension with the field's commonly shared historiographical scope(s) and focus.

Histories of rhetoric and composition traverse an impressive range of subjects and emphases.[13] Still, they might best be, and have been, characterized by their adoption of one of two historiographical scopes: macro-historical or micro-historical.[14] Henze, Selzer, and Sharer offer a succinct characterization of macro-histories: "Histories of composition since 1945 have sometimes represented themselves as Grand Narratives. Such narratives are useful, to be sure, for staking out in broad terms the boundaries of and developments in the field, for defining important trends, and for clarifying those developments that have persisted most stubbornly into current practice" (2008, 4). In sum, macro-histories survey historical developments broadly to present a far-reaching, comprehensive view of the discipline.[15]

In contradistinction, Henze, Selzer, and Sharer argue for more intensely focused histories that preserve "the astonishing range of practices, personalities, and messy particulars that strove for a hearing, however temporarily, within the mixed aggregate that has been known as composition" (ibid.). These kinds of locally focused histories emphasize depth instead of breadth and can generally be grouped under the term *micro-historical.* Rhetoric and composition historians have productively turned to micro-histories in recent years to complicate macro-histories' broadly drawn view of composition education. As one example, in her history of basic writing, Kelly Ritter draws on her drastically varied experiences teaching basic writing at three different institutions and her intensive local, archival research at Yale and Harvard to argue that "basic writing is *exclusively* an institutional construct, a locally specific course designation that stems from, develops from, and ends with the unique culture of each institution" (2009, 9, original emphasis). Ritter's micro-historical research illustrates that basic writing existed even in the most prestigious universities in the country five decades prior to the famed "open admissions" movements of the 1960s and 1970s. As Henze, Selzer, Sharer, and Ritter ably demonstrate, there is much to be learned from sharply narrowing one's historical scope.

In many ways, *Conceding Composition* is a micro-history. It is based on detailed analysis of archival documentary materials; it focuses predominantly, although not exclusively, on the local conditions of a single "obscure" institution; and it carefully considers the situated "movements, moments, mentors, and mandates" (Gannett, Brereton, and Tirabassi 2010, 426) that shaped composition over the course of nearly a century. It could easily be classified among a growing number of disciplinary histories that attempt to illuminate the development of composition "from the bottom up."[16]

However, *Conceding Composition* also aspires to something different than micro-history. For one, *Conceding Composition* examines non-disciplinary institutional exigencies rather than rhetoric and composition micro-histories' principal emphasis: "the history of composition as a teaching subject" (ibid.; see also Enoch 2008, 12). Actually, composition *instruction*—as opposed to composition *education*—plays a relatively limited role in this history, for reasons discussed in the introduction. In addition to my decidedly non-pedagogical emphasis, this study uses concentrated, local inquiry to tell a broadly drawn, even "comprehensive," story about composition education in American higher education.[17]

I hesitate to classify this study as a micro-history for another reason as well. My hesitation is in large part the consequence of an issue raised by Ritter. In arguing for the importance of directed local histories, Ritter concludes that "one cannot speak about composition at the first-year level as if it were always a static, universal course common to all institution types and all institutional missions" (2009, 16–17). She goes on to demonstrate the veracity of this claim throughout the book. She is absolutely correct, especially when one considers the specific manifestations of composition classes, requirements, pedagogies, and more at different sites around the country and increasingly around the world.

However, (1) the prevalence of common composition requirements (2) in radically different sites that (3) exist under common terminological banners such as "first-year composition" or "freshman English" also raises some nagging questions for me: why does first-year composition exist at schools with such widely divergent missions as elite Ivy League liberal arts colleges, internationally renowned research universities, public regional comprehensive universities, and two-year community colleges? And even at non-accredited, for-profit pseudo-universities, such as StraighterLine and the University of Phoenix? This is a point Ritter raises herself when she argues that "composition also desires to be a course that can be 'universally' dropped into any institutional location with some expected degree of conformity—i.e., a 'one size fits all' model, regardless of that institution's history or local needs" (ibid., 6).[18]

Micro-histories of composition practices are certainly important, but I'm left wondering, how can we make sense of the commonplace assertion that "although its title has varied over both time and space (here First Year Writing, there College English), its basic purpose and configuration have not, remaining remarkably stable over a span of 125 years and across the diverse terrain of North American postsecondary education" (Fleming 2011, 1)? To borrow Ritter's introductory comparison, if we imagine composition courses as attuned to locally specific circumstances, how are historians to make sense of courses at both the University of Michigan and Southern Connecticut State University that are designated by some variation of "basic writing" or "first-year composition" despite the otherwise radically different material realities at the two institutions? These are fundamentally questions about how composition is taught, studied, and administered in different institutions, but it should be clear that these questions are rather more broadly drawn than a micro-historical scope can reasonably be expected to answer.[19]

If *Conceding Composition* is not precisely a micro-history, however, it is not precisely a macro-history either. Even leaving aside for a minute the powerful critiques of macro-history in the field, one of the principal reasons *Conceding Composition* is not a bona fide macro-history is that ASU does not fit the commonly accepted parameters of macro-historical subjects. According to Gannett, Brereton, and Tirabassi, macro-histories generally focus on "what can readily be identified as *major* figures, projects, and initiatives" (2010, 426, original emphasis). This is the so-called history of great actors. By and large, macro-histories in rhetoric and composition have been defined, if sometimes indirectly, as histories that focus predominantly on elite institutions (e.g., Harvard, Yale, research universities), "traditional" students (usually young, white, elite, and male), and "traditional" teachers (influential, often recognizable, white, male faculty members from elite institutions who work with traditional students).[20]

ASU hardly fits this description. For most of the institution's existence, it was not elite; the students were decidedly "nontraditional" (ASU students were predominantly working-class and female for many decades, and from the beginning the institution was at least nominally integrated [see Hopkins and Thomas 1960, 180–87]); and although the teachers and administrators were often white, male, and occasionally influential, at least in local and regional matters, it would be a stretch to define them as "traditional" considering that very few of them held any university degrees until the 1910s and even fewer had advanced degrees until the late 1920s. Moreover, ASU can hardly be said to have played a formative role in composition's history before the 1960s or later.

My extended efforts thus far to prove that *Conceding Composition* is neither a macro- nor a micro-history may seem unnecessary. The complementary, if dialectical, relationship between the two would seem to afford plenty of room for a historiographical scope that falls somewhere on the continuum between micro- and macro-, which would allow me to answer my overarching questions.[21] However, my attempts to consider non-disciplinary institutional exigencies have been complicated by rhetoric and composition histories' traditional disciplinary focus. Focus, as noted earlier, is the second concern "genitive history" is meant to address. In the next section, therefore, I continue a bit longer *via negativa* by complicating historiographical scope in relation to disciplinary focus. Following that, I finally turn to a positive definition of genitive history.

FOCUS: ON DISCIPLINE

As Henze, Selzer, and Sharer's definitions make plain, macro-histories effectively define the concerns of the discipline at large by mapping disciplinary borders and limitations, and micro-histories tend to work as finely tuned correctives to the terrain demarcated by macro-histories. In both cases, however, disciplinary issues constitute the common focus. Here I am borrowing David R. Shumway and Craig Dionne's definition of "discipline" as "historically specific forms of knowledge production, having certain organizational characteristics, making use of certain practices, and existing in a particular institutional environment"

(2002, 1–2).[22] In the contemporary academy, disciplines are intellectual "enterprises[s] designed to produce or discover knowledge" based on the distributed cultivation of shared methods, rules, definitions, techniques, tools, and truths (ibid., 2–3).

To trace the contours of disciplinary focus as a "concern," we might briefly consider micro- and macro-historical scopes in terms of Kenneth Burke's rhetorical theory. Burke's work does not function as a major emphasis in this history, but I introduce it here because the method of dramatistic analysis he sets out in *A Grammar of Motives* (1969) affords me some advantageous concepts for elucidating the historiographical stakes of *Conceding Composition*. The first dramatistic concept I want to borrow is Burke's notion of circumferences. "Ideally," Burke writes, "we might locate an act in a set of widening circles, ranging from the uniquely particularized through placements in terms of broad cultural developments to absolute concepts of relationship or ground" (ibid., 86–87). He continues, "We might say that [choices about which circle to emphasize] mark out a circumference by spotlight, while the rest of the stage is left dark" (ibid., 87).

To stick with Burke's analogy, macro- and micro-histories of composition education tend to represent different circumferences. Macro-histories draw broad circumferences, survey widely, and characterize historical developments generally; micro-histories draw more restricted circumferences and complicate or challenge macro-histories through local analyses. Regardless of how a circumference is drawn, however, the spotlight tends to illuminate the performance area of the stage to a greater or lesser degree. In this case, the lighted area constitutes the expanse of the discipline—its shared body of knowledge and its attendant values, practices, and beliefs. Micro-histories may cast light at the edges, but they tend basically to stay onstage.

In effect, regardless of circumference, rhetoric and composition's histories may look at very different parts of the proverbial stage, but they still tend to share a common disciplinary focus—namely, how to draw rhetoric and composition's disciplinary borders in light of the complicating factors they study.[23] This work to define and redefine the disciplinary terrain is what David R. Shumway and Ellen Messer-Davidow call "boundary-work" (1991, 208; see also Vandenberg 1996). According to Shumway and Messer-Davidow, "Boundary-work determines which methods and theories are included [in a given discipline], which should be excluded, and which may be imported" (1991, 209). Despite the number of complex, interanimating variables afforded by the term *discipline* (including theory, practice, pedagogy, material conditions, and the profession) and the infinite number of circumferential choices to be made, the basic guiding question in rhetoric and composition's histories is, what can historical inquiry tell us about the discipline's proper dimensions? Notwithstanding the significant complexity and important scholarly contributions represented in rhetoric and composition histories, by and large the disciplinary focus holds because it helps answer our central questions: What shall we teach? What shall we study?[24]

To be sure, boundary-work in disciplinary histories is not just to establish or protect disciplinary territory. Disciplinary histories are also intended to help scholars and teachers understand the historical causes of our present existence and to reconceive the disciplinary work we do in productive ways. Thomas Miller (1997, 8) points out that the next step for historians after determining the disciplinary limits has been a "pragmatic turn" to study "the institutional practices of the field [of English studies], and then articulating the work of the field to broader audiences"—that is, communicating our disciplinary knowledge. Historians may choose to look at theories, at pedagogies, at cultural influences, at institutional practices, at keywords, at aporias and lacunae even. In some cases, historians cobble various circumferences together, tack back and forth between different circumferences, and bring other disciplines' theories to bear on rhetoric and composition histories to develop interdisciplinary, multidisciplinary, and transdisciplinary insights. And based on what a given historian determines about historical developments, she can make a case for what rhetoric and composition teachers, scholars, and administrators should understand or do differently in the present in hopes of affecting positive disciplinary change in the future.

Identifying disciplinary issues as historians' common focus may seem simply a matter of stating the obvious. Placing disciplinary concerns at the focal point of disciplinary historians' investigative circumferences makes good sense. This is especially the case given rhetoric and compositionists' perennial struggle to earn disciplinary status on par with other disciplines, such as philosophy and literature. What else would disciplinary historians focus on, after all? As Joseph Harris (1997, x) succinctly demonstrates, shared concerns, and the ways they are defined and redefined by members of the field, establish systems of values and enable certain kinds of practices. The discipline constitutes the basic scene in which rhetoric and composition specialists study and teach, and historians establish the shared stories that (1) help teachers and scholars understand the parameters that constitute their professional lives and (2) imagine ways to work collectively toward disciplinary goals.[25]

In his widely cited essay "Writing the History of Our Discipline," Robert J. Connors (1991b, 63) makes the case even more plainly: composition historians "are immediately implicated in their subject . . . From Kitzhaber on . . . composition historians have never had the luxury of scholarly distance. They exist, as composition specialists have for a century, in a world of complex social and institutional problems whose solution is writing teachers' charge." This inability to establish distance may or may not be the common condition twenty-five years after Connors's essay was published. Nevertheless, his basic insight remains unchanged: the sort of disciplinary focus I am raising as a "concern" in rhetoric and composition histories is part and parcel of how rhetoric and compositionists define the field's values, interests, practices, and limits.

It is with this last one, hiding in plain view, that I am presently concerned. As distinguished decolonial scholar Walter D. Mignolo (2012, xvi) puts it, "Disciplines are by definition based on territorial epistemologies," and he heralds non-disciplinary border dwelling as a method to denaturalize the territoriality of disciplines. Mignolo's book is focused on different (much larger) questions than is *Conceding Composition*, to be sure, but his provocative theoretical work underscores my argument about focus. When disciplinary issues are the common conceptual focus, even if borders are continually transgressed and redrawn, it can nevertheless still be hard for historians to establish the kind of radically defamiliarizing perspectives necessary to understand the field's "social and institutional problems" in productively unfamiliar ways.[26]

To be clear, I am not condemning historians' disciplinary focus, much less attempting to demolish and replace it. It has been and remains absolutely vital for helping teachers, researchers, and administrators negotiate the complicated factors that shape rhetoric and composition's existence in the academy. And, of course, I'm attempting to add to it by drawing attention to non-disciplinary institutional exigencies. Nevertheless, such a focus has the effect of privileging disciplinary concerns tied to theory (making disciplinary knowledge) and pedagogy (distributing disciplinary knowledge) in ways that obscure potentially productive lines of inquiry—including, it should be obvious by now, non-disciplinary institutional exigencies—necessary to understand the place of rhetoric and composition in the larger system of higher education. As a result, disciplinary answers to my questions are generally unsatisfying. Changes in composition education are almost always conceived in terms of disciplinary reactions to institutional/cultural contexts.[27] Historians tend to locate these changes retrospectively, by locating effects in the discipline, usually in the form of crises that affected studying or teaching composition, and tracking their causes. Where non-disciplinary exigencies are considered, then, they are generally considered contextual, and we understand them in relation to their effects on teaching and research.

Conversely, without evidence of disciplinary change qua crisis, it can be hard to recognize not-explicitly-disciplinary exigencies that shape our territory indirectly by shaping the institutions in which composition education exists. For instance, changes to a university's accreditation procedures will generally go unremarked unless they directly affect how people teach and study rhetoric and writing. Even then, recognition of crisis might be localized to a particularly troublesome institution without illuminating the effects of similar accreditation standards at 5 or 50 or 500 institutions.[28] In other words, disciplinary constraints establish good (if often imperceptible) reasons for historians to overlook exigencies that were enormously consequential for institutions of higher education but that do not connect easily to perceptible shifts in the discipline.

From a disciplinary perspective, non-disciplinary institutional exigencies might be precursors to, reactions to, or consequences of the discipline's concerns, but they tend not to be the subject of much scrutiny beyond their contextualizing influence because they exist apart from what we teach and research. To casuistically stretch Henze, Selzer, and Sharer's insights, if disciplinary histories stake out the proper intellectual boundaries and developments in the field, by definition non-disciplinary institutional exigencies are categorically exiled.

The common disciplinary focus that anchors histories of composition education and makes them valuable also unavoidably impedes the kinds of questions I want to ask about how composition education existed in relation to institutions of higher education. Thus, while *Conceding Composition* is not an attempt to escape disciplinarity, it is an attempt to temporarily bracket it. To return briefly to Burke's circumferential analogy, if disciplinary histories illuminate the performance area of the stage, the history I am proposing is an attempt to occupy a seat in the audience from which to see the lighted area of the stage, as well as the supports underneath the stage, the rigging, the guy-wires, and the spotlight operators. And maybe even to get a glimpse of the marketing campaigns designed to fill the seats. It is an attempt to develop a more capacious view of the theater. The general question this genitive history is designed to ask, then, is, what might we learn about the existence of composition education in America if we set the history of non-disciplinary institutional exigencies alongside the numerous insights afford by histories of the discipline?

Before I finally introduce the concept of "genitive history" to which I have thus far only alluded, I want to point out two further elements comprised by Burke's dramatistic theories that are particularly useful for my purposes. The first is an assumption of generosity I find especially appealing. Burke is cautious to note that calling terminological assumptions into question does not necessitate "debunking" (1969, 77–108; see also Burke 1984a). That is, looking at the struts under the stage does not require proving that a focus on the performance area of the stage is wrong or bad or insignificant or naive—only that there are other ways to see that can be valuable. In the spirit of Burke's presumptive generosity, I submit that *Conceding Composition* is not an attempt to show that disciplinary micro-histories or macro-histories have been wrong or inferior.

Rather, and second, by calling certain historiographical assumptions into question, I hope to illuminate different issues and concerns in rhetoric and composition's history. Someone at ASU made an explicit decision to change English 1 to English 101. It was, as I describe in later chapters, a decision based on specific institutional needs that cannot be precisely described by reference to disciplinary knowledge. And it happened in colleges and universities all over the country. By considering it carefully, we may not learn how the discipline advanced, exactly, but we do stand to discover formative constraints—and the enduring stakes for teachers, researchers, administrators, and the discipline—we may not previously have thought to consider. With that said, in the next section I delineate genitive history as a methodology for taking in the expanse of the historical theater.

GENITIVE HISTORY: ON EXCEPTIONS AND RULES

Detailing rhetoric and composition histories' common scopes and focus at length, as I have done above, demonstrates some of their limitations for the work *Conceding Composition* proposes to undertake, but it also demonstrates some of their strengths that are invaluable for this study. First, I want to maintain the narrow scope of micro-history alongside the comprehensive scope of macro-history. Second, I want to be able to illuminate disciplinary issues without being inextricably anchored to them. In an effort to retain these valuable aspects of the micro/macro model and to add a new dimension to rhetoric and composition historiography that directs attention to non-disciplinary institutional exigencies, I offer the concept of "genitive history."

As noted, I take the term *genitive* from the field of linguistics, in which it is commonly defined as a grammatical case that refers to possession or close relation. In the English language, the genitive is frequently indicated by the "apostrophe-s" construction. For instance, in the phrase "Helen's face launched a thousand ships," the genitive case signifies that Helen—the possessor—owns the face of Helen—the thing possessed.[29] The possessive quality of the genitive is obviously advantageous for the historiographical theory I am developing (i.e., to talk about Arizona State University's composition education). But what makes the genitive especially appealing to me is the inclusion of a second, interconnected sense of "close relation."

Linguist Kiki Nikiforidou (1991, 151) argues, "The various meanings of the genitive case represent a single polysemous category. This means that they form a coherent unit which relies on systematic connections between all the manifested uses of the genetive [sic]." As Nikiforidou conceives it, the genitive case represents a systematic, "non-accidental" grouping of integrally related components, which can be usefully considered in their particularities, as well as in relation to, and as a reflection of, the larger category. In other words, Helen's face may be unique in its capacity to launch seafaring vessels, but we can only make sense of it because it is one manifestation of "face" that indicates an entire category of visages. Inflected thus, the notion of possession is not a simple claim to ownership. "Helen's face" also indicates a categorical relationship—a group affiliation with identifiable characteristics that maintain across multiple instances of people and faces. Moreover, each individual relationship between person and face may play out in radically differing ways—some may not launch a single ship—without invalidating the categorical association.

More important for my purposes, studying a single relationship between person and face may shed light on important characteristics that concern all person/face relationships. To bring it back to the history of composition, by studying composition education closely at a single institution, it is possible to locate concerns that affected composition education at institutions more broadly. It is therefore possible to understand categorical features and the constitutive limits of the group by studying individual examples and testing them against other categorical constituents. In other words, close examination in one instance requires close examination at additional instances to determine what is common among them and what is not. One additional key to the genitive case as I am using it is that the grouping of components represents strong associational ties without being unavoidably determinative. Put differently, genitive possession indicates close association—possibly even sources or origins—without necessarily rising to the level of genetics.[30]

I adopt the term *genitive* for three reasons. First, it is commonly accepted among rhetoric and composition specialists that terminological choices are inextricably linked to the conceptual parameters in which inquiry can be undertaken. Changing terminology changes parameters. So at the most basic level, genitive history is an attempt to terminologically shift away from the more conventional macro-historical and micro-historical scopes and disciplinary focuses to open up the space for considering non-disciplinary institutional exigencies. Connected to this terminological shift is an attempt to back off, at least to some degree, my claim to "comprehensiveness" above. I take seriously Mignolo's claim that "there are no histories other than local" but that local histories can nevertheless take up "planet-wide and diverse" concerns (2012, x). Genitive history, therefore, is a matter of writing a differently local history than previous disciplinary histories have tended to do.

My other reasons for introducing genitive history are tied to the genitive's specific conceptual attributes. Consider first the possessive genitive aspects of composition education at Arizona State University. ASU was the possessor of its composition education and can be valuably understood as such. ASU's institutional policies, faculty and administrative employees, student body, and so on were specific to the institution in a number of ways. And ASU's composition education (that which is possessed) therefore was intended to meet the institution's (the possessor's) distinct needs. Investigating ASU's composition education as a singular manifestation can enlighten our understanding of composition education in a particular place, in significant detail, with specific evidence.

That said and perhaps more important, *Conceding Composition* is a genitive history because of its associational resonances—because, despite its localized manifestations, ASU's composition education was not atypical. Studying it closely can reveal important non-disciplinary institutional factors that existed across the category. At the broadest level, ASU is "an institution of higher education," and as such it is systematically connected to the group of "institutions of higher education" and may be studied as a component of that category. But it was also a normal school, teachers' college, comprehensive regional college, and research university. It is a state institution in a specific locale populated by specific individuals with their own categorical relations, and so on. The associations/affiliations/expectations around which these categories were structured at particular historical moments are suggestive and allow me to draw inferences from ASU that inform claims about the larger group without being strictly determinative.

The theoretical contours of genitive history involve certain practical considerations as well. Genitive history initially directs historians' attention to issues of *institutional implementation*. Specifically, what institutional mechanisms were necessary for certain kinds of composition education to come into being and subsequently exist at a particular place? What funding sources had to be established or tapped? What deliberative bodies had to take up, debate, and vote on institutional actions? What kinds of political, rhetorical, and promotional campaigns were waged, either prior to or as a result of changes to composition education? Who supported or opposed changes to composition education, how, and why? In short, what concessions were made and why?

These questions and others like them may not seem novel, so let me give one example of how they might inflect disciplinary histories. Connors argues that the escalation of mechanical correctness in nineteenth-century composition classes was a result of cultural concerns about linguistic propriety.[31] He writes that "the beginnings of a structured system of social classes in America" in the late nineteenth century led to "an ethic of 'gentility' and correctness . . . in Americans' attitudes toward speaking and writing" (Connors 1986, 28). This ethic of gentility and correctness, according to Connors, subsequently translated into "the first 'back-to-basics' movement, the first stab at remedial college English," and an eighty-year disciplinary investment in "the single-minded enforcement of standards of mechanical and grammatical correctness in writing" (ibid.). We might say this "first stab" was a concession to concerned citizens.

Connors seems to imagine that nineteenth-century college and university administrators and faculty were universally conscious enough of the linguistic zeitgeist to address it directly through curricular revolution—the introduction of first-year composition—and pedagogical techniques—simplified and instrumentalized instruction in style, grammar, and correctness. Perhaps that was the case. In Connors's history, however, there is no indication of the institutional or extra-institutional mechanisms necessary for coordinating first-year composition at hundreds, perhaps thousands, of institutions across the country. To be frank, Connors circumvents any explanation of how "an ethic of gentility and correctness" materially translated into the first back-to-basics movement because he has no way to explain it without abandoning his macro-historical scope.

A genitive history, on the other hand, would begin by seeking specific evidence at a specific institution about how such translation from cultural zeitgeist to institutional policy occurred. It would attempt to discover what specific actions were undertaken to put first-year composition on the books at Harvard or Howard or Middle Tennessee State.

Researching and writing such a history entails looking for evidence of composition education in local and university archives, English department records, university documents, and more, to be sure. But genitive history also entails looking for evidence of larger non-disciplinary forces that brushed up against composition education in real, if sometimes indirect, ways. Examining such points of contact can help make sense of who conceded composition, how they did so, and why. To revive an example from my introduction, why did ASU transform "English 1" into "English 101"? I can assure you, it was not a consequence of rhetoric and composition's theoretical or pedagogical efforts, nor was it an intuitive administrative response to an inchoate cultural shift.

Colleges and universities are notorious for resisting change, especially radical change. If we mean to understand how and why changes are ultimately made, then, it is necessary to understand specifically what actions were taken. Such investigation requires that historians look beyond disciplinary evidence concerning composition *instruction* to non-disciplinary institutional evidence concerning composition *education.* The investigation might be loosely driven by the possessive genitive questions, "what distinguishes a particular institution's composition education" or "what institutional needs did composition meet." Answering these questions might take historians into presidential papers, board of regents minutes, local newspaper accounts, faculty and administrator interviews, legal and legislative documents, and more. To borrow a phrase from Michel Foucault (1977, 140), genitive history requires "patience and a knowledge of details and it depends on a vast accumulation of source material."

If the initial focus in genitive history is on issues of *institutional implementation,* the subsequent and equally essential focus is on issues of *institutional reduplication.* Here, I am defining reduplication in terms of the associational genitive—the systematic, "non-accidental," integrally related components that indicate larger categorical relationships. In other words, investigating institutional implementation at one institution should help historians identify the reduplication of exigencies at other institutions, even if the responses to those exigencies varied radically from one institution to the next. Discovering that one face has a nose suggests the possibility that all faces may have noses, even if some are aquiline and others are snubbed.

If investigating *implementation* seeks to situate composition education in a local time and place, *reduplication* seeks to discover evidence of "comprehensive" exigencies that existed in specific times at multiple places. This stage of the investigation is also "gray, meticulous, and patiently documentary" (ibid., 139) which do establish shared institutional exigencies and potentially shared responses. To put it more concretely, the genitive history I am proposing in *Conceding Composition* directs attention to the development of a single "writing program" at an "obscure institution" in light of very particular, even seemingly idiosyncratic exigencies without surrendering the associational relationships necessary for considering ASU in terms of "highly structured and motivated" groupings (Nikiforidou 1991, 151) that characterized American higher education more broadly at a given historical moment.

By identifying *Conceding Composition* as a genitive history, I can track complex historical developments in Arizona State University's composition education along various axes while retaining the sense that ASU was inextricably and meaningfully associated with other institutions of higher education—some of which may not have even offered composition courses. In this study, I tracked genitive associations from ASU to five other institutions—the University of North Texas, the University of Indianapolis, Harvard University, the University of Kansas, and the University of California, Berkeley. At each institution, I conducted extensive primary research in the respective university archives and secondary research in books and journals, government documents, and official and unofficial institutional publications. Although it is not always clear in the chapters that follow, my research also depended on illuminating discussions with people at each campus. I use this research throughout *Conceding Composition* to cast ASU's example into high relief.

A brief note on my choice of institutions. The makeup of this list may seem odd, but at least at first, the choices were not odd. I chose ASU because I was a graduate student there. I chose the University of North Texas because it was where I took my first academic job. I chose Harvard because it came up repeatedly in my research. After Harvard, though, my choices became more deliberately odd. On the one hand, I decided that evidence of reduplication should be somewhat random. That is, if my claim that institutional exigencies were often widely shared is sound, then I thought I should be able to track evidence of reduplication at almost any postsecondary institution in the country, given the appropriate historical circumstances.[32] So I picked other institutions based on places to which I was traveling—Lawrence, Kansas, for a Rhetoric Society of America institute, Indianapolis to attend a CCCC convention, and Berkeley for another research project I was working on. To some degree, then, my method of selection was willfully haphazard.

On the other hand, I also tried to choose institutions that are manifestly different—in size, student population, geographic location, funding models, endowments, admissions practices, prestige, religious affiliations, and so on. Harvard is an elite East Coast Ivy. Kansas and Berkeley are land-grant universities—products of the famous 1862 Morrill Act. Kansas was a frontier school when it was founded in 1865, and Berkeley was way out on the West Coast. The University of North Texas and the University of Indianapolis began as normal schools like ASU—North Texas a for-profit, private school that quickly turned public, and Indianapolis a private religious institution founded by the Church of the United Brethren in Christ. Like ASU, both evolved into universities over the course of several decades. Each institution also has a very different relationship to the field. Obviously, some institutions on this list—especially Harvard but also Kansas and UC Berkeley—have been investigated in rhetoric and composition scholarship. Others do not register anywhere in our research and might never register again beyond the covers of this book. This is ultimately a strength of the group, given my claims about the benefits of genitive historiography.

The characteristics of each institution are elaborated in more depth in the various chapters, but suffice to say, each contributes in some way to my overarching claim that first-year composition has long served institutional goals that are largely independent of composition's intellectual aims. In the history I am proposing, then, ASU's composition education is both a genitive entry point and a genitive departure point. The goal is not to determine how composition was taught at every institution in America. Rather, it is to assess how composition education has been broadly and categorically implemented in institutions of higher education and how it has been conceded to institutional ends at institutions across the country.

NOTA BENE

In *Conceding Composition*, I think I am ambitious in arguing that composition has been a concession in American higher education and in developing genitive history to make this case. This book may appear less ambitious in other ways, particularly in my organization of the analyses, which amount to a fairly traditional, chronological long view. I deliberately chose this traditional organization, along with a fairly traditional narrative presentation, to emphasize my central argument about composition in the university. Nevertheless, I consider this study a preliminary endeavor, not the last word on the subject. As such, I readily accept that both my central argument and my methodology will require further investigation to test their persuasiveness.

2

CONCEDING COMPOSITION TO CREATE A NEW NORMAL

In discussing the function of the normal school Dr. [Edwin C.] Hewett emphasized the necessity of a thorough understanding of the subjects to be taught, as well as an understanding of the pupil and the method of instruction. While noting great variation among normals, he classed them all together on the basis of their sole aim to prepare teachers.
—Homer Hurst, *Illinois State Normal University and the Public Normal School Movement*

The work of the normal school is unique. It means more than teaching subjects; it means more than the developing of character; it means the teaching of subjects that they in turn may be taught; it means the development of character that it in turn may be transfigured into character; it means such a preparation for life that it in turn may prepare others to enter fully, readily, and righteously into their environment. Thus to prepare an individual to lead and direct a little child is a grave responsibility.
—National Education Association, "Report of the Committee on Normal Schools"

According to Arizona State University historians Ernest Hopkins and Alfred Thomas Jr., in the last decades of the nineteenth century "Normal Schools . . . were on the main beam of the movement toward universal education and were in high regard" (1960, 44).[1] Normal schools, often called simply "normals," were prominent institutions in American education for the better part of a century, and historians have begun to demonstrate that composition was vital to their systems of instruction.[2] Approximately 200 public normal schools were founded in 46 states between 1839 and 1927 with the express mission of training teachers for the nation's rapidly expanding public school system.[3] Tempe Normal School (TNS) was one of them, and it represented one of the Arizona Territory's earliest attempts to join the movement toward universal education.[4] The first public schools were founded in Arizona in the 1870s, but they were very unstable, generally under-funded, and

DOI: 10.7330/9781607325055.c002

poorly attended. In some cases, schools would open in an area of the territory only to shut down after just one session. In part, this instability was caused by a lack of qualified teachers, and some of the Arizona Territory's early politicians, including Governor Anson P.K. Safford, the so-called Father of the Arizona Public School (McCrea 1908, 101), thought that establishing a territorial normal school would help solve the teacher shortage problem (Hopkins and Thomas 1960, 43–44). It was to this end that Tempe Normal was established.

Founded in 1885, Tempe Normal School came into existence just one year after Harvard's introduction of its fabled first-year composition course, "English A." While Harvard's Adams Sherman Hill was answering the cry for more English in the East, TNS faculty and administrators were attempting to meet a pressing need for qualified teachers in Arizona's fledgling elementary education system. One of my explicit goals in this chapter is to challenge the false equivalence of composition at universities like Harvard and at normal schools like Tempe Normal. I contend that despite composition's importance in normal schools, it was fundamentally different from composition at colleges and universities as a direct consequence of normal schools' unique institutional mission—teaching teachers to teach in public elementary and high schools (Ogren 2005, 32–33). This normal school mission shaped every aspect of Tempe Normal, including who designed curricula, what the appropriate course of study was, what kinds of students would be invited to attend the normal, and more; and those decisions were expressly intended to distinguish the normal school from colleges and universities.[5]

But the timing of Tempe Normal's founding relative to Harvard's introduction of "English A" is suggestive and cannot simply be disregarded. The appearance of composition at both campuses at nearly the same time would seem to indicate a valuable point of historical confluence. The chronological parallel is reinforced by striking intellectual similarities in Harvard's and TNS's composition courses. As I detail below, the intellectual traditions informing TNS's composition courses resonate nicely with what historians have described in first-year composition courses across the country around the turn of the twentieth century. The obvious chronological and intellectual similarities that connect universities and normal schools would therefore seem also to be the appropriate grounds for considering composition as a concession. And yet, as I said, one of my explicit goals is to argue that such a comparison is mistaken. In fact, I contend that the intellectual similarities that make normals' composition instruction appear familiar to historians ultimately obscure institutional qualities that distinguished normal schools as viable institutions in the complicated education landscape of the nineteenth and twentieth centuries.

Given the distinctions it is necessary for me to make, this chapter unfolds somewhat unconventionally. I open the next section by highlighting some of the key intellectual similarities that seem to link composition instruction at Tempe Normal School to the broader history of first-year composition at colleges and universities. Although the intellectual parallels are compelling, however, one complicating factor is that TNS did not offer first-year composition courses. As I demonstrate, the absence of first-year composition is a crucial matter. Following my enumeration of similarities, therefore, I turn to considering issues of *institutional implementation*. Specifically, I consider carefully what specific institutional mechanisms were activated to bring composition education into being at Tempe Normal School such that it strongly resembled first-year composition without ever being first-year composition.

Working from this perspective, I argue that Tempe Normal officials conceded composition to fulfill the institution's mission. In Tempe Normal's case, composition was not a concession in the sense that administrators consciously traded it for other advantages. Rather, being "normal" meant conceding the right to offer courses that duplicated college and university courses, regardless of the nearly identical intellectual traditions informing rhetoric and writing instruction at each. My claim that composition education distinguished normal schools from other types of postsecondary institutions is equally a claim that normal schools conceded opportunities to offer forms of composition—most notably first-year composition—that would have muddied those distinctions.

In keeping with the methods of genitive history, I track the *reduplication* of institutional mission to a second normal school, North Texas Normal College (now the University of North Texas). By weighing North Texas Normal College's example against Tempe's, it becomes clear that composition in North Texas began as a concession on the order of Tempe Normal's—conceding composition to substantiate "normalness." However, at North Texas Normal, composition quickly became a concession in the more conventional sense. As I detail in the penultimate section of this chapter, North Texas Normal's mission was essentially the same as Tempe Normal's at first—training teachers to teach—but it became somewhat more complicated than Tempe Normal's as the result of a series of administrative and legislative shifts in the late nineteenth and early twentieth centuries, which compelled the school to align more closely with the state's colleges and universities. One way alignment was achieved was by conceding new forms of composition education.

North Texas Normal's example reaffirms the lessons I draw from Tempe Normal about composition as a function of the normal school mission. In addition, North Texas's practices of conceding composition to effect institutional transformations highlight composition's institutional, as opposed to intellectual, purposes.

INTELLECTUAL RESONANCES AT TEMPE NORMAL

When the Territorial Normal School at Tempe was founded in 1886, it was located in a complicated cultural, social, and educational scene. The US government passed a series of acts, including the 1862 Homestead Act and the 1877 Desert Land Act, that brought settlers west with the promise of free land for those who claimed and settled it, but in the 1880s the Arizona Territory was still essentially the Old West. Southern Pacific built the first railroad into the territory in 1880, Wyatt Earp and Doc Holliday shot up the OK Corral in 1881, and major battles in the so-called Apache Wars continued throughout Arizona until the Chiricahua leader, Goyahkla (Geronimo), surrendered in 1886. In contrast to A.S. Hill's Harvard, when the normal school was founded in Tempe, it was intended both to train teachers and to augment territorial settlement efforts. Still, there are interesting parallels.

As an important part of its teacher-training curriculum, Tempe Normal had extensive composition, rhetoric, and literacy requirements. Normal school students, colloquially known as "normalites," took a variety of reading, writing, language, and literature classes in nearly every semester they enrolled. TNS's students were rarely as thoroughly educated as elite East Coast college and university students. Nevertheless, composition at TNS bore striking intellectual resemblances to composition at other postsecondary institutions. At a glance, in fact, the intellectual traditions informing composition at Tempe Normal are practically indistinguishable from the traditions informing stereotypical first-year composition classrooms at places such as Harvard. I note five in this section, but this is hardly an exhaustive list.

To begin with, materials from Tempe Normal School exhibit vestiges of the predominant education theories in American education around the turn of the twentieth century. The philosophy of mental discipline—which Laurence Veysey (1970, 21) calls the "traditional philosophy" of learning in higher education throughout most of the 1800s—is evident in catalog descriptions of TNS's English curricula. In 1891–92, for instance, TNS's catalog stated that courses were "arranged in accordance with the order of mental development, and the successive studies were intended to furnish the healthful, educative discipline which the growing mind requires to produce complete and distinctive character as conducive to higher intellectual ability" (Thomas 1960a, 122). According to Sharon Crowley (1998a, 48), theories of mental discipline were grounded in the belief that training and drilling would strengthen the mind, much as muscles were strengthened by regular physical activities.[6] Likewise, Tempe Normal's 1896–97 "Circular and Catalogue" makes the implicit case for mental discipline by describing the aim of instruction in the English department as, among other things, exercising the imagination, giving "proper drills designed to give [expression] greater power, scope, and accuracy," and "train[ing] the muscles into ready submission to mind" ("General Catalogue" 1896, 14).

In keeping with the educative philosophy of mental discipline, the guiding rhetoric and composition theories from the time are also evident at TNS. Descriptions of the composition, rhetoric, and literacy courses at Tempe Normal between 1886 and 1910 rehearse the familiar narrative that composition instruction was progressively separated from rhetoric, formalized, and instrumentalized (Brereton 1995, 3–25; Connors 1997b, 112–70). According to the 1896–97 "Circular and Catalogue," for example, "Composition presents the principles and rules by which the different forms of discourse are constructed from sentences" ("General Catalogue" 1896, 16). Rhetoric, on the other hand, is "anterior to and apart from the superintendence of the student's work in composition" (ibid., 18). This separation of composition and rhetoric proceeds from the philosophy of mental discipline inasmuch as it suggests that strengthening basic foundations (composition) provides the grounds on which advanced work (rhetoric) can be constructed.

Given the apparent separation of rhetoric from composition, it is probably inevitable that both composition and rhetoric courses also evince the prevailing "current-traditional" theories from the period.[7] The modes of discourse—the familiar EDNA model of current-traditional rhetoric[8]—make their first appearance in course catalogs in 1896. Theme assignments, made famous by Harvard's Barrett Wendell, appeared in TNS's composition descriptions soon after. In the 1902–3 catalog, composition course descriptions indicate that "many themes are given, advancing by easy steps from simple narration and description to exposition and construction of argument" ("General Catalogue" 1902, 9). Themes were further institutionalized in 1904 as part of a "theme writing" course added to the junior-year curriculum ("General Catalogue" 1904, 22). In addition, catalogs from this period are rife with the unity-coherence-emphasis (alternatively unity-mass-coherence) model of writing instruction identified and critiqued by Albert Kitzhaber, James A. Berlin, and others.

Mechanical accuracy, correctness, and skills-and-drills also appear more regularly in Tempe Normal's course descriptions over the years. According to the 1901 catalog, the general aim of English instruction was "to secure accuracy and facility in the expression of thought [both in spoken language and written discourse] . . . It is recognized that even a reasonable degree of perfection in all these respects cannot be attained, except by constant drill, extending not over a single year but over a series of years" ("General Catalogue" 1901, 19). A decade later, in 1909, the goal of composition instruction was to provide practice in "sentence structure," "grammar," "logical thinking," "spelling and punctuation," "clear and correct expression," and "literary style, exposition and argument" ("General Catalogue" 1909, 20). "The purpose of composition work," according to the catalog, "is to develop in the sudent [*sic*] the power to express his thoughts not only clearly, correctly, and forcefully, but originally and spontaneously" (ibid.). It is noted that rhetoric coursework also entails composing themes and that "the whole theme and the paragraph are developed; but correctness of grammatical form and sentence structure are [*sic*] striven for especially, while due attention is paid to rehtorical [*sic*] clearness, force and diction" (ibid., 21). There is ample additional evidence to be found, but the descriptions offered thus far should be sufficient to showcase the prominence of current-traditionalism in TNS's English curriculum. If the gradual adoption of themes, modes, and mechanical correctness is any indication, Tempe Normal's rhetoric, composition, and literacy courses closely tracked intellectual developments in the nascent field of rhetoric and composition.

Another indication that composition progressed along familiar lines at TNS is found in textbook adoptions. At various times, Tempe's English faculty adopted textbooks by Adams Sherman Hill, Virginia Waddy, Fred Newton Scott and Joseph Denney, Gertrude Buck, George Quackenbos, John Genung, and others.[9] If we accept David Gold's (2008, 115) argument that "English instructors at normal schools revolted against what they saw as the limitations of traditional university pedagogical practices, especially overreliance on textbooks and lectures," the regular adoption of common composition and rhetoric textbooks at TNS nevertheless indicates faculty members' familiarity with intellectual developments in the field.

In addition, what little explicit pedagogical evidence exists in TNS's archives resonates with "traditional university pedagogical practices." In the only direct description of teaching methods I was able to locate in the archives, a student in TNS's inaugural class, James H. McClintock, describes the system of lectures and recitations around which the classes were constructed. Lecture and recitation were the hallmarks of rhetorical education at colleges and universities prior to 1875. According to McClintock, "Professor Farmer [the first teacher and principal at Tempe Normal] paid personal and especial attention to the recitations in English and Latin" (quoted in Thomas 1960a, 91). McClintock continues, "Principal Farmer believed in rhetoricals. Particularly did he approve of debates. I will remember how I fought for the Chinese exclusion act and for capital punishment, even after the clergy of Tempe had entered the lists on the other side" (ibid., 92). McClintock's description of Farmer's pedagogy is both limited and far removed from McClintock's time as a student, so it might not do justice to the full pedagogical complexity at TNS. Nevertheless, it appears consonant with contemporaneous methods in college and university classrooms around the country.

While combing through the archives, I found scant mention of pedagogy beyond McClintock's reminiscences, but there are occasional glimpses of pedagogical methods in Tempe Normal's course catalogs. In the 1909–10 "Annual Catalogue," for instance, it is noted that "a strong point is made of oral expression and of the correcting of themes" ("General Catalogue" 1909, 20), and "corrections are sometimes made by fellow-students, but usually by class criticism and, especially, by individual consultation with the instructor" (ibid., 21). Again, while limited, these descriptions rehearse familiar pedagogical practices widely discussed in composition histories.

Finally, I discovered one faculty publication from TNS indicating that normal school composition bore strong intellectual similarities to college composition. In 1911 the head of Tempe Normal's English department, James Lee Felton, notes distastefully that contemporary textbooks were beginning to direct students to write themes "varying all the way from sociological and economic discourses to such startling narratives as 'A Trip to Mars,' and the 'Autobiography of a Cat'" (1911, 139). Such topics are perfectly in keeping with those apparently ascendant across the country (see Connors 1987; Kitzhaber 1990, 169–77). Writing and reading themes, Felton notes, usurped previous methods of teaching (which he does not describe but which we might surmise included lectures and recitations) and added heavily to the teacher's labor while simultaneously undermining options for conducting class.

In Felton's view, writing and correcting themes was a waste of everyone's time. Instead, "improvement [in student writing] will come only as a result of mastering the elementary laws of grammar and composition, and applying them constantly in practice" (Felton 1911, 143). From a contemporary perspective, Felton's pedagogical description is a mixed bag. Nevertheless, it is clear evidence that Felton was aware of, and even participating in, professional discussions about composition theories and pedagogies during the so-called current-traditional era. By the time Felton was writing in 1911, his experiences reflected a new paradigm. Lectures and recitations were gone and teaching had devolved into an endless cycle of assigning, correcting, returning, and discussing themes, none of which required teachers to know anything more than what was in the textbook (ibid., 139–40). It should come as no surprise that Felton's essay was published near the beginning of what many rhetoric and composition historians have come to consider a decades-long "period of stasis" in which composition instruction became all but intellectually inert (Brereton 1995, 25).

Without needing to look much further than course catalogs, there are many intellectual parallels historians can draw between composition at Tempe Normal and composition at colleges and universities. Clear parallels in education theories and language and literacy theories emerge; rhetoric and composition were simplified, instrumentalized, and inflected with current-traditional sensibilities; and textbooks, pedagogical methods, and faculty publications seem to be thoroughly products of their time. Add TNS's founding of two literary societies in 1896,[10] the establishment of a school newspaper and literary journals around the turn of the twentieth century,[11] and the inauguration of intercollegiate debates in the early 1900s,[12] and Tempe Normal School's history aligns tidily with histories of rhetoric, writing, and literacy instruction across the country at the time. On intellectual grounds, strong claims can be made about composition at Tempe Normal School as it compares to composition at any number of other American colleges and universities. There are, however, notable institutional reasons to question the plausibility of intellectual comparisons.

INSTITUTIONAL IMPLEMENTATION, OR NORMALIZING COMPOSITION

One distinguishing characteristic of Tempe Normal's composition education was that normalites took courses in, or related to, composition in almost every semester of their coursework. Instead of a single (or even dual) first-year composition course, Tempe's composition education comprised multiple courses, including composition, rhetoric, grammar, and literature. Composition was a fundamental element of normal school education rather than a deficiency to be overcome with a semester of remedial instruction. As a result, the recognizable intellectual traditions noted in the previous section are in wide evidence in TNS's archives because normalites learned about composition and practiced composing throughout the majority of their course of study.

At first, I considered it a distinct advantage that composition was distributed throughout TNS's curriculum. Notwithstanding some theoretical and pedagogical beliefs that seem misguided from a contemporary vantage point, TNS's distributed writing curriculum appealed to me as a writing teacher—something even worth recovering, given the relative paucity of direct composition instruction in many twenty-first-century postsecondary institutions. But TNS's distributed composition curriculum represented a quandary for me as a historian. I struggled to understand Tempe Normal in relation to disciplinary histories, including landmark studies by Berlin, Brereton, Connors, Crowley, and Kitzhaber that claimed first-year composition was all but universal by 1900. It should be clear that composition instruction at TNS is readily recognizable in the intellectual context of first-year composition at colleges and universities. And yet despite all the intellectual trappings of first-year composition, Tempe Normal never offered, much less required, first-year composition throughout its forty years as a normal school.

The disjuncture between intellectual correspondence and institutional absence proved a major sticking point for me when I was in the archives. I found myself trying to account for why first-year composition was not implemented at Tempe Normal School when all the signs seemed to point in that direction. This complication opened up to a series of additional questions, among them: did anyone at TNS advocate for first-year composition, and if so, on what grounds? If TNS's composition education was not based on the deficiency model that apparently informed Harvard's English A, what model was it based on?[13] How could the Normal dedicate so much time to composition instruction and still meet the other curricular goals? And then, what were TNS's curricular goals, and how were they determined? Rather than fixate on first-year composition's absence, I wanted to understand the system of composition education TNS did have and try to explain why it existed. Put in genitive terms, I wanted to determine how TNS's composition was implemented and what institutional goals were served by the school's distributed model of composition.

In considering Tempe Normal's distributed model of composition, it is important to keep in mind that the school's mission and methods were relatively specific. TNS was designed to train normalites as teachers for Arizona's lower schools. This institutional mission was delineated when TNS was founded in 1885 and evoked at least fifty years worth of national discussions about the proper functions of normal schools (see, e.g., Barnard 1851). It is also important to note that normal schools were not second-rate consolation prizes, as some historians have implied (e.g., Butts and Cremin 1953, 449–50; Lucas 1999, especially chapter 2; Lucas 2006, 139–44).

In their history of Tempe Normal's beginnings, Hopkins and Thomas contend that TNS came into being as a result of intense lobbying efforts spearheaded by Tempe's "acknowledged founder and king," Charles Trumbull Hayden (1960, 41; see also Richardson 1964, 10–11).[14] Hayden believed a normal school was a smart economic venture for Tempe because it could be started quickly and would draw investment, settlement, and development to the area (Hopkins and Thomas 1960, 43–44). At the time of TNS's establishment, Hayden was a wealthy landowner, a judge, and Tempe's most prominent business leader, owning both the mill and general store. He profited considerably from Tempe's precipitous growth, spurred by the founding of Tempe Normal. Hayden was probably not entirely opportunistic. He was trained as a teacher, having attended a normal school in Connecticut before moving west to pursue entrepreneurial opportunities. So he may well have had a genuine interest in the educational opportunities for the state. Nevertheless, he was definitely interested in the possibilities for economic development represented by having the normal school in Tempe.

Hayden's belief that the normal was a good economic investment was well founded. According to education historian Christine A. Ogren, normal schools were important economic engines in many small towns (2005, 26). Important enough, in fact, that some towns actively lobbied state legislatures for the right to establish normal schools—efforts that included substantial donations of private tracts of land to influence legislators' decisions. Such was the case in Tempe, where residents George and Martha Wilson donated twenty acres of land to the territory for the establishment of the normal (Hopkins and Thomas 1960, 50–51).

The economic circumstances that occasioned TNS's founding also invite attention to the corresponding legislative circumstances—circumstances that ultimately connect to composition education at the new normal. Charles Trumbull Hayden did not simply found a private normal school, though it was possible to do so. Instead, Hayden and his associates directed extensive lobbying efforts at Arizona's Territorial Legislature to bring a state normal school to Tempe. Hopkins and

Thomas describe a years-long process on the part of Tempe's "leading citizens" to shape public opinion, groom political appointees, and negotiate the political favors necessary to claim the normal for Tempe. The normal school was eventually allotted to Tempe as part of a broad legislative agenda in 1885. Arizona's so-called Thieving Thirteenth legislature, widely considered one of its most intensely corrupt legislatures, distributed generous appropriations throughout the Arizona Territory that year, including funds for the normal school in Tempe, a land-grant university in Tucson (the University of Arizona), a mental health institution in Phoenix, a bridge in Pinal County, a prison in Yuma, and the territory's capital in Prescott (Robinson 1919, 339; Hopkins and Thomas 1960, 54). In this bargain, the normal school was considered one of the most desirable prizes because it came with an ongoing allocation of state funds.

Besides providing a sensational backstory, the legislative process that resulted in TNS's formation had significant effects on composition. One important effect was indirect. At the time the legislature established the normal school, it also established a five-member board of education. Arizona's board of education was separate from Arizona's board of regents, established at the same time to govern the University of Arizona in Tucson.[15] Members of the first board of education included Charles Trumbull Hayden (president) and Robert Lindley Long, the territorial superintendent of public instruction in Arizona. The board subsequently recruited Hiram Bradford Farmer, principal of public schools in Prescott, Arizona, to be TNS's first principal. Farmer's initial responsibilities included designing the normal's course of study. Hayden, Long, and Farmer were all normal school graduates and former schoolteachers.

The establishment of an independent board of education and the appointment of normal school graduates and schoolteachers as its members were of great consequence. For one, this ensured that Tempe Normal was designed and directed by people with interest and experience in the lower schools. Moreover, board members had little or no allegiance to the state university.[16] In fact, none of them had even attended a college or university, which was the case for the majority of normal school officials around the country at the time (see DeGarmo 1893, 411). More to my point, the normal and the university were deliberately designed in contrast to one another because they were intended to address different education needs—teacher training versus research. As such, their institutional missions were fundamentally different, and their curricula were designed with their different missions in mind.

The second legislative effect on composition education at TNS was more direct: the institutional mission defined in TNS's original charter constrained composition instruction to the secondary level. In the legislative act authorizing the establishment of the normal, TNS's institutional mission was defined as "instruction of persons, both male and female, in the art of teaching and in all the various branches that pertain to good common school education; also, to give instruction in the mechanical arts and in husbandry and agricultural chemistry, the fundamental law of the United States, and in what regards the rights and duties of citizens" ("An Act" 1885). Although "instruction in the mechanical arts and in husbandry and agricultural chemistry" was provided for in the charter, the board of education did not commission a curriculum for either mechanical arts or husbandry and agricultural chemistry until the 1910s (Hopkins and Thomas 1960, 84, 191–92). This deferral is noteworthy because the A&M component would have required additional "college" courses the normal proper did not need to offer (ibid., 84–85, 94).[17] In other words, the delay of A&M coursework meant that Tempe Normal's early curriculum was strictly "normal," encompassing two components: (1) "the art of teaching" and (2) "various branches that pertain to good common school education." This legislatively defined mission required normal school officials to implement a split system of instruction, which was characteristic of normal schools at the time.[18] The curriculum comprising the "art of teaching" was postsecondary, and the curriculum comprising the "various branches," including all the rhetoric, composition, and literacy instruction, was secondary.

I will return to "the art of teaching," but first I want to consider the "various branches." The "various branches that pertain to good common school education" in TNS's original charter were more generally referred to as "common branches," and they constituted the standard "academic" curriculum in the vast majority of nineteenth-century American public schools. According to education specialist Larry D. Burton (2010, 128), "There was surprising disagreement, particularly in the early 19th century, as to what these common branches were." In normal school president Alfred Holbrook's 1859 book, *The Normal, or, Methods of Teaching the Common Branches* (a book education historian Wayne Durrill [1997] asserts was the one text virtually all normal school students were obliged to read), the common branches are orthoepy, orthography, grammar, geography, arithmetic, and elocution. The 1903 *Report of the Commissioner of Education* states that earning an Arizona teaching certificate required applicants to pass tests in orthography, grammar, reading, writing, composition, civics, US history, geography, teaching methods, defining, arithmetic, physiology, and hygiene (US Commissioner of Education 1904, 470). Two decades later, education professor Werrett Charters (1924) describes the common branches as spelling, penmanship, language, grammar, reading, drawing, music, handicrafts, geography, history, civics, arithmetic, physiology and hygiene, agriculture, and subject-matter. Despite significant differences between these lists, and although they could be inflected by local conditions and individual instructors' proclivities, the common branches generally revolved around reading, writing, arithmetic, and geography. In the normal school context, "instruction pertaining to the various branches" referred specifically to the widespread practice of reviewing basic subjects that were taught in elementary and high schools.

For practical reasons, many normal schools enrolled students with very little, and in some cases no, prior formal education. Normalites needed to be educated in the same subjects they would eventually be expected to teach, so it was necessary for normal schools to provide instruction in the common branches—in some cases as an introduction to the subjects and in other cases as a refresher course (Herbst 1980, 220; Ogren 2005, 86). In Arizona, territorial schools were scattered and unreliable, so many prospective normalites had no prior schooling. When TNS opened its doors in 1886, the first term of the first year consisted entirely of common branches: reading, writing, geography, arithmetic (Farmer 1886, 2). In fact, "instruction pertaining to the various branches" represented a significant portion of TNS's offerings for a long time. According to Thomas, "For several years after its beginning, the work of [Tempe] Normal was carried on largely at the high school level with a small portion of the program being devoted to teacher training work" (1960b, 315).

TNS's curriculum was permeated with language instruction so teachers would be prepared to teach basic literacy to young students. But as I argue elsewhere, composition was classed among the "various branches" at TNS, meaning it was implemented exclusively at the secondary level (Skinnell 2013). In 1888, normalites took "English Composition" in their first year, alongside grammar, spelling, reading, and word analysis ("General Catalogue" 1888). In 1901, students took "Grammar and Composition" in both semesters of the first year, along with elocution and word analysis, and they took "Rhetoric and Composition" and "Rhetoric and Grammar," respectively, in the first and second semesters of their second year ("General Catalogue" 1901, 17). These years, however, corresponded roughly to the ninth and tenth grades (McClintock 1900). Moreover, there were no additional composition requirements beyond those years.

In 1918, thirty years after the school first opened, Tempe Normal's course of study had expanded and changed in important ways, some of which I detail in chapter 3. One thing that was unchanged, however, was the place of composition in the secondary coursework. The 1918 "Bulletin of the Tempe Normal School of Arizona" notes that required instruction in English includes "word analysis, grammar and analysis, rhetoric, composition, theme writing, reading and literature" and "is based on the requirements for college and university *entrance* as outlined by the American Board of College Entrance" ("General Catalogue" 1918, 40–41, emphasis added). As this description makes plain, composition was one among a number of courses that could prepare students to enter college—it was not pitched as college-equivalent. As a consequence of the normal school mission, composition remained preparatory to postsecondary work. To be very clear, it was not considered "remedial" in the contemporary sense. Rather, it properly belonged in the secondary work, itself a standard component of normal school work.

In contrast to the secondary "academic" coursework, TNS's postsecondary coursework was "professional," and it was exclusively focused on imparting administrative and teaching methods. The "art of teaching" delineated in TNS's charter was widely understood to refer to professional teaching methods—"those principles of our nature on which education depends; the laws which control the faculties of the youthful mind in the pursuit and attainment of truth; and the moral sentiments on the part of the teacher and pupil which must be brought into harmonious action" (Edward Everett, quoted in Ogren 2005, 32). Such a description may seem inflated and ambiguous in the twenty-first century, but in the nineteenth century Everett's description would have been easily recognizable as a reference to "general teaching methods." The provision of "general teaching methods" was the defining characteristic of normal schools.[19] As superintendent of Denver schools Aaron Gove wrote in his contribution to the 1903 *Report of the Commissioner of Education*, "The education covered in the average normal school corresponds well to that of the secondary school, with the increased task of professional work" (1904, 357).[20] The postsecondary focus on the art of teaching—that is, professional methods—was believed to be normal schools' greatest institutional strength, and it often included lessons in subjects such as "school-room duties, study, recitation, school business, recreation, and school government" (Ogden 1879, iii–iv).[21]

At TNS specifically, normalites' postsecondary courses included "Primary Methods," "Arithmetic Methods," "Pedagogy," "School Management," and "Professional Work" ("General Catalogue" 1888). Except for Latin and geometry, TNS's postsecondary curriculum was entirely focused on methods and practice (roughly the equivalent to student teaching). In later years, required courses included "Book-k'ing & Com. Law," "Sch. Law & Sch. Economy," "Methods," and "Practice Teaching" ("General Catalogue" 1904, 21). By the beginning of the twentieth century, normalites at TNS were required to take postsecondary courses in literature, physics, geography, and other courses we might now consider "content courses," but only in service of developing subject-specific pedagogical methods—the "peculiar methods, applicable to each branch of knowledge" (Everett, quoted in Ogren 2005, 32). More to the point, composition was not among them. Any engagement normalites had with composition at the postsecondary level, as part of the "Practice Teaching" for instance, was strictly in the context of acquiring the methods deemed necessary to teach it.

Composition's presence in Tempe Normal's secondary curriculum and its absence from the postsecondary curriculum was not ultimately an intellectual question so much as an institutional one. Composition helped normal schools align with, and contrast to, other institutions by paralleling the common branches typical of secondary education and avoiding the first-year variety of composition at other colleges and universities. The fact that composition at Tempe Normal School bore strong intellectual similarities to first-year composition without ever taking the specific institutional form underscores the value of closely examining institutional implementation. Doing so makes clear that the normal school's institutional mission, as articulated by Arizona's legislature and implemented by Tempe Normal School officials, ensured that composition was a secondary "academic" subject, not a postsecondary "professional" one. The institutional mission constrained composition to certain functions within the curriculum that were all but unrelated to the courses' specific intellectual content. Irrespective of the intellectual traditions informing composition's *instruction*, Tempe Normal School's composition *education* was fundamentally a function of the unique institutional mission.

INSTITUTIONAL REDUPLICATION, OR CATEGORICALLY NORMAL

Tempe Normal School's example goes a long way toward demonstrating the effects of institutional mission on normal school composition education, especially given the relative ease with which parallels can be drawn between Tempe's specific example and broader surveys of normal schools' mutually defining institutional characteristics. A survey of both contemporary and historical literature indicates that TNS was typical with regard to the effects of institutional mission on curricula—normal schools were collectively designed to bridge secondary and postsecondary levels, with "academic" review courses making up the majority of secondary coursework and "professional" methods making up the majority of postsecondary normal school coursework, all with the goal of training teachers for lower schools.[22]

Likewise, specific confirming examples of *institutional reduplication* are readily available. For instance, at the State Normal School in Los Angeles (now the University of California, Los Angeles) in 1887–88, students took English composition as part of the second of a three-year normal course of study, which worked progressively from "elementary work" in the first year to "higher work" in the final year ("Annual Catalogue" 1887, 23). The clear distinctions between academic and normal courses are less obvious in the Los Angeles Normal School curriculum than in Tempe's, but it is clear that the "elementary training" that constituted the early part of the course of study was equivalent to what students should have gotten in "lower grades," and the "advanced classes" were designed as "knowledge required by a teacher." The teacher-training focus is explicitly contrasted in the catalog to work for "one who is merely expecting to become a general scholar" (ibid., 26)—a direct reference to colleges' institutional mission.

Similarly, in the 1907 "Course of Study," Western Illinois State Normal School (now Western Illinois University) differentiated its "Academic Division" from the "Normal School." The Academic Division "correspond[ed] to the 11th and 12th grades in a common school, or the third and fourth years of a good high school." It was designed to prepare students for the Normal School, and it included all the composition instruction offered at the institution ("Course of Study" 1907, 8). The postsecondary Normal School was then entirely focused on teaching methods. At both Los Angeles and Western Illinois, composition was directly affected by normal schools' commonly shared institutional mission, which included the split secondary/postsecondary curriculum. Even granting that some institutions may have represented exceptions to the rule, a profusion of historical evidence, when read from an institutional perspective, reinforces the point: being normal meant offering a curriculum that placed composition securely at the secondary level.

Having shown the important effects of institutional mission on normal schools' composition education, it might seem well and proper for me to end this chapter here and proceed to chapter 3, in which I turn my focus to accreditation. There are, however, additional concerns I need to address before moving on. Readers will likely have recognized by now that TNS's example raises a problem for *Conceding Composition*'s central argument. Specifically, TNS's usefulness for showing that composition was tied to normals' unique institutional mission also introduces a significant limitation.

Although it is clear that normal schools' composition education was aligned with their institutional mission, it is a stretch to characterize the *absence* of first-year composition at TNS as a concession. After all, given the inherently split nature of Tempe Normal's curriculum and given composition's resulting classification as a secondary subject, it seems unlikely that TNS faculty and administrators would have considered first-year composition an appealing option to be weighed, much less a concession to be leveraged. Requiring first-year composition would not have made institutional sense at Tempe Normal School because it would have blurred the distinction between academic and professional coursework that distinguished it from other types of postsecondary institutions. If Tempe Normal is typical—and in many institutional respects it certainly is—it would seem that this limitation is typical as well.

Under these circumstances, I can at best assert a weak version of my claim that composition was a concession inasmuch as normal officials tacitly affirmed that certain forms of composition were suitable for meeting the normal school's institutional mission and others, no matter how prominent, were therefore conceded. Of course, the weak version of my claim raises an additional problem. If I have been successful in my attempt to show that TNS, and by extension other normal schools such as the State Normal School in Los Angeles and Western Illinois State Normal School, were pointedly not colleges and universities, then it would appear that I have also weakened the grounds on which I can make comparative claims about composition in colleges and universities. In other words, by successfully demonstrating that normals like TNS did not offer first-year composition, I have effectively undermined any extension of TNS's example to include claims about colleges and universities and whether they conceded composition to fulfill their institutional missions. Tracking instances of institutional reduplication, however, offers me a way to overcome these obstacles.

I insist on describing normal school composition as a concession because normal schools did not passively base their curricula on institutional mission. Normal school administrators and faculty also (re) shaped normal schools and renegotiated normals' institutional mission over time by conceding composition in the more conventional sense, and in a way that illuminates the practice at other types of institutions. In fact, this is what makes normal schools such useful examples for examining the practice of conceding composition—it is possible to identify concession because many normals did not have first-year composition requirements for many years, and then suddenly they did.

As I discuss in chapter 3, most normal schools were either decommissioned or converted into colleges (usually so-called teachers' colleges) in the first decades of the twentieth century. One way normal schools transformed into teachers' colleges was by introducing new requirements into their curricula, including first-year composition. At Tempe Normal, first-year composition appeared after the institution officially transformed from a normal school into a teachers' college, but first-year composition came into existence at other normal schools under different circumstances.

In the early decades of the twentieth century, many normal schools expanded their curricula to include non-professional postsecondary offerings. There were complex political and economic reasons for doing so, but suffice to say that such expansion generally occurred in concert with institutional attempts to align more closely with colleges and universities. Composition, particularly in courses that paralleled the first year of college, was commonly among normals' newly established "collegiate" offerings. After decades of defining themselves in contrast to colleges and universities, in the first decades of the twentieth century normal schools conceded composition to increase and substantiate their collegiate character. Such was the case at North Texas Normal College (NTNC) in Denton.[23]

North Texas Normal College was founded in 1891 in Denton, Texas, approximately forty miles north of Dallas. NTNC's first president, Joshua Crittenden Chilton, had graduated from National Normal School in Lebanon, Ohio, and taught at the Orleans Graded School and Training Institute in Indiana. In the late 1880s, Chilton's brother was a banker in Dallas, and Chilton decided to move to Texas and open a private normal school to take advantage of the untapped education market in the area. Chilton visited several sites in the greater Dallas area to pitch his idea to local city councils. Ultimately, he decided that Denton was best suited to his goals.

As North Texas historian James L. Rogers (2002) details, despite Chilton's new normal school being a private venture, the citizens of Denton, much like the citizens of Tempe, funded it. The town donated a tract of land to the normal school, and Denton's city council apportioned funds for starting and maintaining the school (ibid., 5–11). In addition, "the citizens of Denton" (primarily local businessmen) provided room and board for NTNC students ("Schedule of Classes" 1890, 15). Rogers also notes, "One other step was involved in the creation of the new college on a formal basis: the issuance of a charter to a group of private citizens who formed a corporation to operate the school" (2002, 10). In other words, the normal school was unabashedly an economic enterprise as well as an educative one. Incidentally, Rogers's choice to call NTNC "the college" is not insignificant, and it is a point to which I return below.

At a glance, comparing TNS and NTNC underscores my argument about the shaping effects of normal schools' institutional mission on composition education. Here again, normalites in Denton took composition, rhetoric, and literacy courses most semesters they were enrolled. Not surprisingly, composition was included in the academic (secondary) curriculum, alongside other "common branches" such as arithmetic, geography, and US history ("Schedule of Classes" 1890, 10). Somewhat more surprising is that the Teacher's Department also included composition, but this exception proves the rule. In North Texas Normal's first catalog, composition is categorized among "Drills in class—Requring [*sic*] no study" (ibid., 10). These drills included penmanship, drawing, vocal music, debating, elocution, and others, indicating they were review courses for students who needed a refresher for academic coursework.[24] Moreover, the catalog describes the teacher's course as focused solely on "methods and principles of teaching" (ibid., 6). Just as at Tempe Normal, any exposure to composition normalites got in NTNC's teacher-training (normal) course was in service of learning how to teach it. In short, the clear institutional reduplications that connect TNS and NTNC reinforce my case that normals' composition education was a function of their distinctive institutional mission. To be properly normal was to offer composition instruction strictly at the secondary, academic level.

When I began tracking reduplication of institutional mission at NTNC, I initially focused on the relationship between institutional mission and composition education. However, in reading through NTNC's course catalogs, I discovered a number of peculiarities that indicated further important, if seemingly minor, variations in its mission. As it turns out, North Texas Normal's institutional mission was not as stable as Tempe Normal's. In fact, NTNC's mission changed radically more than once in the first few decades of its existence—from private normal school and college, to public normal school, to public normal college, to state teachers' college. With each change and with minor changes in between, composition also changed in instructive ways. In retrospect, I recognize that Tempe Normal's mission changed as well, but its relative stability as a state normal school underscored the more dramatic changes at North Texas.

To begin with, some of NTNC's more formative changes: I noted that North Texas Normal College was founded in 1891 as a private institution, not a state normal school. As the name indicates, the institution purported to offer "college" coursework in addition to the academic (secondary) and normal (teacher-training) courses (Rogers 2002, 17–20; "Schedule of Classes" 1890, 6–7). The first two-thirds of NTNC's tripartite curriculum reduplicated Tempe Normal's split "academic" and "professional" curriculum. The college curriculum, on the other hand, focused on ancient languages and general culture ("Schedule of Classes" 1890, 7). It did show evidence of composition in the "Miscellaneous" requirements, which included "themes" and "debates" (ibid., 12). The academic curriculum was a prerequisite for the normal and the normal was a prerequisite for the college curriculum, but beyond those parameters, the structure was very loose. Students could take one or two classes and get certificates of completion. They could take one part of the course and not the others. They could test out of prerequisites or demonstrate proficiency through courses taken elsewhere or professional experience.

The 1890s represented a decade of significant instability for NTNC. In 1893, despite the capacious curricula, NTNC was having trouble attracting enough students to meet its financial obligations. Because it was located approximately forty miles from the population center of Dallas, many potential students were reluctant to attend. One consequence was that a state senator from Denton, Emory C. Smith, introduced a bill to the state legislature in 1893 to allow NTNC to offer state teaching certificates and lend some legitimacy and recruiting power. The passage of this bill marked an early variation in NTNC's institutional constitution by making it a "semi-state school," subject to state teacher-training guidelines and oversight (Crumley 1935). The change to a semi-state school did not solve NTNC's problems, however. The school continued to struggle financially, and it changed hands several times. In 1899, on the efforts of Denton's city council and other state and city officials, North Texas Normal College was officially made a state normal school by the legislature (Gammel 1902). NTNC remained in private control until 1901 when the Texas legislature finally allocated funds to operate the school, and it came under the full control of the State of Texas Board of Education ("Schedule of Classes" 1901, 15).

When NTNC came under the jurisdiction of the Texas Board of Education in 1901, the college curriculum was discontinued altogether. The December 1903 "Bulletin of the North Texas State Normal" states bluntly, "The Normal is neither a college nor a university. The statute creating the institution declares its purpose to be 'For the Special training of Teachers,' and marked deviation from the course thus plainly set forth, would be a violation of legislative intent" (ibid., 3). Accordingly, the entirety of composition instruction was relegated to the first year of the normal curriculum, which as noted repeatedly, consigned it to the secondary level.

The State of Texas's move to eliminate NTNC's college curriculum is notable for two reasons: first, it reaffirms the point I have made throughout this chapter that composition was shaped by normal schools' collective teacher-training mission in a way that bridged multiple normal schools—even when such schools differed in other significant ways. This is especially apparent in the clarification of NTNC's normal school mission in 1901 and the concomitant relegation of composition to the secondary level when the institution came under the state's jurisdiction. The mission and the composition curriculum were inextricable and mutually reinforcing in ways not necessarily visible from an intellectual perspective.

Second, the elimination of NTNC's college curriculum foreshadows normal schools' eventual concession of composition to align with colleges and universities. First-year composition requirements were hallmarks of college and university education in the early twentieth century. If the split academic/professional curriculum branded normal schools as "normal," first-year composition served a corresponding role for colleges and universities. Being a college or university, for the vast majority of institutions, meant offering (and requiring) first-year composition. It was as much a function of colleges' and universities' institutional missions as the distributed composition model was a function of normal schools' institutional mission.

The move to distinguish NTNC from colleges and universities in the early 1900s eventually gave way to concerted efforts at closer alignment. Beginning in the early 1910s, Texas legislators pushed the state's normal schools to become more like the state's colleges and universities. For normal schools such as North Texas Normal, the gradual introduction of composition into the postsecondary curricula over the course of several years served as a crucial link to colleges and universities and eventually contributed to its establishment as a proper college.

To explain this process, a few more steps are worth tracking in NTNC's evolution. After becoming a state normal in 1901, NTNC was obligated to follow the state's requirements for training public schoolteachers. But from 1901 until 1911, NTNC operated under the control of a local board of directors, as did the state's other normals. In 1911, however, Texas's legislature established a State Normal School Board of Regents with instructions to standardize normals throughout the state ("Schedule of Classes" 1912, 9–10).[25] The board of regents removed local control and delineated a uniform standard for all of Texas's normal schools, which included the extension of the normal curriculum from three years to four. According to the July 1913 "Bulletin of the North Texas State Normal College," the four-year curriculum "comprehends two years of high school work and two years of strictly collegiate work, including the professional subjects recognized as necessary to the preparation of teachers" ("Schedule of Classes" 1913, 9). The collegiate portion of the coursework was intended to retain the central mission of training teachers, but it also represented an attempt to increase the status of Texas's normals by aligning their courses with colleges and universities.

This curricular redesign came about in concert with other legislative processes shaping education in Texas. Among them, the legislature endeavored to classify the state's public schools in new ways: first, to designate each public school definitively as a primary, intermediate, or high school; second, to rank high schools as first, second, or third class; and third, to leverage these classifications in efforts to standardize all public schools. One component of the classification scheme dealt with teacher competency: public schools were expected to employ "competent teachers," and the minimum requirement for competence was "a first grade State certificate" (Doughty and Binnion n.d., 6). Such a certificate, good for six years, could be earned at North Texas Normal upon completion of the first two years of the normal school course. A lifetime certificate was granted to normalites upon completion of the four-year course of study ("Schedule of Classes" 1912, 20).

The important thing about the process to classify and standardize Texas's public education institutions is that NTNC and other Texas normals were compelled (and rewarded) in multiple ways to align more closely with colleges and universities. NTNC's move from a three-year course to a four-year course was intended to more closely approximate "collegiate" work. The legislature also encouraged students to take the "college" work by attaching professional incentives to it. This gradual reorientation resulted in the announcement in 1914 that NTNC was on the rank of "full Junior Colleges" ("Schedule of Classes" 1914, 21).

Although the legislative changes to NTNC's institutional mission in the early 1910s were not obviously connected to composition, as NTNC aligned more closely with the colleges and universities in Texas, it should come as no surprise that composition was implicated. For instance, when the "collegiate" curriculum was formalized in 1913, composition suddenly appeared in the first year of college work.

Composition had long been a staple of the pre-collegiate, academic, normal school coursework. The specific course was titled "English 2: Elementary Composition," and it remained in the first year of the normal (high school) coursework even as the college-level curriculum expanded ("Schedule of Classes" 1913, 14). But in 1913, "English 6: Advanced Composition" became a requirement in NTNC's third year—the first "college" year. Advanced Composition is easily recognizable in the intellectual terms I outlined in the first section of this chapter. It was organized around the modes of discourse: description, narration, exposition, and argument (ibid., 15–16). Students wrote weekly themes; they were instructed on the principles of clearness, unity, coherence, and emphasis; and they received "a review of correct grammatical usage" and "capitalization and punctuation" (ibid., 15). It was essentially a proto first-year composition course—both intellectually and institutionally.

"English 6: Advanced Composition" also represents precisely the sort of institutional concession I argue for throughout this book. By offering first-year composition, in the guise of advanced composition, North Texas Normal College was able to address pressing institutional needs—bolstering institutional status, aligning more closely with the state's colleges and universities, and advancing the cause of uniformity—without totally abandoning the distinctive normal school mission. There is no reason to imagine that the pedagogical concerns in the new composition course were unimportant to administrators and faculty. Nevertheless, in North Texas, as in Tempe, composition education was pitched toward solving institutional problems as much as, and I suggest even more than, pedagogical ones. It was a concession.

The institutional value of composition becomes increasingly apparent at NTNC in subsequent years. In 1917, four years after "Advanced Composition" became a requirement, NTNC began offering two additional years of college-level work (so two years of normal school curricula and four years of college curricula). The four-year course of study implemented in 1914 covered two years of high school and two years of college (the junior college model). The two additional years of "senior college" courses were conceived in 1917 as a further supplement, the completion of which culminated in a Bachelor's of Education to complement the various teacher-training certificates and diplomas NTNC had been offering since 1893 ("Schedule of Classes" 1917, 38–39). But it also represented yet another clear move away from the traditional normal school academic/professional curriculum.

In 1920, another gradual readjustment of the curricula and institutional classification was initiated to "correspond to that of the colleges of the first class" (Bruce 1921, 10). This meant, in part, casting off the junior college designation altogether and replacing it with a two-year, pre-collegiate "Normal School" course, which equated to the last two years of high school, and a "Normal College" course, which comprised a full four-year college course ("Schedule of Classes" 1920, 39–44). In effect, between 1917 and 1920 the essential components of NTNC's normal school course of study were re-described in collegiate terms, and what was once fundamental—the normal school education—became the supplement.

Advanced Composition was also redefined in 1920 as three separate courses, "English 30, 31, 32: English Composition and Rhetoric," all of which were required in the first year of the college curriculum. The catalog descriptions of intellectual content in "English 30–32" were virtually unchanged from the descriptions of "English 6: Advanced Composition." But the course description for English 30 did contain the added specification that it was "designed to lay the foundation for a year of practical work in English composition *of college rank*" (ibid., 73, emphasis added). What was implicit before—Advanced Composition paralleled college-level composition—was made explicit in the process of making NTNC's curriculum "correspond to that of the colleges of the first class." In 1922, English 30, 31, and 32 were renumbered as English 101, 102, and 103, again without noteworthy changes to the course descriptions, and the transformation was complete ("Schedule of Classes" 1922, 78). North Texas Normal College had a prototypical first-year composition course: "English 101: English Composition and Rhetoric." The following year, North Texas Normal College relinquished its claim to normal status altogether and officially became North Texas State Teachers' College—a full-fledged college with a four-year course of study and the appropriate composition education necessary to evince its institutional mission.

WHEN CONCEDING COMPOSITION
COMMUNICATES COLLEGE CREDENTIALS

Decoupled from intellectual comparisons, normal schools' composition education challenges a number of well-worn notions about composition education more generally. The common belief among historians is that first-year composition was conceived as a necessary, if temporary, evil given the deplorable state of students' writing skills. In light of the institutional purposes served by composition in normal schools, however, we might begin to rethink this belief. Composition education, in its various forms, enabled individual institutions to situate themselves within broader institutional categories. Normals were normals, colleges were colleges, and universities were universities. Those categorical alignments had complicated political, economic, and educational motivations and equally complicated implications for curricular, pedagogical, and institutional practices.

What is clear from tracking institutional implementation at Tempe Normal School and reduplication at North Texas Normal College is that the normal school mission profoundly shaped composition education. But what also becomes clear is that over the course of two decades, North Texas Normal conceded composition to become more recognizably collegiate. Refusing to do so would have meant essentially forgoing the right to operate.[26] In recognizing this progression, we can also recognize that composition helped shape the institutions by evincing new institutional missions. In other words, changing composition education facilitated larger institutional changes. Surely it was not singular in this regard, but it was indispensable. In the early decades of the twentieth century, many normal schools conceded "normal" distributed models of composition education in favor of "college" first-year composition courses. Such exchanges often occurred in concert with institutional attempts to align more closely with colleges and universities and eventually in normal schools' efforts to officially achieve "collegiate" status. Whether the institutional changes preceded changes in composition education or vice versa, it is clear that specific forms of composition education substantiated institutions' specific (if evolving) missions.

In chapter 3, I return to Tempe Normal School. Like North Texas Normal, TNS abandoned its normal school mission in the first decades of the twentieth century. In 1925, Tempe Normal became a teachers' college, and two years later first-year composition was added to the curriculum. Like NTNC, Tempe's introduction of first-year composition was a concession designed to align the newly constituted Tempe State Teachers' College more closely with other colleges and universities. Unlike North Texas Normal, however, I contend that the pressures in Tempe to become a teachers' college were directly related to regional accreditation. I therefore track composition in relation to accreditation at Tempe Normal School as it became Tempe State Teachers' College. I then set Tempe's example in tension with composition and accreditation at Harvard, the University of Kansas, and the University of Indianapolis.

3

STANDARDIZATION, COORDINATION, AND ALL THAT JAZZ
Conceding Composition for Institutional Accreditation

American education at the end of the last century had come to be a variegated hodgepodge of uncoordinated practices—in school and college alike—which had never undergone any screening from anybody, and many of which were shoddy, futile, absurd beyond anything we now conceive of; and the Age of Standards—as the period of 1890 to 1915 may come to be called—brought order out of chaos.

—Max McConn, "Academic Standards vs.
Individual Differences"

Of the hundreds and hundreds of volumes written about higher education in the United States it is surprising to note that no more than passing reference, if any at all, is made to accrediting, accreditation, or accreditment, as it is variously called. This lack of attention is incongruous when one appreciates how extensively accrediting has influenced the development of higher education in this country. It is even more anomalous when one reflects on the passionate arguments and disagreements it has caused.

—William K. Selden, *Accreditation: A Struggle
over Standards in Higher Education*

In chapter 2 I argued that normal school officials conceded composition in their ongoing efforts to sustain or modify normal schools' institutional mission(s). Despite composition instruction's obvious *intellectual* affinities with rhetoric and composition theories and pedagogies in evidence at colleges and universities across the country, composition education in normal schools was unmistakably shaped by more properly *institutional* concerns tied to the normals' specific teacher-training mission. In this chapter, I turn to a related but distinct institutional concern as it bears on composition's history: accreditation. Unlike normal schools, accreditation remains prominent in American higher

DOI: 10.7330/9781607325055.c003

education in the twenty-first century. In its most basic form, accreditation is relatively straightforward. It is "the process whereby an organization or agency recognizes a college or university or a program of study as having met certain pre-determined qualifications or standards" (Selden 1960, 6). Accreditation is the prevailing form of quality control in higher education. Some organizations, such as the American Medical Association, also use accreditation for certifying the quality of professional programs. But accreditation began and continues principally as a system for coordinating and standardizing institutions.

The vast majority of American colleges and universities are accredited by one of six regional accreditation associations,[1] membership in which entails meeting baseline standards for institutional mission, teaching and learning quality and assessment, financial and material resources, administrative organization and effectiveness, personnel quality, and student services (see, e.g., Higher Learning Commission 2014; Parsons 2003, 32). Although membership in a regional association is technically voluntary, accreditation is mandatory for colleges and universities that want access to federal funds, including student financial aid (Eaton 2001, 3). It is also a prerequisite for joining a number of other influential organizations, such as the American Association of University Professors (AAUP) and the American Association of University Women (AAUW). As such, accreditation is effectively mandatory, and it is consequently ubiquitous in twenty-first-century American higher education.[2] To frontload my argument, institutions need accreditation, and historically, composition has been conceded to secure it.

Accreditation's ubiquity in the current moment, however, can be deceptive for rhetoric and writing specialists. It is easy to imagine, for instance, that accreditation as an institutional concern is far removed from composition as an intellectual one. As Linda Adler-Kassner and Peggy O'Neill point out, accreditation is a centrally important issue on every higher education campus, but "we may not hear these discussions directly in our positions as classroom teachers or program directors" (2010, 27). This sense of distance is reinforced by the suggestion that accreditation has only recently materialized as a potential concern for members of the field. Adler-Kassner and O'Neill direct writing specialists' attention to accreditation in regard to the 2005 Spellings' Commission. Despite meaningful efforts to situate current issues in historical contexts, Adler-Kassner and O'Neill implicitly suggest that accreditation is a relatively new matter for writing teachers, scholars, and administrators in the face of outside forces threatening writing programs and classrooms. Even in pointing this out, however, I should note that Adler-Kassner and O'Neill pay significantly more attention to accreditation than does most rhetoric and composition scholarship.

The suggestion that accreditation is both distant from composition and a relatively new concern is understandable given that accreditation is all but imperceptible in our field's histories. David R. Russell (2002) avers that accreditation is a new frontier for writing specialists. Despite his introduction of an "institutional perspective" (ibid., 31) to study writing instruction during a 120-year period, which included the entire life span of accreditation to that point, accreditation emerges only at the end, as a peripheral consideration when Russell contemplates future directions for the field (ibid., 302). Arthur Applebee (1974) also makes passing reference to accreditation in his landmark study, *Tradition and Reform in the Teaching of English*, but he considers it only briefly in terms of which literary texts were prescribed for college entrance exams by fledgling accreditation associations around the turn of the twentieth century (ibid., 41n30, 50). Other prominent historians, including Thomas Miller (2011, 131–34) and Gerald Graff (1989, 78, 87), likewise allude to accreditation. In most cases, however, the discussion is cursory and focuses exclusively on intellectual or disciplinary consequences for English Studies as a result of fleeting historical encounters with accreditation. There is little sense in the field's historical or contemporary scholarship of the complex institutional causes and effects of accreditation over time.[3] There is even less sense that composition might feed accreditation and vice versa.

In this chapter, however, I contend that accreditation is neither distant from composition nor a new concern. Despite its relative invisibility in the field's scholarship, accreditation has always been intimately linked to composition education. Unpacking this historical relationship makes clear that accreditation and composition were mutually enabling in the last three decades of the nineteenth century (see Skinnell 2014). In fact, accreditation was the most conspicuous cause of institutions conceding composition in the last two decades of the nineteenth century and the first two decades of the twentieth century. Institutions of higher education conceded composition to address the central goals of accreditation, coordination and standardization, which is to say that composition requirements were introduced in many places to provide evidence of coordination and standardization. Composition was a concession par excellence. Consequently, composition became one of the most prominent college courses in the country as accreditation became a dominant force in the twentieth century. Examining the historical connections between composition and accreditation also indicates ways accreditation has persisted into the contemporary moment as a concern for writing teachers, scholars, and program administrators.

In keeping with my initial genitive focus on *institutional implementation*, I begin this chapter by (re)turning to Arizona State University's first institutional manifestation, Tempe Normal School. In particular, I return to its "demise." In 1925, Tempe Normal School was legislated out of existence, replaced by Tempe State Teachers' College (TSTC). Soon after, administrators redesigned the teachers' college courses to correlate with Arizona's other colleges and universities. As a result, first-year composition came into being—to put it baldly, administrators in Tempe conceded first-year composition in efforts to certify the newly formed teachers' college as properly collegiate.

The transformation from Tempe Normal to Tempe State Teachers' College was part of a national trend of normal schools becoming teachers' colleges, and it was closely connected to accreditation. For a number of complexly related reasons that I discuss below, accreditation standards forced normal schools across the country to "upgrade" to teachers' colleges. Normal schools that refused to transform were systematically eradicated because they could not earn accreditation and therefore could not place graduates. Among other consequences, the transformation of normal schools into teachers' colleges required expanding two-year normal school curricula into four-year liberal arts curricula, not unlike what happened at North Texas Normal College as discussed in chapter 2. The expanded college curriculum generally included some version of first-year composition. I argue in this chapter, in fact, that first-year composition was a key concession in the process of becoming a college and earning accreditation. Whereas normal schools previously resisted first-year composition to distinguish themselves from colleges and universities, newly formed teachers' colleges adopted first-year composition to prove that they were properly "collegiate" and worthy of accreditation. First-year composition was conceded to ensure the continued existence of normal schools qua teachers' colleges.

I also contend the act of conceding composition to earn accreditation in normal schools/teachers' colleges was symptomatic of composition's relationship to accreditation at large. Accreditation was designed to achieve two primary aims: institutional coordination (in the form of articulation) and standardization. First-year composition became a key component—in many different kinds of institutions—for achieving these purposes. To make this case, I track *reduplication* of the concession across three additional institutions: Harvard University, the University of Kansas, and the University of Indianapolis. First-year composition served different functions at the different institutions, but each, in its own way, represented a concession to accreditation. Ultimately, I argue that conceding composition was a function of accreditation, even in what were otherwise very different institutional circumstances, with the consequence that composition became relatively ubiquitous as an institutional attribute even in institutions that had little else in common.

FROM NORMAL TO COLLEGE

As mentioned in previous chapters, Tempe Normal School (TNS) never offered first-year composition as such. After forty years, however, the situation suddenly changed. In 1927, "English 101/102: First Year English" was introduced as a requirement, and some form of it has been a requirement at the institution ever since. Viewed through the lens of instruction, there is little to note about the introduction of first-year composition in 1927. At a glance, it appears "English 101/102" was little more than a name change. In 1918, following an exhaustive review of the normal course of study (see Curriculum Committee 1917), Tempe Normal's curriculum included a first-year course, "English 1: Rhetoric and Composition." English 1 incorporated "theme writing" and focused on EDNA—exposition, description, narration, and "very simple argumentative discourse" ("General Catalogue" 1918, 41). "English 2" continued "English 1" but with "higher standards" (ibid., 42). Less than a decade later, in 1927, the "English 101/102: First Year English" description is more sparse but likewise indicates that "exposition and argumentation; theme writing and theme correcting" are the main expectations ("General Catalogue" 1928, 51).[4] Notwithstanding notable stylistic differences in the course descriptions, there is little to suggest English 1 was significantly different from English 101. Even the majority of the teachers were the same.

The relative constancy in TNS's course descriptions is consonant with most composition histories. David Bartholomae (2000) gives a good summation in "Composition: 1900–2000." "As English departments grew into literature departments," he writes, "the composition course was viewed as a burden and a drain and made mechanical and trivial enough to justify the scorn with which it was usually treated" (ibid., 1952). In Bartholomae's concise history, composition instruction was a necessary evil but not a site of vital energy for the first half of the twentieth century. Robert J. Connors (1997b, 203) puts it more dramatically, arguing that composition was "cut off from vital roots in the millennia-old traditions of discourse theory and education" and that it "existed in an intellectual atmosphere that had been increasingly debilitated since 1900." Excepting a few extraordinary individuals such as Sterling Andrus Leonard, Fred Newton Scott, and Theodore Baird (see Brereton 1985; Stewart 1979; Varnum 1996, respectively) and apart from the development of new but relatively minor intellectual approaches (see Brereton 1988), it is commonly accepted that the majority of composition instruction, at least in the first-year course, stagnated for several decades until it was revitalized mid-century.[5] There was little in English 1 or English 101 to cause me to doubt this prevailing consensus.

With this narrative in mind, however, I was curious why first-year composition suddenly materialized after four decades. Sitting in ASU's reading room, poring over whatever materials I could find related to first-year English, I was struck by how little was said about the introduction of the course. It did not help that the 1926–27 catalog was missing when I first started reading the catalogs (the archivists did locate it on my behalf), but even with everything else at my disposal, the introduction of first-year composition seemed to have gone basically unremarked by anyone, including stakeholders in the English department. Since course catalogs constituted the majority of evidence I had that even mentioned the introduction of first-year composition to the curriculum, I started reading them beginning with the first one in 1885. I'll spare readers the grueling details, but I eventually learned a good deal about Tempe Normal School by reading catalog introductions, announcements, courses of study, and so on over an extended period of time.

For the purposes of this chapter, I can boil down my research process to the following revelations. As mentioned, in 1917 TNS administrators reviewed and revised the school's entire curriculum "in conformity with" Arizona's other normal school (founded in Flagstaff in 1901) and "for the purpose of maintaining our accrediting standing with the State of California" (Curriculum Committee 1917). I discuss this form of "accrediting" below, but the upshot of the 1917 curriculum review was that in 1918, Tempe Normal offered six English classes, English 1–6. Students were required to take English each of their first four years:

- "English 1: Rhetoric and Composition" in the first year
- "English 2: Composition and English Literature" in the second year
- "English 3: American Literature" in the third year
- "English 4: Word Analysis, Grammar and Methods" in the fourth year. ("General Catalogue" 1918, 41–43)

What I eventually discovered was that these four years corresponded to high school grades 9–12. "English 1" was a first-year course, but at the secondary level. The majority of Tempe Normal's students earned their high school diplomas and left, but if students stayed for the postsecondary normal school coursework *and* if they elected to pursue the course for aspiring English teachers, they took "English 5: General Literature and Advanced Composition" in their fifth year. Otherwise, English 5 was optional. "English 6: Special English" was also optional. It was a remedial English course offered in the last year of the normal course "for students who are deficient in English in any of the advanced grades" (ibid., 18). "English 5" comes back into the picture below, but when I initially read what I thought were the pertinent archival materials—course descriptions, textbook adoptions, and teaching assignments—it was not apparent to me that English 1–4 were secondary courses. All the evidence I had suggested they were essentially equivalent to college-level composition courses.

What did stand out to me was that in 1918, English 1–6 comprised the entire English curriculum. By 1927, there was a wide variety of literature, drama, and public speaking courses at the 100 and 200 levels. As well, "English 101, 102: First Year English" had been introduced, along with a variation: "English 103/104: First Year English," which was "similar to Engl. 101, 102, but adapted to the students who require more practice in the technique of written composition" ("General Catalogue" 1928, 51). English 1–6 were gone.

My primary concern when I started studying the catalogs was trying to determine exactly which courses of the English 1–6 variety corresponded to what in the English 101, 102 variety. It seemed clear that English 1 was intellectually equivalent to English 101. But English 2 in the 1918 catalog was not evidently equivalent to any particular course in the 1927 catalog. As I parsed the few 1918 courses into the many 1927 courses, I discovered English 1 was disestablished in 1919, English 2 was disestablished in 1920, English 3 was gone in 1922, and English 4 disappeared in 1923. English 101/102 did not replace English 1. It replaced English 5 and became a requirement for nearly everyone instead of just for students specializing in English.

Needless to say, tracking this process interrupted the historical continuity I thought I was examining. What I ultimately discovered is the argument I presented in chapter 2—English 1–6 were normal school courses, comprising secondary subjects (English 1–4) and postsecondary teacher training (English 5 and 6). But even before I began to unravel this process, I had to figure out why English 1–6 gradually disappeared and why they were replaced by English 101/102: First Year English. As it happens, I was looking at a series of concessions related to complicated changes in accreditation in the mid-1920s. Lots of English instruction was conceded in the change from English 1–6 to English 100, 200, and so on. Likewise, similar concessions were made across the campus. But as I explain below, first-year composition was a uniquely complicated concession.

For two decades beginning at the turn of the twentieth century, a particular form of accreditation had existed at Tempe Normal. However, it differed markedly from the form of regional accreditation that currently predominates. Accreditation at TNS consisted of a series of formal agreements, arranged by the Normal's president, with schools and school boards in surrounding areas and states. These accreditation agreements ensured that TNS graduates could teach in those states or districts without having to take qualifying examinations.[6]

In fact, accreditation was one of the principal's (later president's) main charges when the Arizona Board of Education hired Arthur John Matthews to run Tempe Normal in 1900. Matthews turned out to be the longest-serving president in ASU's history, and he was by all accounts a beloved and wildly successful administrator. But when he first arrived, he inherited an institution that was struggling to meet enrollment goals and had faced a series of challenges that threatened to shutter the school permanently (Hopkins and Thomas 1960 97–114; Hronek 1985, 81, 98). He was hired to stabilize and advance Tempe Normal School's standing.

Immediately following his appointment, Matthews stated that the process of building Tempe Normal into a first-rate institution required "two general improvements of immediate necessity—broader accreditation of the Normal and the establishment of comfortable school homes (dormitories)" (quoted in Thomas 1960b, 20). One way Matthews attempted to stabilize Tempe Normal was through negotiating accreditation agreements to ensure some measure of secure employment for graduates. One of his earliest successes in this regard happened in 1902 when he successfully negotiated an accreditation agreement with the California State Board of Education. Subsequently, Tempe Normal's graduates were eligible to teach in California schools without examination, which made Tempe Normal's teaching certificates significantly more appealing to potential students and garnered new respect from interested parties within Arizona, apparently including legislators (ibid., 20–22). Agreements with other states soon followed.

At the same time Tempe Normal was accredited by the state of California, Matthews was notified that graduates would also be given full transfer credit to Berkeley and Stanford for work completed at the postsecondary level and that transfer would be without examination. Alfred Thomas Jr. comments, "This was indeed gratifying to the Normal students for it not only gave them recognition, but it showed the people of Arizona that the Normal was rapidly reaching a high educational standard in which they could have confidence. This confidence made them willing to invest more money toward building-up the institution" (ibid., 22). Thomas's commentary is telling in that it recognizes the importance of agreements like those negotiated by Matthews for making the case to Arizona's legislature that the normal school was valuable and worth funding. Many Arizonans, especially politicians who supported the University of Arizona in Tucson, were skeptical of Tempe Normal's value until other states expressed appreciation in the form of accreditation and transfer agreements.

Negotiated accreditation agreements were common among normal schools in the early twentieth century (as were transfer agreements). In these agreements, the entire curriculum served as a concession in the transactional sense—the curriculum was offered as evidence of good faith in exchange for reciprocity. California schools got a new supply line of "appropriately trained" teachers, and Tempe Normal gained important credibility. Services were rendered, and goods were exchanged (in this case, graduates). But this transactional concession was relatively short-lived.

By the beginning of the 1920s, individual accreditation agreements were beginning to lose favor. The circumstances that occasioned this change were exceedingly complex, but the causes are comparatively straightforward—while normal school officials were making individual accreditation arrangements, college and university faculty were collectively developing regional accreditation associations, which had more economic and political power. In short order, the regional accreditation associations subsumed all education institutions in broader pursuits of coordination and standardization.

In 1922, California's State Board of Education notified President Matthews that their twenty-year-old accreditation agreement would expire unless Tempe Normal's teacher-training curriculum was expanded from a two-year "professional" course to a four-year "collegiate" course "to place [TNS] on the college basis" (Thomas 1960b, 319–21).[7] In keeping with a national trend, Tempe Normal School had already begun to reduce the amount of high school courses offered with the intent of focusing strictly on teacher preparation (ibid., 315–16; see also Hopkins and Thomas 1960, 200; Ogren 2005, 202).[8] This was the reason English 1–4 were gradually eliminated. As Thomas editorializes the process, "In order to keep pace with the growth of the state, the establishment of high schools, and the advancement of the Normal School standards in the United States, all the high school work was abolished at the Tempe Normal School in 1923" (1960b, 315). The entire secondary curriculum was conceded to the cause.

But the elimination of high school coursework was not sufficient to retain TNS's accreditation agreement with California. That required Tempe Normal to offer additional postsecondary coursework of a "collegiate" nature (Swetman 1933). The normal schools in California had recently been "upgraded" to teachers' colleges (Merlino 1962), and other states had also started restructuring their normal schools into four-year colleges (Thomas 1960b, 319, 429–30; Maxwell 1923; Felmley 1923; Ogren 2005). According to a document titled "Arguments for the State Teachers' College, 1925," circulated by Tempe Normal's Alumni Association in 1925, "75% of the states have converted all or part of their normals into state colleges" (Alumni Association of the State Normal School Tempe 1925). Tempe Normal followed suit, becoming Tempe State Teachers' College, replete with "a teachers' training course of four years" and authorization to "award the degree of Bachelor of Education" ("An Act Changing Tempe Normal School to Tempe State Teachers College" 1925).

The conversion of normal schools into teachers' colleges was a direct effect of the increasing influence of accreditation associations. The loss of California's accreditation was the tipping point for Tempe Normal, but accreditation by association had been on the horizon for several years. In 1917 the American Association of Teachers' Colleges (AATC) was formed to recognize and promote high-quality normal schools and teachers' colleges. Over the next several years, the AATC became increasingly involved in formal accreditation for teacher education. In 1918 the North Central Association of Colleges and Schools (NCA) introduced its own set of accreditation standards for teachers' colleges (Brown 1918, 92–93).[9] The NCA is especially noteworthy because it was (and still is) the largest and most influential regional accrediting body in the country.

Moreover, the NCA began accrediting Arizona's secondary schools in 1916, and it began accrediting the University of Arizona in 1917. It is not clear if these particular advances affected Tempe Normal in the last half of the 1910s, but it is inconceivable that administrators were unaware of them, especially since President Matthews was actively involved in local, regional, and national education associations with interest in accreditation.[10]

In the 1920s, the pressures of regional accreditation became more acute. Most regional accrediting associations were working to establish a system whereby teachers in accredited high schools would be required to earn credentials from regionally accredited institutions of higher education—that is, colleges and universities (Felmley 1923, 44; Geiger 1970, 186). The NCA indicated its desire to do so in the 1910s (Clark 1912, 29), though it required compliant state legislatures, and Arizona's legislature did not comply until 1930 ("North Central Approves State College at Tempe" 1932–33; Thomas 1960b, 630–31). Nevertheless, regional accreditation (or national, in the case of the AATC) gradually supplanted individual accreditation agreements throughout the country, and TNS was no more sheltered from these pressures than any other institution. By the time California threatened to rescind TNS's accreditation agreement in 1922, Tempe Normal was already suffering by comparison to upgraded teachers' colleges elsewhere. Becoming a teachers' college, then, was quite literally a requirement for Tempe Normal School's survival. Without establishing a "collegiate" curriculum, normal school graduates would eventually have been barred from teaching even in Arizona, and Tempe Normal would have been barred from training teachers altogether.

CONCEDING FIRST-YEAR COMPOSITION IN TEMPE

The elimination of English 1–4 at Tempe Normal was a direct consequence of administrators' push to eliminate high school–level coursework and "devot[e] its entire efforts to teacher training courses" (Thomas 1960b, 315). This push was an unmistakable effect of the school's efforts to meet standards being enforced by accreditation associations. The direct and indirect pressures of accreditation, furthermore, caused normal school administrators to expand the remaining postsecondary curriculum from two years to four and to seek teachers' college status. This brings me back to "English 101/102: First Year English." Using just this general context, it is possible to make a reasonable, if circumstantial, case that Tempe State Teachers' College administrators conceded "English 101/102: First Year English" to become a college, and indeed they did. This process was not entirely dissimilar from the process I described in chapter 2 by which North Texas Normal College gradually aligned with Texas's state colleges and universities, the major difference being that in Texas, the state compelled institutional alignment before a regional accreditation association could do so.[11] However, there are circumstances unique to TSTC that bring composition's concession into higher relief.

The progressive effects of accreditation no doubt had far-reaching implications for the entire curriculum at the newly christened Tempe State Teachers' College, as I point out below, but the composition curriculum was noticeably shaped by two particular occurrences: first, in 1926 TSTC administrators were informed that the University of Arizona in Tucson would no longer accept transfer credits from TSTC students. The university had long had a process for accepting transfer work from the normal school, but when the teachers' college was legislated into being (an act university officials opposed), university administrators agreed to accept transfer work from TSTC only "when the courses established by this act shall have been accredited by the University of Arizona" ("Statement of President Marvin" 1925). However, university administrators asserted that the teachers' college courses were not equivalent to the university courses, and it was on these grounds that they refused to "accredit" TSTC's courses in 1926 (Thomas 1960b, 415–30). One of the important differences was TSTC's lack of a first-year composition requirement.

The second occurrence that shaped TSTC's composition education was that the American Association of Teachers' Colleges became a formal accreditation association in 1926. Tempe Normal had become a member of the AATC in 1923, the same year the AATC developed its first set of accreditation standards. For all intents and purposes, though, there was no mechanism for enforcing the AATC's standards at that point, which made them little more than strong recommendations. In 1926, however, the AATC developed new standards and, more important, enforcement mechanisms, which were adapted from standards defined by the North Central Association of Colleges and Schools (Keith 1926, 107). The NCA connection becomes important later, but the immediate implication of the AATC's revised standards was that Tempe State Teachers' College needed to further revise its curriculum if it wanted to retain AATC accreditation. In the transformation from normal to teachers' college in 1925, TSTC's curriculum essentially became an expanded form of the normal school curriculum. It still focused primarily on methods and pedagogy with additional coursework in "college subjects" such as literature, history, economics, biology, and mathematics (Arizona Board of Regents 1925). Under the new guidelines in 1926, TSTC administrators had to redesign the teachers' college curriculum as a two-part course of study with the first two years consisting of "elementary" courses and the second two years consisting of "advanced" courses—what we might now recognize as general education and major courses, respectively.

The University of Arizona's refusal to accept transfer credits from TSTC, combined with the new standards required for accreditation by the AATC, left Tempe State Teachers' College little choice but to redesign the curriculum to conform to "collegiate standards." TSTC administrators therefore deliberately designed the new curriculum to correlate with the university's requirements (Thomas 1960b, 422–30) and meet AATC guidelines (ibid., 453, 620). In theory, "collegiate standards" did not prescribe specific courses, but in practice, as TSTC's new curriculum signals, "collegiate standards" mandated first-year composition. This de facto mandate is underscored by other sources as well. In a survey published in the *North Central Association Quarterly* in 1927, for instance, the authors noted that of the forty-five NCA accredited postsecondary schools surveyed, all of them required first-year composition (Sub-Committee on English 1927; Davis 1926).

At no point did the accreditation associations state outright that first-year composition was a requirement for accredited colleges and universities, but over and over they provided models that made the veiled but unmistakable case. Given the realities at hand, TSTC administrators had little choice but to concede first-year composition in the most direct sense—administrators yielded one thing (first-year composition) to attain another desirable thing (accreditation). What this meant in Tempe was that, beginning in 1927, TSTC's curriculum conformed to collegiate standards and students were required to take "English 101/102: First Year English." As a result, the transfer agreement with the University of Arizona was reinstated, and TSTC retained its accreditation by the American Association of Teachers' Colleges.[12]

In the ensuing years, English 101/102 continued to be a concession where accreditation was concerned. In 1928, as a result of events to which I can only gesture here, it became clear that Tempe State Teachers' College needed accreditation from the NCA (Hopkins and Thomas 1960, 213). In short, NCA accredited secondary schools would only hire teachers educated at regionally accredited colleges and universities. The teachers' college in Tempe therefore had little choice but to seek NCA accreditation, which was more stringent than AATC accreditation. According to Alfred Thomas, "Accreditation in the North Central Association of Secondary Schools and Colleges as a class A institution of higher education required improvement and up-grading throughout the institution" (1960b, 620). This included (1) dismissing faculty members who could not "measure up to the new requirements of the Doctor's degrees necessary for respectability as faculty in an accredited Teachers College" (ibid., 620);[13] (2) ranking faculty members as

assistant, associate, and full professors based on their academic qualifications;[14] and (3) significantly reducing class sizes across the institution.[15]
Administrators undertook these "improvements and upgrades"—sometimes ruthlessly—and TSTC was provisionally awarded NCA accreditation in 1931, pending re-inspection in 1932 and 1933 to monitor some
"issues of concern" that threatened to undermine the school's fitness.

The general attempts to bolster the newly formed teachers' college's
quality and reputation affected different areas of the campus community in different ways. Some programs, such as the agriculture program,
were dramatically reduced in size and stature—a concession to efficiency. Composition, however, was not reduced. In fact, the NCA inspector determined that TSTC's writing program in particular needed to be
expanded and upgraded to meet NCA standards.[16] Composition became
a concession to "standards."

In the NCA's 1933 inspection report for Tempe State Teachers' College,
two recurring concerns with regard to composition were specified. The
first was that TSTC's writing courses were too uniform. According to
the report, "The faculty is, for the most part, well trained. [However,]
the inspector cannot feel that the work in English Composition is satisfactory. The students are not separated according to ability or previous training. This criticism rests with the organization and not with the
instructors" ("Inspection Report" 1933, 4). The distinction between
composition's organization and composition instruction is telling—the
inspector was not concerned with the intellectual content of composition courses. He was concerned with its institutional structure, which I
explain below.

The inspector's second concern was that class enrollments were well
above the NCA benchmark of thirty students. In his report, the inspector
notes that English composition classes enrolled approximately fifty-five
students, and other departments had similar over-enrollment problems
(ibid., 4). "It is sufficient to state," the inspector writes, "that either some
of the departments are under staffed or too many students are sched-
uling certain courses" (ibid.). English was one of the worst offenders.
Demonstrating fitness for NCA accreditation meant specifically addressing these two concerns, and in so doing, TSTC's administrators repeated
composition's concession in the ongoing pursuit of accreditation.

Administrators attempted to address the second issue—large class
enrollments—in a rather predictable manner. First-year composition
was required of almost all students in accordance with TSTC's collegiate status,[17] and the institution was consistently increasing enrollments
each year.[18] Therefore, the only way to reduce class sizes was to add new

composition faculty. Faculty across the institution were being fired in droves—according to Hopkins and Thomas, "the axe fell upon 31 faculty members—more than half of [the] 56-person faculty"—between 1930 and 1933 (1960, 216). Nevertheless, the English department faculty expanded from three in 1930–31 to eight in 1932–33, all of whom were ranked and all of whom taught first-year composition every semester (in many cases, they taught only composition courses, irrespective of rank). Although increases in enrollments during the Great Depression overwhelmed some of the faculty expansion, class sizes gradually began to drop toward the end of the decade.[19]

Administrators' responses to the inspector's first concern, about differentiating course levels, were perhaps also predictable, but they illustrate in small measure the complexity of the relationship between accreditation and composition. As noted, in 1927 TSTC offered a variant of "English 101/102" called "English 103/104: First Year English," which was essentially designed as a remedial version of the course with more focus on "techniques" (read: grammar and usage drills) ("General Catalogue" 1928, 51). Soon after English 101/102 and English 103/104 were introduced, a third version, "English 105/106: Literary Appreciation," was launched. English 105/106 was for "freshmen who, by standard test, show special skill in English composition and aptitude for intensive study of literature" (ibid., 52). No surprise here: "remedial" students got extra skills and drills, "regular" students got regular current-traditional composition practice, and "advanced" students got literature. These three versions of first-year composition were available at TSTC for at least five years before the inspector's report was filed in 1933.

The inspector's concern about differentiating students based on ability or training may seem curious given the existence of 101/102, 103/104, and 105/106; but steps administrators had taken in preceding years suggest a way to understand the criticism. Prior to 1931, TSTC students were enrolled in one of the three available writing sequences based on placement test scores. Upon satisfactory completion of any sequence, students fulfilled their composition requirement. In other words, each sequence satisfied exactly the same requirement as the others. This was before the NCA's first inspection in 1931. Soon after that inspection, English 103/104 was officially declared remedial ("General Catalogue" 1931, 93). English 103/104 could no longer be substituted for English 101/102 but instead preceded it. "If, however, a student makes exceptional progress in the special course," the catalog explains, "he [*sic*] may be transferred after one semester to the regular course, and in such circumstances will be considered as having fulfilled the requirement" (ibid., 93). English 105/106 remained equivalent in credits to 101/102, but it was what we might consider an early version of an honors course. This is described in ASU's archives in very vague terms. Decisions were made, changes were implemented, grievances (if any) are unremarked. In fact, there is no explicit explanation for the change in English 103/104's status or of the process, but it is reasonable to infer that English 103/104 was amended to satisfy NCA standards.[20]

However, the NCA's 1933 report called for more differentiation. The hierarchicalization of English 103/104 and English 101/102 was apparently not sufficient. Again, the inspector did not specify what the concern about differentiation was, nor does his report make suggestions for correcting the issue. Nevertheless, in 1934, administrators surrendered English 103/104, evidently in deference to NCA standards.[21] In its place, "English A: Special First Year English" was introduced "for freshmen whose ratings in the preliminary standard test indicate a need in the mechanics of language" ("General Catalogue" 1934, 95). Whereas English 103/104 carried six units toward graduation—three units per semester—English A carried no credit and was not specified for a required time. It could take one semester or two (maybe more), and students matriculated into English 101/102 on the department chair's recommendation. The introduction of English A represented a real differentiation in levels of writing instruction: anyone who did not meet the minimum requirements for written communication as determined by test scores was prevented from joining the college community altogether until students could prove they were "fixed."[22]

A striking aspect of the three-year process of differentiating writing instruction at TSTC is that accreditation was inextricably connected to the institutional structure of composition. That is, composition education—as an institutional construct—was profoundly transformed in the institution's pursuits of accreditation, but conceding composition was also a vital element of those pursuits. In other words, conceding first-year composition unmistakably helped facilitate the institution's existence, growth, and development. It was not singular in this function—other changes had to be made to the institution as well—but it was essential.

ACCREDITATION: REDUPLICATION

The circumstances in which Tempe Normal administrators conceded composition to become Tempe State Teachers' College are idiosyncratic in a number of ways—the punitive suspension of transfer agreements by another state institution, for instance, is probably not widely generalizable. But the pressures of accreditation were by no means unique to Tempe. In fact, accreditation was already pervasive by the time TSTC came into existence, and I contend that the concession of composition at TSTC is emblematic of composition's connections to accreditation on a much broader scale. Faculty and administrators at institutions across the country conceded composition in general, and first-year composition in particular, in connection to accreditation beginning as early as the 1880s. What becomes very apparent very quickly when studying the connections, however, is that the effects of accreditation are virtually impossible to recognize by focusing on composition instruction alone because accreditation's links to composition were not primarily intellectual—they were primarily institutional. As a matter of fact, both accreditation and composition changed in a number of ways over the years (changes in the latter are documented at length by rhetoric and composition historians), but the connection between the two was so durable as to be nearly invisible because their institutional functions were not bound to intellectual concerns.

From an institutional perspective, it is impossible to overlook the fact that accreditation was a momentous force that profoundly shaped American education. In fact, accreditation is among the most important and consequential forces in the history of American education, particularly in the development of higher education in the last two decades of the nineteenth century and the first three decades of the twentieth century. As I show below, accreditation affected different institutions in very different ways, but there are some common elements: institutional coordination, standardization, legitimation, and first-year composition. Therefore, rather than offer a detailed comparison of institutional reduplication at one institution, as I did in chapter 2, in the remainder of this chapter I offer three limited instances of concession at three institutions (Harvard, the University of Kansas, and the University of Indianapolis). My intention is to offer a sort of evidentiary scatterplot to emphasize the fundamental connection of first-year composition to accreditation, even in what are otherwise very different institutional circumstances.

Regional Accreditation (Harvard)

As convention has dictated since Albert Kitzhaber completed his dissertation in 1954, I begin my historical examination at Harvard. Harvard is widely recognized to have instituted one of the first and most widely copied first-year composition requirements in the country. The teachers and scholars who populated Harvard's writing courses over the year are among the most famous names in composition's history: Adams Sherman Hill, Barrett Wendell, and LaBaron Briggs, to name a few. These men and others produced textbooks adopted across the country, and according to Kitzhaber, James Berlin, Sharon Crowley, Donald Stewart, and any number of other historians, Harvard's people and intellectual products spearheaded a revolution in the way rhetoric and composition existed in the academy. It seems only fitting to return to the scene of the revolution.

My reasons for doing so, however, are not simply based on disciplinary convention. In fact, my decision to return to Harvard in this chapter is the result of tracking accreditation—not composition—in the archives. When I was researching Tempe Normal School's transformation into a teachers' college, I came across a number of supplicating correspondences from Tempe's presidents to the North Central Association of Colleges and Schools asking for standards, inspections, re-inspections, and so on. Although Tempe State Teachers' College did not receive full NCA accreditation until the mid-1930s, the NCA was nevertheless the most influential body in the creeping dominance of accreditation standards that began decades earlier. By the 1920s, when Tempe's administrators were feeling the full weight of accreditation, the NCA was already a powerful force in secondary and postsecondary education throughout most of the western United States.[23] And the NCA's wide influence helps explain why Tempe's administrators were eventually compelled to change the normal school into a teachers' college, replete with first-year composition curricula.

Since the NCA was ultimately responsible for Tempe's introduction of first-year composition, I started researching the history of the organization to see if I could determine how first-year composition came to be a de facto NCA requirement. In fact, the NCA's English standards were adopted when the association was founded in 1895. The NCA, along with the Middle States Association of Colleges and Schools (founded in 1887) and the Southern Association of Colleges and Schools (founded in 1895), grew out of, and borrowed English standards from, another accreditation association: the New England Association of Colleges and Preparatory Schools (NEACPS) (Davis 1945, 3; Geiger 1970, viii; VanOverbeke 2008b, 176). The NEACPS was the country's first accreditation association. It was developed in 1885 under the auspices of several secondary and postsecondary New England education officials, including Harvard's long-serving president, Charles W. Eliot. In short, the

NCA's (and every other accreditation association's) English standards began under the auspices of the NEACPS.

My goal in this section is to argue that Harvard officials conceded composition in the service of accreditation, which is the case. However, Harvard's example is not as straightforward as Tempe's because first-year composition was not adopted at Harvard to gain accreditation. Rather, Harvard officials (including Eliot and Adams Sherman Hill) and others used first-year composition to invent and develop accreditation. As I argued in "Harvard, Again" (Skinnell 2014), Harvard's now-infamous English A requirement—which Kitzhaber called "the parent of all later courses in freshman composition" (1990, 61)—started out as a concession to articulation. I do not intend to elaborate the entire history of articulation here, but it does bear some explanation to explain how first-year composition ultimately became a concession to accreditation.

In 1869, Charles Eliot assumed Harvard College's presidency. One of his main objectives was to turn Harvard College into Harvard University, which entailed raising tuition, expanding the faculty, attracting philanthropic donations, and, most important, increasing enrollments (President of Harvard University 1887, 46). Eliot's master plan for increasing enrollments was to reorient Harvard's curriculum away from the prescribed classical curriculum to an elective system in an effort to attract new crops of public school students. Public schools in the nineteenth century generally did not offer classical training, focusing instead on modern training designed to prepare students for the workforce. As a result, most public school graduates were not trained in Greek and Latin languages and literatures, a major obstacle for anyone who wanted to attend a college like Harvard. Public school students were therefore hard for colleges to recruit. In recognition of this disjuncture, Eliot advocated strenuously for elective curricula at Harvard because he believed reforming the postsecondary curricula to include both classical and non-classical subjects would free secondary schools from what he considered the unnecessary and undesirable choice of providing education either for "life" or for "college" (Eliot 1876, 1892, 1893, 23, 1903; see also President of Harvard University 1887, 7–9). In turn, elective curricula would allow students trained in classical and/or modern subjects to matriculate to Harvard.

It was in these circumstances that first-year composition was first conceded by Harvard's faculty and administrators. English A, Harvard's first-year composition requirement, was put into place as part of the move toward elective curricula. Given the varied secondary preparation of the new populations the elective system was designed to attract,

Harvard's administrators and faculty felt it necessary to retain a small number of required courses that every matriculant would be required to take. English composition was one of them, and, in fact, it was the only required course that Eliot did not suggest belonged in the secondary school. When the elective system went into full effect in 1884, Harvard's only required courses were rhetoric, English composition (themes and forensics), German or French, and lectures on chemistry and physics (President of Harvard University 1885, 5; Harvard University 1884, 73). According to Eliot, all the courses except English composition were "obviously matters which properly belong to the secondary schools" (President of Harvard University 1885, 5). In the drive to institute elective curricula and attract public school students, Harvard offered first-year composition as a concession to students who came from very different backgrounds.

When English A was first conceded in 1884, it was in the service of articulation—of connecting Harvard's curriculum to the public high schools. It was expressly intended to be a concession inasmuch as it created a bridge from public high schools to Harvard that had never existed before. The prevailing belief in rhetoric and composition histories is that first-year composition was intended as a temporary remedy until secondary schools finally accepted responsibility for writing instruction, but this belief overlooks the institutional functions the requirement was supposed to facilitate.[24] The first-year requirement was less about whether students could write and much more so a concession to the institution's needs to make Harvard responsive to high schools and to non–classically trained students. In fact, Eliot repeatedly reaffirms his belief that "the English language and literature are, or should be, studied from the beginning of the primary school to the end of the university course" (1894, 35). Composition was a major part of this vision.

If first-year composition began at Harvard as a concession to articulation, it soon became a concession to accreditation. Eliot's vision of elective curricula was coming into being at many institutions. As a result, even as Eliot was looking to attract new students from public schools, New England's traditional preparatory schools were "press[ed] somewhat severely" by the burgeoning number of entrance exams at the various New England colleges ("Editorial" 1892, 548; Brown 1903, 570). As elective curricula grew and expanded, classical preparatory schools were struggling to appropriately prepare students to apply at different schools with varied entrance requirements. In 1884, the same year English A came into being at Harvard, officials at the Massachusetts Classical and High School Teachers' Association in Boston reached out to Eliot to propose "closer co-operation" between New England's secondary and postsecondary schools in an effort to relieve the pressure of increasingly divergent entrance exams ("Editorial" 1892, 548; Tetlow 1886).

The result of these meetings in 1884 was the development of America's first accreditation association the following year. The New England Association of Colleges and Preparatory Schools was formed for "the advancement of the cause of liberal education by the promotion of interests common to college and preparatory schools" (quoted in Broome 1902, 129; Eliot 1904, 771). Among the first members of NEACPS were most of New England's elite colleges and universities, including Amherst, Brown, Dartmouth, Harvard, and Yale. Almost immediately, NEACPS established a subcommittee, the Commission of Colleges in New England on Admission Examinations, to study the wide variety of entrance requirements among colleges and universities and devise options for streamlining it (Commission of Colleges 1887, 5–6).

NEACPS's Commission of Colleges began by studying English standards because it "was clearly the question of most urgent importance in the conviction of the preparatory teachers" (ibid., 11). In 1887 the commission published its first set of recommendations, which included a recommendation for association members to redesign the last year of preparatory schools and the first year of colleges to articulate more closely. Specifically, the commission recommended that "Vergil [*sic*], Latin Prose Composition, Homer, Greek Prose Composition, Geometry, French, and English Composition" be offered in the last year of secondary schools to "assist the preparatory teachers in reserving work for their pupils as shall make a symmetrical course of study for the year immediately preceding admission to the college" and "prevent interruption in the study of subjects which will be continued after admission to college" (ibid., 8).

In short, the commission's recommendations encouraged both secondary and postsecondary schools to offer composition, and the form of composition it advocated at the postsecondary level was modeled on Harvard's English A. In a 1904 speech, Harvard's president Eliot reflected on the development and effects of accreditation in New England: "In no department has the influence of the work of the Commission been more marked than English. It early secured a recognition of its recommendations in many colleges and schools all over the country, and for the past five or six years the improvements which it has introduced, chiefly determined by the principles formulated by Harvard College twenty-five years ago, have been adopted by the [accreditation] associations" (1904, 764). If English A was originally a concession in the sense of Harvard officials yielding or surrendering composition in exchange for closer relations to public high schools, by the time NEACPS adopted it as part of accreditation recommendations, it was beginning to morph into a concession in a different sense—an unchallenged premise on which other arguments could be built. Specifically, first-year composition allowed the accreditation associations to advance arguments about the importance of standardization.

A lot of ink has been spilled on the tumultuous education reform efforts in the last decades of the nineteenth century, so I won't rehearse it all here.[25] Suffice it to say, American education was poorly articulated and almost completely unregulated in the 1800s. According to Marc A. VanOverbeke, the lack of institutional coordination in the nineteenth century meant secondary schools, colleges, normal schools, women's schools, and more competed with each other for students and resources (2008b, 17–20). In the absence of a national education authority with the power to define and regulate education, college, university, and secondary school officials attempted to devise mechanisms for streamlining and standardizing the education system themselves.[26] To make a long story short, accreditation by association, which began with NEACPS, provided a model for coordinating and standardizing large numbers of institutions to (1) reduce competition between secondary and postsecondary institutions, (2) standardize institutional objectives, and (3) formalize articulation. Within a very short period of time, accreditation associations were established to cover the entire country, and each one adopted the English standards laid down by NEACPS's Commission of Colleges.

By the turn of the twentieth century, hundreds of secondary and postsecondary institutions had joined accreditation associations. And more important, most members happily acceded to the associations' recommendations—which meant, among other things, conceding composition for the privilege of membership.[27] In short, Harvard's concession to articulation paved the way for Tempe's administrators to concede composition in pursuit of accreditation forty years later.

University Accreditation (Kansas)

Regional accreditation eventually became the dominant force for coordinating American education institutions, but early on there were rival accrediting systems as well. My next institution, the University of Kansas, became an accredited member of the North Central Association of Colleges and Schools in 1913, but its connections to accreditation prior to that evince a different version of conceding composition. The University of Kansas is an apt subject for my study because, like Harvard, it has been the subject of much discussion in rhetoric and composition histories as a result of the work of English professor Edwin M. Hopkins (see Berlin 1987, 53; Connors 1991a, 71–72, 1997b, 192–95; Popken 2004; Russell 2002, 140–42). Hopkins is best known for his work detailing the labor conditions of composition teaching, which resulted in a series of publications in the 1910s and 1920s (e.g., Hopkins 1912, 1923). He was a tireless teacher, scholar, and administrator, and according to Randall Popken (2004), Hopkins suffered both physically and professionally for his commitment to composition.

Notwithstanding Hopkins's important contributions to composition research in the twentieth century, I am more interested in an earlier period. When Hopkins was hired in 1889, the school was in a period of major institutional reform designed to make the University of Kansas into a "true university" (Griffin 1974, 121). The University of Kansas was one of the first land-grant universities, founded in 1866 with funds established four years earlier by the Morrill Land-Grant Act of 1862. Although it was a university from the time it opened in September 1866, according to University of Kansas historian Clifford S. Griffin, "The only things it had in common with an actual university were a name, a charter, and a large measure of faculty factionalism. In every other way, the University of Kansas was merely a preparatory school for an institution of higher learning that did not yet exist, and an undernourished preparatory school at that" (Griffin 1966, 1). According to one of the school's first professors and eventual presidents, Francis H. Snow, the state of the early university was a reflection of education in Kansas more generally. Snow recalled in his 1890 presidential inaugural address, "When Professors Robinson, Rice and myself met each other for the first time to plan for the opening of the institution, we found not a single genuine High School in existence in the entire State of Kansas. It therefore became necessary to begin the University as a High School" (1890, 22–23; see also Griffin 1966, 1).

For several years, the University of Kansas worked at the level of the state's students, but by the late 1880s the campaign to turn it into a "true university" was well under way. The process of becoming a true university involved the University of Kansas in an alternate form of accreditation than the one adopted at Harvard. This second form of accreditation, university accreditation, was initially designed to motivate Kansas's high schools to reform their curricula to align with the university's (Griffin 1974, 122–23). This form of accreditation was first developed at the University of Michigan in 1870 to "accredit" Michigan's high schools (VanOverbeke 2008a, 2008b). In Michigan's pioneering version of university accreditation, university faculty members visited state high schools to determine if the teachers and curricula were sufficient to prepare students for university-level work. Graduates from accredited high schools could then enter the University of Michigan without taking entrance exams. One goal of the Michigan model was to clearly differentiate the two types of institutions (standardization), and another goal was to ensure the quality of high schools preparing students to enter the university (coordination). Kansas adopted similar accreditation procedures.

The University of Kansas, in fact, based its original charter on Michigan's, so it is not terribly surprising that it also adopted the university accreditation model. Although the University of Kansas maintained a preparatory department until 1891 when the "true university" reform efforts were in full effect, the university had long used its curricula to try to shape secondary curricula in the state. Griffin notes that the 1876 "standard curriculum" for accrediting the state's high schools was "practically a duplicate of the University's own preparatory curriculum" (1974, 123).[28] In other words, the university used the preparatory course to effect standardization of secondary schools by way of accreditation; then, as with the Michigan model, accredited schools could send students to the University of Kansas without examination ("Annual Catalogs/Reports" 1889, 44–45).

The preparatory course was also a mechanism for coordination in that "the Preparatory Department had three separate courses parallel to those of the college: a Classical Course, a Scientific Course, and a Modern Literature Course" (ibid.). Since the university's primary goal was to provide postsecondary education and since it was able to shape the state's secondary curricula by coordinating the state's high schools through accreditation, it is no surprise that the secondary and postsecondary levels were explicitly designed to articulate with one another. The connection is similar, in fact, to the articulation efforts under way at Harvard in the same period.

The attempts to articulate, coordinate, and standardize that characterize Kansas's efforts to direct education in the state relied on, among other things, the concession of composition. In Kansas, "accredited" secondary schools were expected to offer composition courses to help students prepare for jobs and college alike. The parallel college courses, when accreditation was first offered by the university in 1876, all included English composition courses in the first year as well.[29]

My goal here is not to give an exhaustive history of the University of Kansas but to note again the convergence of accreditation and composition. In the 1870s and 1880s, when the university maintained the preparatory department and the classical college organization, accreditation was primarily designed to ensure that Kansas high schools were offering a (relatively) standard curriculum that coordinated with the university's postsecondary work. This included composition at both the secondary and postsecondary levels, just as it did in Harvard's regional accreditation model.

But many of the state's schools opted not to seek accreditation from the University of Kansas because "the University requirements for admission to the Freshman class were so far in advance of the capacity of the average High School as to produce an impassable chasm" (Snow 1890, 39). Moreover, beginning in the 1880s, the university moved to become a "true university," which entailed "the abolition of the Preparatory Department, the introduction and development of the elective-major-minor system, and the establishment of new schools in addition to the College" (Griffin 1974, 121). In the process of reorganizing along these "true" lines, the university relinquished its primary tool for recruiting postsecondary students, which was the preparatory department. In its absence, accreditation retained the basic aims of standardizing, but given the university's disconnection from many state schools, accreditation also took on additional coordinating responsibilities in the burgeoning university. Under these circumstances, conceding composition became even more important.

In 1890, incoming university president Snow noted in his inaugural address, "The most important step towards making this institution in reality, what it is in name, a genuine Kansas University, is the establishment of a closer and more vital connection with the entire public-school system of the State" (1890, 35). In effect, university administrators came to realize that if accreditation was to have any lasting influence on the secondary schools, it was necessary for the university to "bridg[e] the chasm of separation" (ibid., 39). University administrators did so by instituting a split curriculum: in 1892, after "the first major curricular reform" (Griffin 1974, 304), the first two years consisted of set requirements that proceeded from the secondary curricula. In the freshman year, these requirements included mathematics, English 1 ("English composition, with themes and exercises"), hygiene, a foreign language, chemistry, botany, and English 2 (literature) ("Annual Catalogs/ Reports" 1893). The final two years consisted wholly of electives. A decade later, in 1903, a new undergraduate curriculum was instituted

that "integrated with that of the high schools" but allowed more flexibility (Griffin 1974, 306). The new curriculum retained requirements
in the first two years based on units completed but allowed students to
make choices within certain categories ("four units in English; six in
foreign languages"; and so on). There were two caveats: "All freshman
[still] took English rhetoric and attended hygiene lectures" (ibid.). Put
otherwise, composition was among the first of the university's concessions to advance the goals of accreditation in the 1890s, and it remained
as the last uncompromised concession into the twentieth century, when
Edwin Hopkins earned his reputation studying labor conditions in the
course. Even as other requirements shifted, changed, and disappeared,
composition remained an important concession to the goals of coordinating and standardizing Kansas's education institutions. By the time
the University of Kansas joined the regional accreditation movement
in 1913, composition was a mainstay that provided ample material for
Hopkins's research.

The examples of Harvard and Kansas provide a glimpse into the long
and complicated process of developing America's education hierarchy
through accreditation in the late nineteenth century[30]—a process in
which conceding composition played an important role. Composition
proved especially useful for "bridging the chasm" between secondary
and postsecondary institutions—in Harvard's case, to attract new populations of students; and in Kansas's case, to maintain connections that
were weakened when the university eliminated the preparatory department—because it contributed to the symmetry of secondary and postsecondary work. As such, both of the prominent forms of accreditation (by association versus by universities) sponsored postsecondary
composition requirements in the broader pursuit of coordinating and
standardizing American education institutions. By the early twentieth century, American education's now-familiar hierarchical structure
was mostly in place as a consequence of accreditation's prominence
(VanOverbeke 2008b, 2).

Marketing Accreditation (Indianapolis)

Once articulation was well established, accreditation by association
slowly took precedence over other forms because it was the least oner-
ous of the procedures. As regional associations became more dominant, accreditation took on additional functions. William K. Selden,
former executive secretary of the National Commission on Accrediting,
argues that "in addition [to the articulation function], accreditation was

developed so that the better institutions could identify themselves publicly and protect themselves collectively against their shoddy competitors of the academic market place" (1962, 320).

In the late nineteenth century, associations developed a set of common standards, definitions, and procedures that various education institutions could follow to align—more or less officially—with other institutions.[31] Institutions could also choose not to align with the recommendations laid out by accreditation associations, but opting out became increasingly difficult after the turn of the twentieth century (see Ravitch 1978; Tyack 1978). Moreover, the focus on standards, then as now, carried with it certain political and rhetorical advantages. Beginning in the early twentieth century, with the education hierarchy well established and composition firmly established as a tool of articulation, accreditation took on the role of legitimizing education institutions by certifying that they met minimum standards for quality. As accreditation became less and less optional for schools that wanted to demonstrate their "quality," composition became more thoroughly entrenched as a concession for the purposes of accreditation. One additional example should be sufficient for demonstrating the point.

About 500 miles east of the University of Kansas, Indiana Central University (now the University of Indianapolis) was founded in 1902 in downtown Indianapolis. Indiana Central was a religious institution founded by the Church of the United Brethren in Christ "to afford the best possible opportunities for securing a liberal education, where all the instructors are scholarly, Christian men and women, and where the influences are conducive to the best and highest development of the social, moral, intellectual, and religious nature" (Indiana Central University 1906, 11). Indiana Central was a private institution like Harvard; it enrolled primarily working-class students from the surrounding area like Tempe Normal School; it offered secondary, postsecondary, and normal school courses of study—in part to facilitate articulation like the University of Kansas; and accreditation was one of the chief concerns for Indiana Central's administrators for at least the first three decades it existed.

Accreditation took several forms at Indiana Central because the school's administrators were desperate to access accreditation's legitimizing functions as a way to recruit students and donors alike. From its inception, Indiana Central's academy (secondary) courses were arranged in accordance with the accrediting requirements of the Indiana State Board of Education, and "in 1908 the academy was accredited by the state and thus declared to be equal to a commissioned high school" (Hill 2003, 16). State accreditation, while never as dominant as other forms of accreditation, nevertheless played an important legitimating function for schools in states where it existed. Accordingly, admission to Indiana Central's regular college was determined by whether an applicant attended an Indiana State Board of Education accredited institution. Several Indiana schools were among the first schools accredited by the North Central Association of Colleges and Schools in the early 1900s. According to Indiana Central's first annual catalog, issued in 1905 when the school officially opened its doors: "Graduates from any of the high schools commissioned by the State Board of Education will be admitted to the Freshmen Class without examinations. Graduates from accredited private schools and public schools in other states will receive a like privilege. Graduates from noncommissioned high schools or students otherwise deficient in their entrance work will be permitted to enter suitable classes in the Academy and remove such deficiency" (Indiana Central University 1906, 14). In short, Indiana Central University was oriented around accreditation as a series of legitimizing standards from its founding onward.

Moreover, the founding of the Teachers' College at Indiana Central was "urged by the State Superintendent of Public Instruction" and designed in line with the expectations of same (ibid., 12). The Teachers' College was officially accredited by the state in 1908, and the university was accredited by the Board of Education of the Church of the United Brethren the same year (Hill 2003, 17). Over the next thirty-five years, Indiana Central University (ICU) pursued various forms of accreditation from the Church of the United Brethren, the Indiana State Board of Education, the Association of American Colleges, and the North Central Association of Colleges and Schools. ICU did not officially earn accreditation by a regional association, the omnipresent North Central Association, until 1942 because of persistent problems with the school's financial status. Basically, the North Central Association required that schools carry a certain amount of available operating funds to qualify for accreditation, and ICU could never manage to raise sufficient capital for inclusion. Nevertheless, ICU administrators oriented the school around the prevailing standards of the various accrediting bodies, and they continued to pursue different forms of accreditation from different accrediting bodies to have the legitimizing credentials that made recruitment and fund-raising possible.

As ICU's president, Irby J. Good, explained in his 1926 report to the board of trustees, "To succeed, the college must have good student attendance or it will fail in its income and purpose and appeal. To win students we must appeal to them on the basis of high college standards, good facilities, splendid associations, Christian environment, recognition by the State Board of Education as a standard college and for its recognition of superior work by Indiana University" (1926, 4). It is clear from this statement that Good is well attuned to the legitimizing functions of "recognition" by official organizations, but he raises the specter of regional accreditation even more specifically a few paragraphs later: "We cannot gain membership in the North Central Association of Colleges or in the Association of American Colleges and Universities without having a productive endowment of $500,000 above indebtedness. As long as we cannot hold membership in these organizations our students who go out to teach or to various universities are seriously handicapped and it will soon become very difficult for us to overcome this handicap." He concludes that if ICU fails in its pursuit of accreditation, the institution "is inviting failure and disaster to the college enterprise" (ibid., 4). Although regional accreditation was still more than a decade and a half away for ICU, it is clear that Good is well aware of the importance of accreditation for the life of the institution, and any number of minor changes and major transformations were undertaken in subsequent years in its pursuit.

The point here is that Indiana Central University was designed to meet curricular objectives that aligned with various forms of accreditation. It was less important for the purposes of articulation because articulation concerns had been largely settled by the time ICU was established. And although accreditation helped facilitate the coordination of standards at the different levels of education, it was less instrumental in changing them than it had been for Harvard or Kansas. Nevertheless, accreditation was the predominant frame of reference by which ICU's administrators made decisions about curriculum, school organization, funding, graduation requirements, and more. In effect, accreditation was particularly important as a legitimizing tool for ICU, which had neither the endowment of an elite Ivy League school like Harvard nor the state sponsorship of a land-grant institution like Kansas. Accreditation, therefore, helped strengthen ICU's reputation as a valid education institution. The importance of accreditation at ICU is reinforced throughout the university archives because administrators knew that legitimation through accreditation would facilitate student recruitment and fund-raising (e.g., Good 1921; Hill 2003, 191). It is within this general orientation to accreditation that we can read the concession of composition at the institution.

For one, students in accredited secondary schools (including Indiana Central's academy) were required to take composition courses to meet college entrance requirements. As should be obvious by now, this was a long-standing and wide-ranging concession at the secondary level. In Indiana Central's catalog, the purpose of composition in secondary schools was "to train the student to write clear, simple English" (Indiana Central University 1906, 15). As well, first-year composition was a requirement (a concession) in the college coursework. In 1905, all of ICU's matriculants had to take English 1, 2 and 3: "Rhetoric and Composition. Two hours a week throughout the year. The work consists of class discussions and themes. Required of all candidates for the degree of Bachelor of Arts" (ibid., 20). They also had to take Math 1–3 and Philosophy 1–3, but all the other requirements beyond English, math, and philosophy offered students a modicum of choice. In later years, only the English and math requirements dictated specific courses—a pattern in keeping with that at other schools where most requirements continually changed, sometimes dramatically, but composition was a steadfast concession to connect postsecondary institutions to their secondary counterparts.

Here again, I do not intend to provide an exhaustive history, but given Indiana Central University administrators' fidelity to accreditation standards, both when the school opened and in later years, we can infer that composition was a relatively conservative requirement by the time ICU opened its doors in 1905. Truthfully, there is almost nothing in the university archives that specifically discusses composition. But given the administration's sustained attention to the demands of accreditation, coupled with statements in official documents such as the one in several annual catalogs indicating that curricula were designed to fulfill the "partial pursuit of several recognized standard lines of college work" (Indiana Central University 1914, 28), it seems clear that composition advanced Indiana Central's institutional aspirations—it was a necessary concession—with regard to accreditation. Put even more directly, the first-year composition requirement was a minimum institutional concession for securing accreditation.

CONCLUSION

Accreditation occasioned a lot of serious disagreement in the last decades of the nineteenth century and the first decades of the twentieth century. Few issues, if any, were more prominent and contentious in American education at the time.[32] But by the 1920s, schools at all levels were increasingly reliant on accreditation from regional agencies (Harper 1970, 138–40). This was certainly the case at Tempe Normal School, Harvard, the University of Kansas, and Indiana Central University. Schools that were not regionally accredited, both at the secondary and postsecondary levels, gradually (but relatively quickly) saw their influence wane and their resources sapped.

As accreditation expanded throughout American education, spurred by legislatures and education reformers, so too did first-year composition requirements. It was one of the most evident curricular concessions in institutional pursuits of accreditation because it was one of the few requirements that bridged almost every postsecondary institution. Although institutions regularly introduced and removed other curricular requirements—math, hygiene, literature, philosophy, pedagogy—the one curricular certainty across a wide range of institutions over a long period of time seems to have been some version of first-year composition. It proved a useful tool for achieving the purposes of coordinating and standardizing institutions in the nineteenth century, and it therefore eventually stood as a clear concession by which institutions could advance, preserve, or secure accreditation in the twentieth century. By the time accreditation came to Tempe, it had been instrumental in advancing the concession of first-year composition for nearly four decades.

It should be clear by now that conceding composition was not a particular form of hostility on the part of administrators and faculty across the country. There is little or no indication at most of the schools I surveyed in this chapter, and many others that I've spent time researching, that administrators and faculty conceived of first-year composition as a way to punish underprepared students or to put composition in its rightful place as a "transient" necessity, for instance. Nor, for that matter, is it clear that first-year composition was adopted primarily because faculty and administrators deemed it the most efficacious model of writing instruction, though they may well have believed it to be so. What mattered most, though, was composition's role within, and relative to, an institution's institutional—as opposed to intellectual—needs. This condition existed for many years prior to accreditation's invention and it has, not surprisingly, persisted ever since.

Despite the passionate disagreements that occasioned accreditation's rise in the nineteenth century, in the decades after the turn of the twentieth century accreditation became mundane, and new pressing concerns rose to the educational forefront. In chapter 4 I turn to the relationship of conceding composition to federal funding. In the 1930s, 1940s, and 1950s, the United States government invested substantial resources in postsecondary education in the form of research grants, student loan programs, and education subsidies. Beginning in the early 1930s, administrators across the country systematically reoriented postsecondary institutions to attract these new sources of federal income. Drawing on archival research from Arizona State University, the University of North Texas, and the University of California at Berkeley, I argue that conceding composition was linked to postsecondary campaigns to attract new students and new sources of income. I contend that developments in composition education allowed administrators to make arguments about access, selectiveness, fitness to receive students, and capacity for high-level research, all with the goal of attracting federal funds.

4

OF FUNDING, FEDERALISM, AND CONCEDING FIRST-YEAR COMPOSITION

*Two great impacts, beyond all other forces, have molded the modern
American university system and made it distinctive. Both impacts have
come from sources outside the universities. Both have come primarily from
the Federal government. Both have come in response to national needs.*
—Clark Kerr, *The Uses of the University*

*In the years since the Second World War the Federal Government has
utilized the facilities of higher education to a much greater extent than
is usually realized . . . These federal activities have had a considerable
effect upon the programs and finances of the colleges and universities.*
—Richard G. Axt, *The Federal Government
and Financing Higher Education*

As I argued in chapter 3, education officials at a large majority of American postsecondary institutions conceded composition in the last decades of the nineteenth century and the first decades of the twentieth century to accomplish the goals of accreditation: specifically, coordination/articulation, standardization, and legitimation. In many cases, maybe most cases, conceding first-year composition was integral to institutional efforts to earn accreditation proper. Of the issues I examine in this book, none was more instrumentally involved with the nationwide development of first-year composition than accreditation, and accreditation continued to have important reciprocating effects on American higher education and first-year composition for decades. In fact, it still does. But accreditation is not the only major institutional exigency that bears attention in a history of composition's concessions.

Even as accreditation agencies were strengthening their influence in American education at the beginning of the 1930s and as two-year normal schools were transforming en masse into four-year teachers' colleges as a result, federal funding almost instantaneously became a central concern in postsecondary institutions. Beginning during the

DOI: 10.7330/9781607325055.c004

Great Depression, the US federal government allocated vast new sums of money to institutions of higher education—allocations that grew sharply throughout the twentieth century (Axt 1952; Bloland 1969; Fass 1982; Geiger 2008; Graham and Diamond 1997; Orlans 1962).[1] Over the course of several decades, postsecondary officials' attempts to secure federal funds resulted in a system of higher education that was very different from what existed just a few decades earlier: more people, more programs, more political influence. At the turn of the twentieth century, higher education was haphazard and somewhat arbitrary, but by the mid-1970s American higher education was "a marvel, if not the envy of the world" (Cohen and Kisker 2010, 306). Composition's prominence only grew during this period, and I argue in this chapter that its growth was connected to, and conceded in the pursuit of, federal funding.

The monumental effects of federal funding on higher education have not been lost on rhetoric and composition historians. Edward P.J. Corbett, for instance, connects composition's "dragoon[ing]" of graduate students and increasing reliance on adjuncts after World War II to the federally funded GI Bill (Corbett 1993, 65). Joseph Harris (1997) argues that the National Defense Education Act (NDEA, 1958) shaped disciplinary disputes about the proper subject matter in college English classrooms (see also Strain 2005).[2] And James Berlin (1987), Sharon Crowley (1998a), Diana George and John Trimbur (1999), John Heyda (1999), Thomas Masters (2004), and others have carefully demonstrated that the communications movement, the general education movement, and various practical skills movements were all connected more or less directly to federally defined needs during and after World War II.

For all historians' awareness about the increasing importance of the federal government in composition classrooms mid-century, however, there is very little sense in most histories that first-year composition served any role but a reactive one before, during, and especially after the war. Take, for instance, Richard Lloyd-Jones's (1992) "Who We Were, Who We Should Become," which is indicative of more generally held beliefs in the field. According to Lloyd-Jones, "In a single year—1946—college enrollments had doubled. Faculty with clout could justifiably shift to teaching upper-level literature courses, but even so, what with teaching six or seven or eight courses a year, most people still taught a first-year course and shared in the anxiety about who was being recruited to teach the extra sessions in church basements at odd hours. The lighter loads of the 'Research University' were generally yet to come, but the implicit specialization of composition had begun by default" (ibid., 487). One way to parse Lloyd-Jones's observation is that the *effects* of federal funding on first-year composition beginning in 1946 are relatively easy to see in retrospect because they triggered responses that rippled throughout the discipline. The end of World War II was a watershed moment. It is clear in rhetoric and composition histories that first-year composition was fundamentally remade by the war; and there is little, if any, sense that composition was part of a larger institutional agenda apart from the war.

Rhetoric and composition historians' reactive orientation to the effects of the war has set the terms for much of what specialists know about "who we were" in the twentieth century. This may be demonstrated by reference to another brief example. In Edward P. J. Corbett's history of writing program administration—apparently the first of its kind—he sets out to place composition and writing programs in broader institutional contexts, but like most historians, he begins with colleges and universities being overrun in the 1940s by GI Bill recipients and then narrows his focus to English departments. Echoing Lloyd-Jones, Corbett notes that "college enrollments took a quantum leap" in 1946 and "English departments especially bore the brunt of that tidal wave of students" (1993, 65). For Corbett, the GI Bill represents a crisis point in first-year composition's history that colleges and universities, and, more important, English teachers, had to cope with (likewise, Lloyd-Jones repeatedly casts it as a matter of survival or triage). Over the course of time, the "tidal wave" has proved professionally and intellectually salutary. Corbett and others have argued that the GI Bill's effects on first-year composition were uniquely responsible for redefining rhetoric and composition's professional existence in the second half of the twentieth century. But there can be no mistake that the initial exigency was a crisis that can apparently best be understood by appraising the unique effects on English departments and writing programs.

Lloyd-Jones and Corbett's portrait of higher education in general, and first-year composition classes in particular, as suddenly overwhelmed in the immediate aftermath of World War II is common enough, and perhaps it is even demonstrably true. But it also obscures efforts by higher education faculty and administrators to attract the tidal wave of students and the federal funds that accompanied them. In other words, if colleges and universities were *suddenly* overwhelmed in 1946, they were not *unexpectedly* overwhelmed; nor were administrators and faculty entirely unwilling participants in the process. Moreover, because Corbett hones in on English departments and writing programs in a moment of crisis, he isolates the GI Bill as an exceptional exigency. But, in fact, the GI Bill was less a singular crisis point than a new iteration of the federally funded normal that began more than a decade earlier during the New Deal era. The difference, at the most basic level, is one of perspective. Viewed from Lloyd-Jones's and Corbett's intellectual perspectives—that is, in light of the consequences of GI Bill enrollments for English teachers—composition was undoubtedly overrun and transformed. But viewed from a positive institutional perspective—which is to say, viewed in terms of composition's role(s) in achieving certain institutional goals—composition was revitalized as a concession in the campaign spanning the majority of the twentieth century to direct new students (and new dollars) into higher education.

In this chapter, I again examine composition's concession, this time in relation to federal money. Using evidence from three schools—Arizona State University, the University of North Texas, and the University of California at Berkeley—I argue that college and university administrators, and to a lesser degree faculty, conceded composition throughout the mid-twentieth century to reshape higher education and attract federal money. As in previous chapters, I begin by tracking institutional implementation at Arizona State University in the 1930–50s, and then I track reduplication at North Texas and Berkeley. During this period, federal funding significantly increased as a proportion of higher education budgets, and I argue that composition was a key institutional concession that allowed postsecondary institutions to meet evolving federal funding requirements, beginning with the New Deal in the 1930s, continuing with the GI Bill in the 1940s, and expanding with various federal research programs in the 1950s.

THE TIDAL WAVE

The pressing exigencies of accreditation I discussed in chapter 3 were largely managed at Tempe State Teachers' College by the early 1930s. Therefore, when I started researching for this chapter, I was chronologically positioned to recognize prominent discussions about the institutional effects of the Great Depression in the materials I was reading—that is, newspaper clippings, institutional histories, and administrative reports, mostly. For reasons that will become clearer later, however, I initially passed over the 1930s without finding much to discuss where composition was concerned. Instead, I focused my attention on the next major institutional transformation in Tempe—when the school was converted from a teachers' college to a regional comprehensive college—in 1945.

In March 1945, Tempe State Teachers' College officially became Arizona State College in Tempe (ASC), just in time to welcome the tidal wave of returning GI Bill–eligible veterans who were "demanding every variety of higher education the newly re-made College could provide" (Hopkins and Thomas 1960, 265). In the fall of 1945, just as Japan was formalizing its surrender following the US bombings of Hiroshima and Nagasaki, the newly constituted Arizona State College enrolled 553 students; four months later, in the spring semester of 1946, the school's enrollment more than doubled to 1,163 (Richardson 1964, 18). Course catalogues show that the number of composition courses more than quadrupled as a result. The momentous growth continued apace in subsequent years, such that 4,794 students were enrolled at ASC in 1949–50 ("General Catalogue" 1950; Hopkins and Thomas 1960, 263–65).

The enrollment numbers are perfectly in keeping with the story rhetoric and composition historians have long told about the historical moment. The ASC English department's responses to the precipitous growth are also familiar. For one, new faculty were hired: beginning in 1945, the department had three faculty; in 1946, there were five faculty; in 1947, there were fourteen; and in 1948, ASC's English department employed nineteen faculty. The English chair's reports to ASC's president directly demonstrate that faculty were engaged in trying to meet the students' needs despite the overwhelming numbers. And, of course, English faculty were overloaded. This is the "tidal wave" of which Corbett writes. In some ways, postwar conditions at the new state college in Tempe typified postwar conditions in first-year composition programs everywhere around the country.

When I started writing this chapter, I followed the disciplinary convention of tracking the post–World War II tidal wave into composition classes—surveying the flood damage, as it were. But, as in previous chapters, I hit a snag. To make a long story short, the timing of the Tempe State Teachers' College's transformation into Arizona State College gave me pause. To wit, Tempe State Teachers' College became Arizona State College in March 1945—just nine months before enrollments doubled. Beginning in fall 1945, for the first time in the institution's existence, students could earn a bachelor degree in the liberal arts and sciences, in addition to the BA in education that had been available since 1928. The transformation from teachers' college to state college is especially noteworthy because administrators at Tempe State Teachers' College had been trying to get Arizona's legislature to make the school a multipurpose state college with liberal arts degrees since at least 1936 (Thomas

1960c, 495). But the change had been repeatedly blocked in the legislature on the grounds that it would duplicate, and thereby undermine, the University of Arizona in Tucson (Hopkins and Thomas 1960, 249). Frankly, I was curious why Arizona's legislators suddenly changed their minds (of which they are rarely accused).

The simple answer is that Arizona's legislature was finally moved to act because of the GI Bill. According to Harold D. Richardson, an upper administrator at Arizona State College (and eventually Arizona State University) in the 1950s and 1960s, "Soon after the passage of the GI Bill in 1944, it became evident that the State of Arizona could not participate effectively unless all three of its institutions were able to educate and graduate returning war veterans" (1964, 18). In her history of Arizona State's English department, Katherine C. Turner provides additional clarification: "The GI Bill helped to motivate the change [from teachers' college to multipurpose institution] because, to take advantage of it, institutions had to grant degrees in other fields as well as in education" (1979, 60). In short, Arizona's legislature made a major, controversial institutional change—one it had been refusing to make for nearly a decade—because failing to do so would have reduced the amount of federal dollars for which the state's institutions would be eligible. Franklin D. Roosevelt signed the GI Bill into law in June 1944, and TSTC became ASC just nine months later. Another way to say this is that Tempe State Teachers' College administrators, as well as Arizona's state legislators, openly courted the flood of new students with federal money to spend. They were certainly not caught off-guard by the tidal wave, as composition historians have insinuated. The official change from teachers' college to state college effected at the highest levels of state government proactively paved the way for college composition to "bear the brunt" of GI Bill enrollments in Tempe.

As with the change from normal school to teachers' college, the change from teachers' college to state college was not simply a name change. Fulfilling the expectations of a regional college entailed, among other things, a prompt reorganization of the college curriculum. To ensure that Arizona State College satisfied federal requirements for GI Bill eligibility, Arizona's Board of Regents (which supplanted the Arizona Board of Education when TSTC became ASC) commissioned a report by US Office of Education officials "to study the degree proposition and render advice" (Hopkins and Thomas 1960, 261). Within less than a year, ASC administrators used the recommendations from the federal "Works Report" to implement twenty arts, sciences, and pre-professional majors, each with its own subject-specific curricula. These majors extended from a newly established general education program, which included first-year composition.[3]

I return below to the process of curriculum development, but first I want to briefly tease out the role of first-year composition in the new general education program. A report issued in 1944 by TSTC's Committee on the Liberal Arts Curriculum explains why first-year composition was to be required for all students: "The first of our objectives is the development of communicative skills. This is, of course, a major function of the elementary and secondary schools. All that the college can hope to do is to extend this training to a level of competence considered adequate for college-trained individuals. We have indicated for this purpose the year course called First Year English already in the curriculums. This is to be required of all students" (1944, 7). The committee's report rehearses a number of well-worn commonplaces about the appropriate place for composition education (viz., prior to college), but what is most striking to me is that the committee prioritizes institutional needs (i.e., "our objectives") by reaffirming the requirement of first-year composition. First-year composition had long been a fixture in the Teachers' College, and in redesigning the curriculum to make the school a regional comprehensive college with twenty new major tracks, one of the first acts was to revitalize and reinforce the first-year composition requirement. In other words, first-year composition was the inaugural concession to the new institutional cause. Composition smoothed the transition from teachers' college to state college by addressing the state college's "first objective."

Specifically, first-year composition addressed ASC's first objective by contributing to the new, unified general education program. Prior to 1945, when TSTC students selected a major, they took a discrete, unified, four-year course of study (though it allowed for a number of electives). In other words, the program of study for an English major at the teachers' college was a four-year course; the program of study for history majors was technically a separate four-year course; likewise for elementary education majors, and so on. Although there was significant overlap in the actual classes students took, TSTC's courses of study were attached to a specific major. In this organizational scheme, English 101/102 was a single yearlong course that could be (and generally was) required as part of each major at the discretion of administrators and faculty.

The regional comprehensive curriculum reorganization, however, expanded the course of study and the possible choices students could make. Majors were no longer unified, four-year plans. They consisted of two years of general education, which everyone took, and two years of major-specific coursework, which resembles the curricular structure at most institutions to this day. This new curricular organization was supposed to provide students with more individualized options without abandoning the breadth of learning that is the cornerstone of liberal education. In the process of developing the general education course, English 101/102 became two separate courses, "English 101" and "English 102," so students could select sections that fit their schedules.

It is hard to say what the intellectual consequences of dividing 101 from 102 might have been, if any. Course descriptions for the separate semester courses were little changed from descriptions of the yearlong version of 101/102, suggesting that the intellectual content was essentially unchanged by the institutional reorganization. Moreover, other intellectual efforts were undertaken during the same period—the division of students into one of three "ability groups" from 1941 to 1952, for instance. But even as the departmental reports report these other efforts, there is no mention of concerns or effects related to the 101/102 split beyond the fact that it happened.

The separation of 101 and 102 was nevertheless a critical institutional concession. Splitting first-year composition into two, semester-long courses was necessary for the general education program and actively facilitated changes to the institution in keeping with federal guidelines for GI Bill eligibility.

To be clear, changes to both the institution and composition in 1945 were interrelated efforts in Arizona State College officials' attempts to recruit new students in the wake of GI Bill legislation. But they were explicitly institutional—as opposed to intellectual—changes. From the evidence I have discovered, changes to composition were not informed by, much less predicated on, developments in composition research or pedagogy at all, despite the fact that the program was run by Louis M. Myers, by then a nationally respected writing specialist. Nor is there any indication that Myers had strong feelings about the change or any input at all, for that matter.

This is hardly surprising given what I have been arguing throughout this book—the concession of composition to meet institutional needs was a regular occurrence in Tempe by the 1940s. It should come as no surprise, then, that reorganization of first-year composition at Arizona State College in 1945 indicates more than a discrete concession in response to a unique federally instigated exigency. Rather, it was one point of reference in a decades-long pattern of conceding composition that responded to an assortment of institutional exigencies.

More specifically, though, composition's concession to ensure ASC's GI Bill eligibility was part of an ongoing process of orienting the institution to federal funding that had begun several years earlier. In other words, what may seem like a relatively insignificant alteration to first-year composition in 1945 was also one point of reference in a long process of institutional reorientation to federal expectations.

Before I elaborate this point, the speed with which the change from TSTC to ASC was instituted, both in composition and in the curriculum at large, is worthy of remark. Arizona's legislature changed the teachers' college into a state college to ensure GI Bill eligibility less than nine months after the GI Bill was signed into law—an extraordinary rate of accomplishment in legislative matters. Administrators of the newly formed state college commissioned a federal review of their curricula and subsequently implemented the federal recommendations in less than a year—again, an inconceivably swift achievement for a large, state-controlled, bureaucratic institution. In fact, the remarkable speed with which Arizona's legislators and Arizona State College's administrators moved was only possible because TSTC administrators and faculty had spent the previous eight years reorganizing the course of study to mirror the work of a regional college within the teachers' college framework (Hopkins and Thomas 1960, 248–49; Thomas 1960d, IV–19). This included large-scale curricular reorganizations in the late 1930s intended to garner legislative support for the institutional change from teachers' college to state college long before World War II started. When the change was eventually made official, Arizona State College administrators were well prepared to make what small concessions were still necessary to realize their goals. In short, the concession of first-year composition in 1945 represented the realization of a long process of institutional change, not a first reactionary response to the tidal wave of burgeoning enrollments.

BEFORE THE TIDAL WAVE

In gesturing here to the long process that proceeded composition's concession at Arizona State College in 1945, I mean to direct attention away from the narrative of "urgent wartime need" that characterizes the lion's share of composition's histories (Finnegan and Wallace 2014, 402). Splitting composition into two courses was not so much a crisis response as a kairotic response, and one for which administrators had long been preparing. As such, it directs our attention to the process that prepared the ground for the 101/102 split to occur—a years-long institutional reorientation to federal funding, which began long before the tidal wave was even on the horizon.

The first iteration of federal funding at Tempe State Teachers' College was part of the New Deal response to the Great Depression, and it is toward the New Deal that I am moving, but I want to proceed by turns because I think the process I followed in tracking the 101/102 split is instructive. I said earlier that prior to 1945, TSTC majors were discrete, unified, four-year courses of study leading to a Bachelor of Arts in education with specializations in the teaching of a particular subject (e.g., English, math). This is technically true, but the courses of study at TSTC, organizationally discrete though they were, were intended to mirror as closely as possible the organization of most liberal college/university courses of study. What this means is that each of TSTC's courses of study was ideally intended to mimic the work a student would have done to earn a Bachelor of Arts or a Bachelor of Science degree at a traditional college or university, even though the teachers' college could not officially offer those degrees.

These unofficial courses of study might best be considered "aspirational," inasmuch as they were supposed to attract students who wanted a BA or a BS but could not for one reason or another attend an institution that actually offered them. When the 1945 college curriculum was formalized, the existence of this curricular structure smoothed the transition from teachers' college to regional comprehensive immeasurably. In fact, the federal "Works Report" drew on TSTC's existing aspirational courses of study to formulate its final report for the regional comprehensive recommendations.

These courses of study were aspirational in another way. As early as the mid-1930s, TSTC administrators were lobbying for the teachers' college to become a regional comprehensive college. In 1936, Tempe State Teachers' College's president Grady Gammage commissioned a survey of TSTC's student body, which revealed that the majority of students had little or no interest in becoming teachers.[4] As many as two-thirds of the survey's 689 respondents reported that they were place-bound and had only enrolled at the teachers' college because there were no other options for four-year college degrees in the area (Thomas 1960c, 495; Hopkins and Thomas 1960, 246–47).

Drawing on these survey results, TSTC administrators sought to reorient the teachers' college curriculum to reflect a regional comprehensive curriculum. It was, not coincidentally, a double concession on the part of administrators—it was a concession to attract potential students and a concession to legislators in that TSTC administrators hoped that resembling a regional comprehensive college would influence legislators to make it official.

The desired institutional transformation was stymied for nearly a decade by politicians who supported TSTC's institutional rival, the University of Arizona. Nevertheless, the legislature and the Arizona State Board of Education did sign off on the curricular reorganization. In 1937, TSTC administrators introduced a masters degree in education, expanded course offerings to approximate liberal arts curricula even though students could still only technically earn a BA in education, and put the beginnings of a general education program into place (Thomas 1960d, IV–19). Composition requirements were still technically subject to implementation by the administrators of the individual majors, but English 101/102 was a de facto universal requirement. These early efforts at institutional transformation ensured that by the time the US Office of Education produced the 1945 "Works Report," TSTC administrators had been more or less preparing to meet the report's objectives for the better part of a decade.

The 1937 curriculum expansion was intended to address student needs, and no doubt it did. But it was also predicated on a series of other institutional measures. For one, to reorganize the curriculum as administrators wanted, they needed to expand the faculty. Expanding the faculty, however, required an expanded budget after years of economic devastation. 1936–37 seemed to me a curious time to attempt to increase TSTC's operating budget, given the effects of the Great Depression that supposedly lingered until World War II. According to Hopkins and Thomas, however, "In 1937, the Legislature provided more liberal funds, and further important faculty additions followed" (1960, 241). Five new faculty were hired in 1937, including English department chair and eventual Conference on College Composition and Communication executive committee member Louis M. Myers, and four more in 1938. It is worth asking, where did the money to hire new faculty come from?

The recommitment of state funds in 1937, after years of economic depression, came about in large part as a result of federal New Deal funds that had helped restore the state's economy. In fact, although many people were still reeling from the Depression in 1937, the state of Arizona and especially Tempe State Teachers' College were starting to emerge from the worst economic conditions as a consequence of New Deal aid. The infusion of state funds to hire faculty at TSTC in 1937 represented a significant advance in the school's economic circumstances.

The point worth making is this: the reorganization of Tempe State Teachers' College's curriculum in 1937 had lasting effects at the school that we can trace into composition education in the 1940s. But this reorganization was only possible as a consequence of the teachers' college's institutional reorientation to federal New Deal funding beginning even earlier. New Deal funds were credited with rescuing the state of Arizona from collapse, and it turns out that a significant amount of the New Deal funds allocated to Arizona were channeled through TSTC beginning four years before the curriculum was redesigned.

In 1933, after Tempe State Teachers' College had secured accreditation, Grady Gammage was hired as TSTC's new president. His predecessor, Ralph Swetman, made the painful changes necessary to earn accreditation and then left for a job in New York. Gammage was hired to recuperate the "half-wrecked" institution (ibid., 223), and he was particularly interested in discovering ways to attract more students and reduce the economic consequences of the Depression, which included significantly reduced state allocations.

Hopkins and Thomas provide an appropriately dramatic recounting: "In that hot summer of 1933, the new President of [Tempe] State Teachers College sat in his office on the vacant campus, appraised the situation of the institution that was now under his care, and explored the possibilities of a single, all-inclusive recovery-plan for the College, to which his reading of the news from Washington had given him the clue . . . Title Two of the newly-signed National Industrial Recovery Act provided Federal funds for public building purposes—that was the clue" (ibid., 234).

In August 1933, Gammage applied for federal Public Works Administration funding for TSTC, which was granted and which was just the beginning of federal funds flowing to the institution. Between 1933 and 1940, more than $1.7 million worth of federal funds went to relief efforts at TSTC (ibid., 238). According to ASU's institutional historians, TSTC's receipt of New Deal funding "proved to be a symbol of recovery which not only restored high morale at the College, but did much to lead Arizona upward and out of depression" (Richardson 1964, 17). For most historians of Arizona State University, the 1937 curricular expansion touched off by Gammage's survey of student attitudes was, in fact, inextricable from the preceding physical expansion of the campus funded by federal money. Securing federal funds, it turns out, was one of TSTC's major institutional exigencies in the pre–World War II era (on par with earning accreditation), and we cannot understand the ensuing World War II "tidal wave" in first-year composition without first considering this major institutional shift.

CONCEDING COMPOSITION FOR THE FLOOD OF FEDERAL FUNDS

My goal here is not to trace all the funding sources and New Deal–era policies that shaped Tempe State Teachers' College. My goal, rather, is to demonstrate that TSTC's 1945 campaign to attract GI Bill money was part of a much longer campaign to orient the institution to federal funding. This campaign began in 1933 when TSTC was first awarded over $400,000 in development loans by the Public Works Administration to repair, upgrade, and expand the physical campus. Over the course of the next six years, New Deal funds from the Public Works Administration (PWA), the Works Progress Administration (WPA), the National Youth Administration (NYA), and the Reconstruction Finance Corporation (RFC) went to construction wages, materials costs, and student labor at TSTC. "The campus became a beehive of activity," according to Hopkins and Thomas (1960, 238). By the time the GI Bill was conjured into being, TSTC had been oriented—and orienting—to federal funding requirements for more than a decade. When composition was conceded in 1945 to make Tempe State Teachers' College into Arizona State College, federal money was a mainstay in the institution's budget.

The obvious question at this point is, whither composition? What, in other words, was composition's role in the 1930s when TSTC progressively oriented to federal funding? Unfortunately, the answer is not exactly straightforward. On the one hand, composition was where it had been ever since first-year composition was differentiated and stratified to earn accreditation in the first years of the 1930s. In fact, there is no indication that TSTC's composition courses saw any significant changes as a result of the Great Depression or the New Deal. Nor, for that matter, was the institution's response to the Depression and federal funding obviously shaped by composition in those years. Composition was relatively constant as an institutional entity throughout the 1930s. This might seem to undermine any claim that TSTC's administrators and faculty conceded composition to attract federal funds in the decade and a half leading up to the GI Bill tidal wave.

On the other hand, however, I think it would be a mistake to imagine that composition's constancy in the 1930s was unconnected to the turmoil of the Depression or to federal funding in the New Deal era. Rather, I suggest that if we consider composition in terms of the major institutional exigencies of the 1930s, composition's stability is precisely the reason to consider it in terms of concession. In a decade of profound instability, I contend that composition was a concession to business as usual and a sign of Tempe State Teachers' College's reliability and steadfastness amid the cultural chaos of the Depression. In this sense, composition might be productively thought of as a "weak concession."

My evidence for claiming that composition was a weak concession in the 1930s, which I detail below, is admittedly circumstantial. I think this helps explain why, when I was searching for institutional exigencies to investigate in the years after accreditation, I initially overlooked the New Deal era—there was almost no evidence in the archives of direct connections between federal funding and composition at TSTC, and there certainly do not appear to have been any changes that rippled throughout the discipline as the GI Bill enrollments would a few years later. The invisibility of the Depression in composition's history is in keeping with scholarship in rhetoric and composition at large. As Cara A. Finnegan and Marissa Lowe Wallace (2014) point out, there is virtually no scholarship in rhetoric's disciplinary histories that examines the 1930s closely.[5]

Nevertheless, I maintain that the institutional link between federal funding and composition is significant because of five interanimating factors:

1. According to historian Paula S. Fass, "In the process of administering relief, the New Deal discovered not only massive illiteracy but also a population with outdated and inadequate skills. The relief projects became actively involved in underwriting a practical vocationalism and helped to define this as a deeply educational issue and responsibility" (1982, 46).

2. A portion of the New Deal funding was earmarked for adult education to help prepare relief employees for better jobs. Adult education, which commonly took the form of reading, writing, and vocational skills, comprised 3.4 percent of all federal aid distributed in Arizona between 1933 and 1938 (Arizona State Committee 1938, 24).

3. New Deal funding, particularly in the first phase of PWA relief, was distributed to state, county, municipal, and district authorities to coordinate assistance as broadly as possible. To that end, postsecondary institutions like TSTC were the recipients of hundreds of millions of dollars in stimulus money in the 1930s, which was used to provide direct aid to students, fund part-time employment for students, hire educators, and employ construction workers to expand and upgrade college and university grounds (Fass 1982; Grieder 1945). According to the 1938 "Report of the Arizona Appraisal Committee," which was charged with surveying the effectiveness of New Deal funding in Arizona, these various units "had the responsibility of bringing local unemployed and local needs together under Federal relief machinery" (Arizona State Committee 1938, 3).[6] This meant that the units had to demonstrate that they were stable enough to distribute relief from the federal government to needy individuals.

4. Part of TSTC's evidence of institutional stability was its recently secured regional accreditation. Regional accreditation was one of the factors

federal agencies considered as they judged applications. An additional aspect of TSTC's accreditation was that it was a state institution, which meant it was eligible for state and federal funds that private and non-accredited institutions could not access.

5. Public Works Administration funds, like the majority of those received by Tempe State Teachers' College, were primarily loans that had to be underwritten by material assets in case the receiving organizations were eventually unable to repay the loans (ibid, 25).

Taken individually, these five factors do not amount to much for composition's history, though some may invite further investigation. But taken together, it is possible to draw some tentative conclusions about the nature of composition's weak concession during the Great Depression. Remember that first-year composition was instrumental to earning and maintaining accreditation at TSTC. Accreditation helped demonstrate institutional stability, one of the most important characteristics for relief-eligible institutions. As an accredited, state-supported institution with close ties to local communities, Tempe State Teachers' College fit the bill as a stable institution. It is hardly a direct causal link, but without composition, TSTC would not have been accredited and might therefore have been ineligible for PWA funds.

Composition was also implicated, if again indirectly, in the needs of the communities New Deal funds were supposed to serve. As I discuss in more detail below when I examine the University of North Texas, education institutions that received federal funding were encouraged, at least to some degree, to support adult education. The goal was to address the American workforce's "massive illiteracy" so that people earning federal relief could develop skills that would make them better equipped for the job market. It is unclear from the materials I examined exactly what adult literacy programs TSTC facilitated. What is clear is that TSTC administrators and faculty were involved in adult education and the expanded vocational training associated with New Deal goals. It is noteworthy that several of the problems Fass (1982) identifies as the most pressing happen also to be problems first-year composition was long supposed to have been aimed at addressing.

One additional indication that composition contributed to the stability of TSTC was that even amid the devastation of the Depression, the English department exploded in size and scope. In 1930–31, TSTC's English department had three faculty members; in 1932–33, there were eight faculty (Hopkins and Thomas 1960, 216). As well, TSTC's new literature-heavy English major was installed and expanded, literary societies were put into place, several literary magazines and journals were established, and the department was expanded to include specializations in dramatic arts, speech, and journalism (Turner 1979, 22–30). And composition offerings grew, with the majority of faculty members teaching at least one section every semester. Even as faculty members throughout the institution were being fired in droves, the English department was substantially bolstered.

Drawing any sort of direct causal link between composition and federal funding in this period would be speculative, but this much is certain: literacy was a major concern of New Deal administrators, composition (and other forms of literacy education) was a central concern of TSTC's English department, and composition was an essential requirement for regional accreditation. Speculative though the links may be, they're nevertheless highly suggestive. Inasmuch as accreditation demonstrated TSTC's fitness for federal funding and the English department helped TSTC address the goals of federal relief, it seems reasonable to claim that composition was conceded to the cause of institutional stability—both its maintenance and demonstration. It was not yielded in the first sense of concession I outlined so much as it was assumed in the second sense. Composition was steady when everything else was disordered. The intended effects of composition's weak concession were undoubtedly to help students, to prepare them for jobs, and to carry on the long tradition of advancing students' literate development. But composition was also a key, if indirect, concession in orienting Tempe State Teachers' College to federal funding in the 1930s.

By 1937, when TSTC's curriculum expansion began and new faculty were hired, the teachers' college had been subsisting partly on federal money for four years. In the subsequent years, aided by continuing federal support, composition became an increasingly evident concession to TSTC's institutional campaigns. In his 1937–38 report to the president, newly hired English department chair Louis M. Myers outlined six changes he wanted to undertake to improve the work done in first-year composition.[7] These included demanding "a higher standard of mechanical accuracy than has heretofore been enforced," "demand[ing] more actual written work with enough of it done in class to serve as a check against cheating," "giv[ing] more training in reading," and "prepar[ing] models of written forms and a system of minimum essentials of mechanics which we would like to have adopted throughout the college" (ASU Department of English 1938). For Myers, these changes were intended to strengthen students' writing in TSTC's composition classes, but they were also supposed to strengthen the teachers' college as an institution by coordinating writing instruction across departments and strengthening English training "throughout the state" across secondary and postsecondary institutions.

Moderate though Myers's recommendations may seem, it is clear that they were intended to facilitate the liberal arts–style curriculum that underwrote administrators' appeals to transform the teachers' college into a state college. By the time Myers was hired, composition's stabilizing functions were less necessary. The institution was ready for change, and Myers's first annual report indicates the relatively minimal concessions necessary to begin to move the school away from the holding pattern of the Depression era and toward the growth patterns that became so obvious by World War II. Minimal concessions of composition stacked up in the 1930s and 1940s, and by the time the GI Bill tidal wave crested, the institution was well oriented for the ensuing flood. The small concession of splitting 101 and 102 was a drop in the proverbial bucket.

AFTER THE FLOOD

I have spent a good deal of this chapter arguing that first-year composition was a concession, in various degrees of strength, for attracting federal funds to Tempe State Teachers' College and then Arizona State College. Before examining institutional reduplication at the University of North Texas and the University of California at Berkeley, I want to draw attention to one more instance of implementation at Arizona State. This instance, what I call the university-status movement, represents the strongest form of concession at Arizona State College, and, as such, it will be somewhat shorter than the New Deal and GI Bill cases. But it is useful for demonstrating the increasing comfort with which administrators conceded composition to attract federal dollars in the twentieth century, such that it indicates a (continuing) trend rather than a series of discrete exigencies.

To begin, some brief context: Richard G. Axt (1952) notes in his landmark study that "before the Second World War, federally sponsored research at colleges and universities was practically nonexistent, with the notable exception of agricultural research . . . In 1950, on the other hand, at least fourteen Federal agencies sponsored research at colleges and universities" totaling at least $150 million annually and representing more than a 1,000 percent increase during the previous decade (ibid., 85–86; see also Geiger 1986; Graham and Diamond 1997). During World War II, the US government began to invest substantial funds in higher education to support research and development programs. Many were defense-related contracts, but there was also a significant rise in basic research programs. As Axt details, the Atomic Energy Commission, the US Department of Defense, the Public Health Service, and a number of additional federal agencies developed robust research collaborations with universities in the late 1940s. However, even as federal research funds rapidly expanded in scale during and after the war, the vast majority was concentrated at just a handful of institutions (Axt 1952, 94; Graham and Diamond 1997, 28). As Axt puts it, in 1949, "Well over 90 percent of Federal research was accounted for by the 121 institutions listed as 'universities' in the classification used by the Commission on Financing Higher Education" (1952, 94).

Because of the limited scope of federal research funds during the 1940s, most postsecondary institutions, including the newly established Arizona State College, saw the largest federal benefit from the GI Bill. College composition courses, as is well documented, also saw the largest direct consequence of federal funds in higher education.

At the beginning of the 1950s, however, GI Bill enrollments were beginning to wane, even if total enrollments remained much higher than they had been before World War II. Many schools faced a serious dilemma about how to continue to provide for the expanded number of matriculants given the general reduction in GI Bill funds. At roughly the same point, however, new forms of federal research funds came into existence with the establishment of prominent federal programs such as the National Science Foundation in 1950 and the expansive National Defense Education Act in 1958. Since the majority of federal research funds were earmarked for "universities" with established research programs, it may come as no surprise that efforts to achieve "university-status" were soon under way in institutions around the country.

During the period 1951–58, Arizona State College administrators began a concerted effort to upgrade the college into a university. In 1951, there were nearly six times as many students enrolled at ASC as there had been in 1945, and, according to Hopkins and Thomas, the "old Teachers College form of organization—14 Departments, each with its own head, all reporting directly to the President" was "far outgrown" (1960, 280). President Gammage appointed a committee to study the problem of institutional organization, and based on the committee's recommendation, the school was reorganized into a "university-structure" in 1953 (though "university-status" was still five years away). The university-structure established three things: (1) a College of Arts and Sciences, comprising fourteen departments and a dean; (2) a School of Education, also with a dean acting as intermediary between the faculty and president; and (3) a doctoral degree, the DEd in education.

At the same time this reorganization was undertaken, the Arizona Board of Regents made a second request to the US Office of Education for a survey of the institution (see Richardson 1964, 20–23). In 1953, the federal Hollis Commission surveyed ASC and found that the institution was "rapidly becoming a University" in function, size, and complexity. The Hollis Commission Report recommended that "orderly steps should be taken" to make ASC an official university in light of the state's expanding education needs (quoted in Hopkins and Thomas 1960, 287). Following this report, the university-structure was further expanded. The development of the university-structure was intended to make administering the school more efficient as enrollments grew, but it was also intended to eventually achieve university-status, including a research program with graduate degrees and research faculty, in order to access federal research funds.

Achieving "university-status" entailed a number of institutional concessions where composition was concerned. For one, in accordance with the introduction of the university-structure, the school's commitment to general education was reaffirmed and five distinct sections of general education were established: communications, humanities, social studies, science and mathematics, health and adjustment. First-year composition was designated a communications requirement, to be "required of all students so that the needed skills in reading, writing, speaking, and listening might be developed" (General Education Committee 1954). This reorganization meant a major administrative shift for first-year composition. For all intents and purposes, the classification of first-year composition as a communications course rather than a humanities course separated composition at an administrative level from the more literature-focused English curriculum (which *was* in the humanities section).

The importance of general education notwithstanding, the realignment of first-year composition was aligned with the university-status movement. According to Louis Myers's 1953 report to the president, "The [new first-year composition] plan is roughly similar to the one already in force at the University of Arizona, but has some modifications which we believe are improvements" (ASU Department of English 1953). This new plan included revisions to basic ("remedial") writing instruction that relegated "the lowest fifteen percent of students" into non-credit-bearing remedial writing courses. Remedial instruction was explicitly conceded to emulate what proper universities (in this case, the University of Arizona) did. Myers seems to have been encouraged by the intellectual effectiveness of the change for writing instruction, but his reports throughout this period remain fixed to varying degrees on institutional concerns.

In 1956, for example, despite noting that the results of the new reme-dial program were "highly satisfying," Myers also notes that "the aver-age scores of our entering students and the cut-off point for Remedial English . . . are dangerously low. If we are to achieve university standards we should raise our admission requirements in such a way as to elimi-nate most students of the sort now assigned to remedial English" (ibid.). This comment rehearses the institutional/intellectual split I have been arguing for throughout *Conceding Composition*. Regardless of intellec-tual effectiveness, Myers conceded that remedial English needed to be rethought because it was an impediment to upgrading the school from a college to a university.[8]

As Myers's reports to the president also routinely indicate, conceding composition—in this case, remedial composition—to achieve university-status was not left solely to the English department. Composition was conceded at the highest administrative levels. In 1958, Academic Vice President Harold D. Richardson sent a memo to President Gammage stating that the Coordinating Committee for Curriculum Development recommended that remedial English courses be discontinued. "If you concur," wrote Richardson, "we shall prepare an announcement to the faculty and students and a publicity piece for the newspapers" (1958). In the course of just five years, remedial writing instruction went from being a vehicle for showing ASC's quality in relation to the University of Arizona to being terminated to show standards were being raised.

The intended effect of discontinuing remedial writing instruction was not wholly realized, as is apparent in a letter from Gammage to Richardson and other administrators worth quoting at length:

> The *Tucson Citizen* said that Arizona State had seized academic leadership when we recommended and the Regents passed the program of eliminat-ing bonehead English or high school English or whatever you want to call it. The saving in faculty salaries, etc., was pointed out.
>
> Now the University representatives are saying that this, simply, is a watering down of all of our English. It does not mean raising standards but lowering standards, and that we are putting the poor students in with the others and giving them college English.
>
> I think in carrying this program out it should be made very clear that it is a tightening up, and the plan should prove this. (Gammage 1958)

As Gammage points out, the program to eliminate "bonehead English or high school English or whatever you want to call it" was ultimately made by the Arizona Board of Regents and was manifestly concerned with raising the school's stature to earn university-status.[9]

At the same time remedial writing instruction was undergoing radi-cal changes, graduate study was becoming a more prominent aspect of

ASC's offerings, and it also required conceding composition. The teachers' college had introduced a masters degree in education in 1937 (as a consolation for not receiving authorization to grant a wider selection of bachelor degrees [Thomas 1960c, 495]), and it remained the only graduate offering until 1953 when the Doctorate of Education was introduced along with the university-structure.

The establishment of the DEd represented an opportunity for the English department. As enrollments grew after World War II, some English faculty members were paid stipends to teach overloads. Beginning in 1954, however, Myers arranged to have DEd students teach remedial English courses (before they were discontinued) for practice teaching credit instead of cash. "Aside from the economy," he writes, "we believe this will make for rather better instruction" (ASU Department of English 1954). Myers does not comment on the quality of teaching by DEd students in subsequent reports, but once the system was established, it apparently stayed in place.[10]

In 1956, with the introduction of masters-level work in English, teaching responsibilities in composition increasingly passed from full-time faculty to graduate students.[11] Although some full-time faculty continued to teaching writing courses, the most senior members of the department were freed from composition classrooms, and their efforts were redirected to graduate training. As part of the proposal for the graduate English program, teaching assistant positions and part-time faculty appointments were requested and granted. In his annual report in 1955–56, Myers wrote:

> The greatly increased freshman enrollment, together with the prospect of an M.A. in English, and the possibility of a DEd in English, have made advisable a modification in our staff set-up, which is now underway. Hitherto we have aimed at a single permanent staff. Next year we shall have six graduate assistants teaching two sections of First Year English apiece, as well as several temporary instructors. Thereafter we hope to have even more graduate assistants . . . The size of the permanent staff can thus be somewhat reduced, even in the face of growing enrollments. (ASU Department of English 1956)

Myers believed the combination of graduate students and part-time faculty, plus the introduction of teaching seminars, would improve the department in four ways: (1) more highly trained faculty members could be used more effectively than they currently were teaching first-year composition, (2) it would afford "sound training for apprentice teachers," (3) the budget could be reduced or reallocated, and (4) the graduate program could be improved.[12] Each of these changes represented, in some way or another, conceding composition. "Highly trained" faculty were pulled out of composition courses and put in charge of graduate teaching, graduate apprentices were given composition courses to prepare them for university teaching, overload stipends for composition teachers were reduced, and improvements in the graduate program built on all the other concessions. Although these concessions did not necessarily draw federal funds directly into the English department, they strengthened the institution's comprehensive efforts to achieve university-status and attract federal research funds.

The development of graduate programs was intended to bolster the university-status movement in the larger effort to attract federal research funds. In 1961 six doctoral programs were developed at ASU to take advantage of available federal research grants (Sabine 1992, 15).[13] President G. Homer Durham actively encouraged faculty research by providing in-house research grants and developing grant-writing support for faculty applying for federal and private grants (ibid., 89–90). According to former English faculty member and department chair Nicholas A. Salerno (2005), beginning in the 1960s new faculty were suddenly recruited for their scholarly credentials as opposed to their teaching credentials. In the early 1960s a new policy was introduced whereby "all assistant professors would have their teaching loads lightened from twelve hours per semester to nine, thus freeing them for research" (Nebeker 1985, 42). At the beginning of the 1960s, ASU had virtually no access to outside research funds, but by the end of the decade "research burgeoned as millions of research support dollars flowed in from government and business foundations" (Sabine 1992, 199).

Graduate study symbolized an important upgrade in the quality and status of ASC and a necessary one to qualify for federal funds. To build the graduate programs in English and education, it was necessary to attract students by offering funding and teaching assignments, and it was necessary to free full-time faculty to direct the new graduate students. Hence Myers's belief that literature faculty should teach graduate courses instead of writing courses. It was yet another in a long line of concessions. Graduate study directly caused writing instruction to be conferred from the most experienced members of the English department to the least experienced as a concession to "university-status" and the pursuit of federal funds.

Although the dissolution of remedial writing instruction and the transfer of first-year composition teaching to graduate students are prominent concessions in the pursuit of federal funds, one additional change is worth noting: the introduction of ASC's first writing program administrator. Teaching assistants and part-time faculty gradually took over writing instruction in 1956, and it was assumed that they needed supervision and training. As well, in 1957 the General Education Committee determined first-year students should be exempted from first-year composition in the event they took four years of high school English and performed well on a departmentally administered examination. The feeling was that higher-quality students would be more willing to attend ASC if they could avoid some of the less pleasant curricular requirements (Turner 1979, 221–22). In prior years these tasks had fallen to the department chair, but the addition of administrative tasks associated with changes to composition education, alongside the expansion of administrative tasks associated with the university-structure, required a dedicated director of composition. Funds for the position were sought and allocated by the Division of Languages and Literatures in 1957.

Although the establishment of a dedicated writing program administrator was a consequence of conceding composition, not a cause of it, I gesture to it here because it actually served to weaken the link between English and composition and strengthen the link between composition and institutional needs. The director of composition reported to the division head, not the English chair. In subsequent years, a number of college and university committees considered the proper role of writing instruction in the curriculum. This reinforced the intellectual/ institutional split by taking first-year composition's oversight away from people who had at least some investment in composition as an intellectual subject (i.e., Myers) and putting it in the hands of people with more explicitly institutional responsibilities. What was taught in composition courses—the intellectual content—was apparently still dictated primarily by writing teachers and the program director, but first-year composition was by then a thoroughly institutional creature. In short, the interconnected efforts to achieve university-status and attract federal research funding to Arizona State College powerfully reinforced composition's value as an institutional concession.

A RISING TIDE LIFTS ALL SHIPS

Thus far, I have analyzed Arizona State's concessions of composition in relation to federal funding at length, and what remains for this chapter is to track reduplication to other institutions. Given how involved and technical my argument about Arizona State has been to this point, I intend to track reduplication as briefly as possible at two additional institutions: the University of North Texas (UNT) and the University of

California at Berkeley (UC Berkeley). I argued in chapter 2 that UNT developed in very similar measure to Arizona State when both institutions were normal schools and then teachers' colleges. They continued to track very closely in many ways throughout the majority of the twentieth century. I look at UNT briefly because its example reinforces the reorientation to federal funding I have described at Tempe.

I intend to spend slightly more time with UC Berkeley. As a land-grant university founded in 1868, UC Berkeley was established as a direct result of federal education funding, and it has long been the recipient of substantial federal funds. According to Hugh Davis Graham and Nancy Diamond, UC Berkeley was one of the sixteen universities that dominated federal research funding before and throughout World War II (1997, 28). In other words, UC Berkeley was never not oriented to federal funding. I chose UC Berkeley because, although it might seem to provide a disconfirming example of my thesis that postsecondary institutions conceded composition to orient to federal funds, it turns out that Berkeley administrators also conceded composition in the mid-twentieth century to attract federal research funds, though in ways that differed from ASU and UNT. Specifically, in the late 1950s Berkeley administrators conceded composition, along with other "basic courses," to protect their established access to federal funds, to attract additional federal funds, and to attract other research grant funding. Berkeley's example, therefore, helps demonstrate the flexibility of composition for aligning institutional behaviors with federal funding.

But first to UNT, long before it became a university. In 1923 North Texas Normal College changed its name to North Texas State Teachers' College (NTSTC) as part of the wave of normal school to teachers' college transformations I discussed in chapter 3. The school was NTSTC in the 1930s when the Depression hit, and the details of NTSTC's development are strikingly similar to those of Tempe State Teachers' College. According to UNT historian James L. Rogers (2002), Texas's state budget was slashed in 1931. Nearly $300,000 in building, operations, and maintenance funds were originally allocated in the state budget to NTSTC, but those funds were vetoed by the governor (ibid., 176). 1932 was no better, and in 1933 every college in Texas took a 25 percent across-the-board budget cut. Curricula were reduced, faculty pay was cut, and tuition was raised to offset some of the state budget reductions.

Also in 1933, North Texas State Teachers' College administrators struck on a grand plan to apply for federal Public Works Administration assistance. The following year, NTSTC received a $160,000 loan and a $50,000 grant from the PWA to build a dormitory. In subsequent years, additional federal funds were funneled into NTSTC for dorms, recreation buildings, a library, a theater and speech building, an addition to the hospital, and more (ibid., 228–29). All told, NTSTC took in nearly $1 million in federal loans and grants between 1933 and 1940 ("Schedule of Classes" 1939). As a consequence, NTSTC grew precipitously even during the Depression's bleakest years. In 1934 the physical campus was 24 acres, with 10 buildings and 50,000 volumes in the library ("Schedule of Classes" 1934, 30–31). By 1942, largely on the strength of federal money, NTSTC had expanded to 160 acres, with 45 buildings and 120,000 volumes in the library ("Schedule of Classes" 1942, 38–39).

If NTSTC's relationship to federal funds closely mirrored Tempe State's, so too did composition education. During this time, composition's institutional existence at NTSTC was essentially stable. It changed once in 1933, when the school went from a quarter system with three composition classes (English 101, English 102, and English 103) ("Schedule of Classes" 1932, 67) to a semester system with two classes (English 131 and English 132) ("Schedule of Classes" 1933, 70–71). It is unclear why the change from quarter to semester was undertaken, but the timing suggests federal funding and semester hours may have been related. More to my concern, composition's course descriptions were condensed in the conversion, but composition was otherwise essentially unchanged. At the risk of oversimplifying, it seems apparent that composition was dutifully fulfilling its role at NTSTC as a weak concession through the 1930s and early 1940s—even as NTSTC was otherwise in turmoil, composition was steady.

Throughout the New Deal era, NTSTC continued to track closely with Tempe State Teachers' College. In 1935 NTSTC introduced an education MA, and in 1937 it introduced a liberal arts undergraduate degree, just as its counterparts did in Tempe. As the degree offerings changed, curricula were expanded, enrollments grew, and faculty numbers grew as well. Then in 1944, following a conference with some of the same federal officials who eventually visited Arizona and produced reports for the newly established Arizona State College, NTSTC president Joseph McConnell "told the faculty that he wanted a study of possible reorganization of the college to meet changing postwar conditions" (quoted in Rogers 2002, 224). The outcome is unsurprising—the teachers' college became a state college "in all but name" in 1945 (ibid., 263; "Schedule of Classes" 1946, 29). The "state college in all but name" was, not coincidentally, eligible for GI Bill recipients just in time for the tidal wave of students to arrive on campus. After the war ended, enrollments ballooned at NTSTC, and English faculty were quickly under water.

The issues worth considering during this process are basically reduplications of issues I discussed at length when considering implementation
at Tempe State Teachers' College above. At North Texas State Teachers'
College, administrators repeated many of the same attempts to attract
federal funds as TSTC administrators did. So did administrators at many
other teachers' colleges—by 1945, a significant number of teachers' colleges were becoming state colleges, either in name or in institutional
organization.[14] There are, however, two peculiarities worth mentioning.

First, in President McConnell's archived papers, there is a treasure
trove of materials documenting negotiations in the 1930s and 1940s
between teachers' college officials and federal officials about reim-
bursements, federal education expectations, community engagement
programs, adult education programs, and more (McConnell 1937;
Research Division 1943). These negotiations are far too numerous to
detail here, and many are only tangentially related to composition. But
one thing is abundantly clear—NTSTC administrators and faculty were
deeply engaged in orienting the school to federal funding throughout
the 1930s and 1940s. It was an extended campaign, not just a few iso-
lated instances. To offer one relevant example, beginning as early as
1936, NTSTC administrators and faculty developed a series of community education programs, especially literacy programs, that depended
on federal guidelines and funding (McConnell 1937). Faculty from the
English department, and other departments as well, offered reading
and writing classes and workshops in public libraries, community centers, and other civic arenas. These were not college composition courses
precisely, but they were close in spirit. Considered broadly, these community literacy programs—developed using federal Emergency Adult
Education money—represent another form of "conceding composition." Although the community literacy programs were undoubtedly
a service to people who would otherwise have had no access to formal
education, the programs also represented attempts by NTSTC administrators and faculty to attract federal money and buffer the institution
from some of the most devastating effects of the Depression.

The second peculiarity is more directly a concession in the main
sense I have been arguing for throughout this book. In 1944, as NTSTC
administrators began preparing for the flood of new students with GI Bill
benefits, a committee was established called the Committee on Student
Use of English ("Schedule of Classes" 1944, 61). The Committee on
Student Use of English was charged with assessing students' writing in
their junior year to ensure proficiency before they would be allowed to
graduate. Any student found to be "deficient" was required to retake

"English 131: Grammar and Composition." The committee only lasted until 1950, ending at roughly the same time GI Bill enrollments started to tail off, which is perhaps suggestive. But in any case, for at least six years, including when the so-called tidal wave was cresting, composition was doubly conceded at NTSTC—first as part of the general education requirements and then again for treating "deficient" students. If composition classes were overwhelmed after World War II, it was at least partly the result of a new, if short-lived, requirement that made some students take first-year composition twice.

The instances of reduplication at UNT carry on—the school officially became a state college in 1949, administrators installed a doctorate in 1950, the state college became a state university in 1960, and research grants became an increasingly important component in the institution's existence throughout this period (Rogers 2002, 263). Composition played a role, if generally a small one, in these continuing administrative attempts to orient to the new federally funded norm, but minimal concessions followed minimal concessions. Composition was a reliable institutional concession throughout the mid-century in Texas, just as it was in Arizona and elsewhere.

Rather than continue to rehearse additional instances of reduplication in North Texas, I want to finish this chapter by examining composition's concession in rather different circumstances at the University of California—particularly at the flagship campus in Berkeley. As noted, Berkeley might seem to offer a counter-narrative to the story I have been telling because it was federally funded throughout its existence. Of course, I intend to argue the opposite—the UCs generally, and UC Berkeley specifically, conceded composition in the pursuit of federal dollars, just like the other institutions I have considered up to this point.

UC Berkeley was founded in 1868 as California's first state university, which means it did not endure the same growing pains many normal schools, teachers' colleges, and state colleges endured—or at least not in the same way. Berkeley's example is noteworthy, however, in part because of other California institutions' developments along these lines. In the late nineteenth century, to complement the state university in Berkeley, California officials developed a number of state normal schools (including the first state normal school in the western United States, which is now San José State University). In keeping with the national trend, the majority of California's state normal schools became state teachers' colleges in the mid-1920s (Merlino 1962). The one exception was the Los Angeles State Normal School, which was converted into UCLA and became the southern branch of the University of California in 1919. In

1935, California's state teachers' colleges officially became multipurpose state colleges—succeeding at a time when Tempe State Teachers' College and North Texas State Teachers' College failed to achieve the same conversion. In 1944, on the brink of the GI Bill tidal wave, one of California's foremost state colleges, Santa Barbara State College, became a third branch of the UC system against university administrators' wishes (Stadtman 1970, 340–48). All the while, additional public higher education institutions were founded throughout the state. By the mid-1950s, there were three competing systems of publicly funded higher education in California: (1) two-year state colleges, (2) four-year state colleges (now the California State University system), and (3) four-year state universities (now the University of California system).

The complicated history of California's higher education system is documented in volumes of readily available histories. The important point for this chapter is that by the mid-twentieth century UC Berkeley found itself competing with other state institutions for resources, including federal research and development funds, once its exclusive domain. "Particularly disorderly," writes Jane Stanley (2010, 93) in her history of composition at Berkeley, "was the 'growing political aggressiveness' . . . of the state colleges in their pursuit of the PhD and the right to conduct research." In a passage Stanley also quotes, former Berkeley chancellor and UC system president Clark Kerr recalls that in the late 1950s, the fight over research money among California's colleges and universities was a pitched battle: "The state colleges wanted research university status. They had earned it. They expected to get it. And all the Federal R&D money, after *Sputnik*, was out there for the asking, and they wanted their share of it" (2001b, 176). Kerr is not particularly cagey about UC officials' possessiveness where research funds were concerned: "The strategy of the university was clear . . . We did not want to share resources with sixteen additional 'university' campuses (the 12 established state colleges and four more then being developed) . . . And we did not want to watch the state colleges abandon their highly important skill training functions for teachers in the hot pursuit of the holy grail of elite research status" (ibid., 178). The actions taken by UC officials to safeguard resources—particularly federal funds—and elite research status ended up being closely, if indirectly, connected to conceding composition.

In 1960, after years of complex political maneuvering on the part of UC officials, California's Master Plan for Higher Education was passed into law. Naturally, the process was complicated and contentious, but the effects are relatively straightforward. The master plan defined the proper roles of California's three systems of higher education as follows:

(a) junior colleges could "offer instruction through but not beyond the fourteenth grade level" for associates-level degrees and transfer credits (California State Department of Education 1960, 3); (b) state colleges (now the California State University system) could offer liberal arts and sciences degrees, including at the masters level. In addition, it was specified that in the CSUs, "Faculty research, using facilities provided for and consistent with the primary function of the state colleges [i.e., pedagogy and teacher education], is authorized" (ibid.; Stadtman 1970, 394; Stanley 2010, 94). Finally, (c) the University of California was granted sole responsibility for basic research among California's higher education institutions, sole responsibility for training PhDs, and therefore nearly exclusive access among California's postsecondary institutions to federal research funds (Kerr 1957, 3).

In their efforts to secure resources and elite research status exclusively for the UCs, administrators, including Kerr, made sustained arguments throughout the 1950s and 1960s that the UCs should "emphasize graduate and upper-division levels of teaching" and "reduce proportionately their lower-division components" (Kerr 1961, 7). By the same token, however, University of California officials had "no intention of withdrawing from undergraduate or lower-division [levels of teaching]" (ibid.). The reasons for emphasizing upper-division and graduate work are fairly obvious—UC faculty were increasingly required to produce research and secure grant funds, so faculty and administrators felt that teaching specialized courses to majors and graduate students would be advantageous for meeting these objectives.

The retention of lower-division courses merits more unpacking. For starters, when the master plan was being negotiated among the various stakeholders, one of the primary talking points among university officials was that such a plan was necessary to reduce redundancy among the three higher education systems (Stanley 2010, 93).[15] On one hand, reducing redundancy was the justification for apportioning research exclusively to the UCs, which required the emphasis on upper-division and graduate work. On the other hand, the multi-tiered postsecondary system was designed so students could transfer between the tiers, depending on their ultimate goals. This meant that students had to have a baseline of courses, generally the first two years' worth, which would transfer easily among systems and across campuses (Kerr 1964, 71, 1966, 8). In fact, the "basic courses" were a primary concession in the master plan to connect the three systems but especially to connect the universities to the community colleges.[16] This was one way UC officials garnered the political support from community college officials that was necessary to overcome state college officials' attempts to obtain research responsibilities. Not to put too fine a point on it, but the universities strengthened their political alliance with community colleges by conceding composition. The promise of the UCs to accept transfer students who satisfactorily completed the basic courses in California's two-year colleges was a significant political leverage point. Although composition was not unique as a concession to "unity" among systems, by virtue of the fact that it was the most comprehensive requirement within the "basic courses," it was one of the largest concessions in California higher education.

Composition, along with other "basic courses," was also a necessary concession to fulfill UC Berkeley's graduate education commitment. In a June 1957 report to the UC president, Clark Kerr (1957, 2) argued for retaining lower-division curricula at Berkeley because, among other things, "a full undergraduate program provides employment as readers and teaching assistants to many self-supporting graduate students . . . and it gives many teaching assistants valuable training for future college or university teaching careers." Much as at Arizona State College, Berkeley's first-year composition courses were a funding source and a training ground for graduate students. Suffice to say that the basic courses in Berkeley were an important component in efforts to orient the university to attract (and retain) federal funding. And since Berkeley was the flagship of the UC system, its policies in such matters held significant weight throughout the system—influence that grew when Berkeley's chancellor Kerr became UC system president in 1958.

Not to be lost in the details is that basic courses, including composition, were conceded to bring "post-Sputnik" funding to the UCs, particularly to Berkeley where administrators fought even other UC campuses for federal money. As Stanley puts it, "Berkeley stood in relation to the other campuses of the university [with regard to federal funding] as the university as a whole stood in relation to the state colleges" (2010, 96). Berkeley was the largest beneficiary of federal money (see Kerr 2001a, 2001b; Seaborg and Colvig 1994), and it had the largest vested interest in "unity" across campuses and institutions necessary to protect its federal largesse.

But if the UCs conceded basic courses in general, they conceded composition in particular. As Stanley details at length, first-year composition at UC Berkeley especially was routinely the subject of hand-wringing, reform efforts, and public deliberation about the roles and responsibilities of higher education institutions: "Complaining that the university's standards have been breached is a way of reminding all concerned just how high those standards are" (2010, 84). As Stanley carefully documents, first-year composition and its associated apparatuses routinely came to Berkeley administrators' aid. Over and over again, composition was the most visible concession in continuing efforts to demonstrate Berkeley's institutional standards, improvement, and goodwill.

CONCLUSION

It should be clear by now that composition routinely served as an institutional concession throughout the mid-twentieth century in federal funding campaigns at schools around the United States. Composition's precipitous institutional growth during this period, then, suggests it was not just a common concession but one of the most important concessions schools could make to orient to federal expectations. As such, first-year composition became increasingly institutional in character and, counter-intuitively, increasingly flexible as institutional needs evolved. But obviously, composition also grew as an intellectual concern during the same period, as evidenced by the rise of rhetoric and composition as a discipline. The two are not exactly unrelated. It is not surprising, to me at least, that two of the most prominent dates in the field's history— the 1949 founding of the Conference on College Composition and Communication and the 1963 "birth of modern Composition" (North 1987, 15)—are so proximal to important dates in American higher education's important institutional moments (the GI Bill tidal wave and the university-status movement, respectively).

Still, I am inclined to believe that the institutional/intellectual split I have developed throughout this book remained important during this period. UC Berkeley offers one final example that highlights the fundamental—and growing—distinction between composition's intellectual and institutional roles that was characteristic of the era of burgeoning federal funds. In 1967, following years of pitched battles over UC Berkeley's first-year composition requirement—battles carried on at the local, state, and even national levels, including direct interventions by California governor Ronald Reagan and FBI director J. Edgar Hoover—UC Berkeley hosted its ninth annual Chancellor's Conference on English Composition (Flanagan 1967). The conference drew over 800 participants from area high schools, community colleges, state colleges, and local universities (Berkeley, UC Davis, and Stanford). It was funded by Berkeley's Office of the Chancellor and was organized by a five-member standing committee drawn from the Berkeley and UC Davis faculties. It appears to have been a pretty big deal. In the 1967 post-conference report to the chancellor, conference committee chair Thomas Flanagan declared that "the Conference strongly persuades me that it serves a most useful pedagogical service, and deserves our full-est support" (ibid.). It is unclear to me how much longer the confer-ence carried on after 1967, but for nearly a decade at least, UC Berkeley administrators funded a gathering for hundreds of composition teach-ers to talk about composition teaching.

What makes this conference such a striking example is that it was carried on during the period in Berkeley's history when composition's institutional existence was most hotly contested. Berkeley administrators were apparently committed to the intellectual work of the course even as they were arguing about its possibilities and its failures in institutional campaigns to prove Berkeley's quality, prestige, and qualifications as a federal research site. The *intellectual* work evidenced by the ninth annual composition conference and the *institutional* work evidenced through-out this chapter and in Stanley's book might have been taking place in two different worlds. So, too, in Tempe and North Texas.

This split is perhaps to be expected given the political and economic realities of higher education in the twentieth century. In 1969 Harland G. Bloland pointed out, "As the costs of higher education soar, the national government emerges as the only agency capable of sustaining adequate support for this massive enterprise" (1969, 15). By 1969, of course, the national government had been directly subsidizing higher education in various ways for at least four decades. And as the federal government took increasing responsibility for funding colleges and uni-versities, they became increasingly oriented to national interests (see Squire et al. 1961). The fact that composition programs strengthened mid-century rather than weakening is telling. Still, Berkeley's composi-tion conference highlights the possibilities inherent in the intellectual/institutional split. UC administrators and non-composition faculty may well have been ambivalent about or hostile to composition, but they nev-ertheless allowed—and funded—the people most responsible for com-position's intellectual direction to carry on their work. Put differently, higher education administrators and faculty were then, and are now, at pains to balance institutional exigencies with the intellectual com-mitments that should inform teaching and learning. It is not a perfect system, to be sure, but it bears repeating that conceding composition is not necessarily in conflict with theoretical or pedagogical best practices.

In the years since Flanagan's report to Berkeley's chancellor, much has changed in the intellectual terrain of rhetoric and com-position. Nevertheless, institutions of higher education remain ori-ented to federal expectations, as does composition in various—even imperceptible—ways.

Conclusion

CONCEDING (IN) RHETORIC AND COMPOSITION
On Questions of Seeing and Being Seen

Only the most purblind and creeping academician struggling to turn
out some quantity of pages could completely dismiss the question of
whether his [sic] work might do some good for the world. But what can
our field, generally obsessed by problems of the moment or looking to the
revelations of the future, learn from such study of days past?
—Robert J. Connors, "Historical Inquiry
in Composition Studies"

This book has presented an alternative portrait of composition's early institutional fortunes than the ones that predominate in our field. As any teacher, scholar, or administrator in the field knows, composition serves many complex, even conflicting, roles in the academy and even, for that matter, in the field itself. I have been arguing that one of the most prominent, if nevertheless unfamiliar, roles composition has served is as an institutional concession. As the most required course in modern American higher education, first-year composition proved critical to the development of higher education as such, from an unregulated system of disparate institutions serving discrete populations of students in the early nineteenth century to the relatively homogeneous system of institutions serving massive populations of students across the country by the mid-twentieth century.

Rather than lament the inextricably institutional nature of composition education, however warranted that may seem, it is worth remembering that composition's institutional value does not preclude good teaching and good learning—only that they are not necessarily coextensive. Still, first-year composition's value as an institutional concession helps explain why the course endured in American higher education and why it thrived, despite a steady procession of complaints from all quarters that composition did not (and does not) meet its ostensible purposes of remediating

DOI: 10.7330/9781607325055.c005

underdeveloped matriculants, preparing students for subsequent college writing tasks, or helping students to write better more generally.

My decision to conclude this history in the late 1950s is undoubtedly conspicuous given the seismic shifts in the field of rhetoric and composition that began in earnest in the subsequent decades. It has been well-established by historians that the 1960s marked the real intellectual turn of the discipline, including the development of distinct research methodologies, peer-reviewed journals and books, scholarly societies and conferences, and graduate programs (Goggin 2000; Hairston 1982; North 1987). The temptation may be to presume that the development of rhetoric and composition as a discipline, and the concomitant development of our disciplinary knowledge about the intellectual work of composing and teaching, has gradually reduced composition's uses as an institutional concession. I believe the opposite to be the case.

Composition has not been freed of its institutional value(s) in subsequent decades, and in fact, its institutional value has probably been strengthened as the requirement has become virtually unassailable. Even if influential members in the field could agree that the course should be abolished, for instance (see Connors 1997a; Crowley 2002), the notion that disciplinary specialists could make that decision unilaterally is impossible to maintain. If times have changed where conceding composition is concerned, it seems to me largely because composition is now such an indispensable expectation in institutions of higher education that the kinds of major national changes to composition that accompanied the rise of accreditation are relatively less sweeping. Moreover, each of the non-disciplinary institutional issues discussed in this book has continued uninterrupted into twenty-first-century higher education, though their forms and names have sometimes shifted. Composition is still routinely conceded to address them all, and it is regularly conceded to address other institutional exigencies as well.[1]

It seems only fitting to return to Arizona State University, to a moment well after the disciplinary turn, for a final example. When I first started the research for this book in 2008, I arranged to interview David Schwalm, ASU's writing program administrator during the period I initially planned to write about. That interview was a crucial entry point for what this project has become, even though I have largely moved away from the original incarnation.[2] Still, one of the things that stayed with me from that conversation was a part of the discussion we had about what Schwalm called ASU's "Basic Writing Wars."

In 1987, just a year after Schwalm was hired to direct the writing program, ASU's upper administrators contracted with a local community college to offer English 071, a basic writing course for ASU students who scored below a certain number on the SAT or ACT tests.[3] As part of the 071 deal, South Mountain Community College provided full- and part-time faculty to design and teach sections of English 071 on ASU's campus. Students who were placed into English 071 paid ASU enrollment costs but did not receive ASU degree credit for the course. Still, they had to pass English 071 to enter ASU's required first-year composition course, English 101. In reflecting (not enthusiastically) on the English 071 agreement, Schwalm (1989, 21) observes: "The conflict here is not between the university and the community college. The 'turf' issues are intramural, and they are not trivial when the contestants are university faculty and administrators and when curriculum is the contested ground. In this instance, administrators largely uninformed or misinformed about the field of composition and the writing needs of students have made decisions that have an enormous impact on the composition curriculum in itself and as an integral part of the larger university curriculum." In subsequent years, for various complex reasons, ASU withdrew from the contract with South Mountain Community College and returned developmental writing instruction to ASU's English department (see Glau 1996).[4]

Given the arguments I have been making throughout *Conceding Composition*, university administrators' unilateral decision to farm out ASU's basic writing courses to the community college is not especially remarkable, except inasmuch as it happened thirty years later than the other examples in this book. In fact, the English 071 example is perfectly in keeping with a long history of ASU's institutional representatives' efforts to concede composition in general. In some ways, the decisions about English 071 were consequences of a much earlier concession that falls squarely within my historical gaze. In 1958, as Arizona State College administrators campaigned to have the school "upgraded" from a regional college to a state university (which would make the institution eligible for additional forms of research funding), the Arizona Board of Regents passed a rule prohibiting the state's public universities from offering remedial English courses for credit. That rule is still in effect nearly sixty years later, and it has been subsequently reinforced by Arizona's legislators. Concessions feed concessions.

The English 071 episode is a gratuitous reminder that composition has continued to be a concession in American higher education in the years after my study leaves off. In fact, one of the most obvious implications of *Conceding Composition* is that composition has always been institutional and therefore always available as a concession in any and all of the three senses I outlined in my introduction. This is as true for the decades since 1960 as it was for the decades prior. At Arizona State University alone, there are plenty of examples, historical and contemporary, that reinforce my central claim that composition is perpetually configured and reconfigured, yielded, assumed, or emphasized to meet institutional needs, regardless of whether it also meets intellectual needs or best practices. In some cases, composition's institutional value parallels, and even powerfully reinforces, what rhetoric and composition specialists know to be the best intellectual circumstances for teaching students to write (Lester and Glau 2008).[5] In other cases, as in the case of English 071, composition's institutional value diverges dramatically from the field's established intellectual values.

The easy conclusion I can draw from this final example is methodological. In considering the practical implications of this study, the institutional perspective I have been advocating is a ready tool for examining how composition education has been implemented in institutions of higher education. Paired with the genitive method I have employed for tracking institutional exigencies across multiple institutions, we stand to learn a lot about how people at myriad institutions of higher education have conceded composition and why. By investigating the institutional conditions in which composition has existed at any given time, we stand to learn a tremendous amount about how composition's institutional circumstances enable and limit our disciplinary knowledge. The field's disciplinary histories have gone a long way to help teachers and researchers understand how writing has been taught and studied in the modern university, to say nothing of what it has helped us learn about rhetoric and writing education for more than two millennia before Harvard was even a dream. But our histories have not been able to explain how composition has lived in institutions of American higher education and why it has thrived, even (maybe especially) in ways we find troubling.

Even as I assert the methodological prospects, however, there is another implication patent in the English 071 example, as well as in the other examples in the book. Whatever else composition may be to institutions of higher education, we must begin to acknowledge that it is not invisible and never has been. Given the history of composition as a concession, we can no longer rely on rhetoric and composition's constitutive narrative of intellectual marginalization to drive our understanding of what we teach and study.

Obviously, this is not an innocuous point. A good deal of the field's scholarship is predicated on the idea that rhetoric and composition and all the things it stands for are essentially off the radar. Take, for example, the conveniently named "Visibility Project," spearheaded by Louise Wetherbee Phelps. Phelps's indefatigable efforts to get rhetoric, composition, and writing studies listed in the National Research Council's taxonomy of research disciplines is based on the fact that such listings affect how programs, graduates, doctorates, and more are counted for various official purposes (see Phelps and Ackerman 2010). On the other hand, the efforts directed at getting rhetoric and composition recognized in official channels build from the notion that the field is "hidden in plain sight" (Rodrigue 2013), which I have been arguing is not entirely accurate.[6]

In the case of English 071, Schwalm likewise asserts that "uninformed or ill-informed [upper] administrators continue to make curricular decisions that have been and continue to be detrimental to composition programs" (1989, 21). The commonsense that follows from this narrative is that if people—administrators and faculty from other disciplines, legislators, and the public—will just get to know the field better, they will be persuaded of our intellectual value. Visibility is billed as a proxy for appreciation. One of the long-standing missions of the field, in fact, has been to produce disciplinary ambassadors to bring rhetoric and composition into view. Other attempts to grow the field and its curricula, sometimes precipitously in a particular locale, have traded on the implicit belief that size will eventually translate into recognition. The insinuation, though not generally voiced, is that informed or better-informed or at least marginally aware administrators would make better decisions about composition.

Over and over, however, the field's research shows that more information in the hands of institutional decision-makers does not guarantee more composition-friendly decisions. Even at places where rhetoric and composition specialists have migrated into top administrative positions, composition's place in the academy is fairly consistent (even as its functions may change with the needs of the institution). Notwithstanding some very important work carried out on the assumption of composition's invisibility, an important implication of *Conceding Composition* is that rhetoric, composition, writing instruction, literacy education, and so on are not invisible. Far from it. This book suggests, to the contrary, that composition is, and always has been, highly visible to administrators, other faculty members, and other interested parties. It may in fact be one of the most visible aspects of higher education. Composition's very visibility is what makes it valuable as a concession.

Reconsidering composition's "invisibility" (or marginality or any other number of synonyms) in terms of concession suggests that visibility in institutions of higher education is rather more complex than our scholarship has often acknowledged. Visibility can serve some teachers and researchers even as it seriously harms others; it can result in more funding and support for writing programs even as it results in more meddling from non-specialist parties; and visibility may result in disciplinary commitments intended for split audiences—student writers and administrative "bean counters." In other words, the consequences of rising to the attention of the institutional community are unpredictable at best.

Ironically, many of the efforts undertaken in the past half-century to make rhetoric and composition more intellectually sound—including expanding into basic writing, writing centers, writing across the curriculum, writing program administration, writing assessment, and so on and so forth—have also resulted in more visible indicators of composition's institutional value. Which is to say, composition's broad applicability is a central aspect of its institutional flexibility and therefore its institutional appeal. But as I have been arguing, more intellectual visibility does not guarantee composition's disciplinary security, and, in fact, it may have the unintended consequence of making composition more valuable as a concession. Likewise, better teaching, more savvy composition administrating, and more curricular innovation do not protect composition from institutional concession. In some cases they may paradoxically draw the kind of institutional attention that results in more (and more dubious) concession.

How to proceed in the face of this institutional reality is unclear to me. I certainly do not have easy conclusions to offer, and during the course of writing this book, I have become increasingly skeptical of easy conclusions whenever they are offered. What I do know is that rhetoric and composition teachers, scholars, and administrators cannot continue to assume that composition's intellectual life is the central value of composition for institutions of higher education. Even as rhetoric and composition scholarship grew increasingly sophisticated in the nineteenth and twentieth centuries and now into the twenty-first century, the theoretical and pedagogical developments rhetoric and writing specialists use to mark sea changes in the field have often been of little consequence to faculty and administrators who conceded composition to solve pressing institutional problems.

In short, we cannot continue to imagine that composition instruction, or the pedagogies and theories that influence instruction, somehow exists on a separate (intellectual) plane from the institutions that require composition education, but then again, neither can we imagine that pedagogy and theory are necessarily persuasive in arguments over composition in the university. Simply put, the intellectual/institutional relationship, at least where composition is concerned, is far more complicated than the field has generally conceded. I can therefore only think to end this book with a call to pursue the methodological implications described above so we can begin to discover and describe composition's institutional value—both historical and contemporary—and so we can, to borrow a phrase from Robert J. Connors (1984, 158), "come to understand more clearly the power we hold and constraints upon us." This will not stop institutions from conceding composition—nor would we even want it to if we genuinely believe that composition is an important part of what takes place in institutions of higher education. Still, if and when rhetoric and composition teachers, researchers, and administrators undertake the complicated task of discovering how composition serves complex institutional needs, perhaps we may discover new ways to act that support strong institutions as a reciprocal function of strong writing instruction.

NOTES

Introduction

1. Arizona State University was founded in 1885 as the Territorial Normal School at Tempe, and during its first seventy-five years in existence it had no fewer than eight different names. To minimize confusion, I refer to the school in subsequent chapters by one of four names that reflect its institutional character at the time under consideration (Tempe Normal School, Tempe State Teachers' College, Arizona State College, or Arizona State University, respectively). When referring to the institution's collective history, as I do throughout this introduction and chapter 1, I refer to the institution as Arizona State University or ASU because it is the name that will be most familiar to my readers and is therefore the most useful for representing the institution across periods in which it was more than one type of institution.

2. Many notable rhetoric and composition scholars have been connected to ASU's writing program in one way or another over the past few decades, including Roberta Binkley, Jennifer Clary-Lemon, Sharon Crowley, Frank D'Angelo, Chitralekha Duttagupta, John Gage, Greg Glau, Maureen Daly Goggin, Peter Goggin, Bonnie Lenore Kyburz, Elenore Long, Paul Kei Matsuda, Keith Miller, Susan Miller-Cochran, John Ramage, Rochelle Rodrigo, Duane Roen, Shirley Rose, David Schwalm, and Michael Stancliff, to name just a few. In addition, several prominent rhetoric and composition scholars have worked at ASU without any direct connection to the English department or the writing program on the main campus (there are four ASU campuses, each with its own majors, departments, and programs): Akua Duku Anokye, former chair of the Conference on College Composition and Communication, is associate professor of Africana language, literature, and culture in the Division of Humanity Arts and Cultural Studies at ASU West; Joseph Comprone served as dean of Arts and Sciences at ASU West, among other positions, in the 1990s; Barry Maid is professor and former head of the Technical Communication program at ASU's Polytechnic Campus; and Elaine Maimon was provost at ASU West and vice president of ASU in the late 1990s and early 2000s. None of them have, to my knowledge, taught in or administered directly the writing program on the Tempe campus, where the majority of students take courses. It seems very likely there are others I have not discovered in the course of my research.

3. To limit myself to just two examples, the WPA-L listserv, which boasts as many as 3,000 rhetoric and composition specialist subscribers at any given time, was developed at ASU by David Schwalm and Barry Maid in the 1990s; and ASU's writing program faculty, including John Ramage and Greg Glau, helped pioneer the Stretch model for basic writing instruction, which stretches English 101 over two semesters to give basic writers additional time to practice and develop their writing (see Glau 1996). Stretch has become a national model for basic writing. ASU also enrolls more than 80,000 students on four campuses as of fall 2014 (Keeler 2014), and ASU Writing Programs' is "the largest college writing program in the United States" (Rose and Skeen 2010, 1).

DOI: 10.7330/9781607325055.c006

4. See, for example, Donahue and Moon (2007); Gold (2008); Henze, Selzer, and Sharer (2008).

5. In contrast to the common belief within composition studies that writing program administration gained status in higher education as the field of rhetoric and composition professionalized (see, e.g., Connors 1999; Corbett 1993; Heckathorn 1999, 2004; McLeod 2007), my research strongly suggests that writing program administration at ASU, such as it was, garnered considerable status for many years after the position was introduced in 1957, at least with respect to faculty tenure. Writing program administration was considered a service assignment at ASU from its inception, to be sure. However, tenure and promotion decisions in the mid-twentieth century were based predominantly on teaching excellence and service to the university and community (see, e.g., "Faculty Personnel Policy" 1956). Teaching and service were the primary criteria for promotion and tenure at ASU until well into the 1960s, and their prioritization lingered in faculty evaluation decisions until well into the 1970s, even after research became the official coin of the realm. As long as this was the case, writing program administration, which was university-level service, was considered a significant professional contribution and worthy of tenure consideration. As research expectations in higher education increased throughout the 1960s, 1970s, and 1980s, however, and as administrators at Arizona State University sought "major research university" distinction (see Arizona Board of Regents 1980), respect for writing program administration effectively decreased in tenure decisions. By the early 1980s, writing program administration at ASU was apparently no longer a tenurable effort in the absence of academic publication and therefore became a burden without rewards for untenured faculty.

6. After Guinn's departure, ASU's English department chair, Nicholas A. Salerno, attempted to recruit Edward P.J. Corbett from Ohio State (Corbett 1984). It is not clear whether Salerno intended for Corbett to run the writing program, but it seems likely. In the absence left by Guinn, the writing program was run from 1984 to 1986 by a series of interim directors, including M. Clare Sweeney (then director of the Writing Center), John Mateja (a temporary research fellow in the education department), and at least one graduate student.

7. Archer also tried to recruit Ed Corbett to ASU (Corbett 1984).

8. Louis M. Myers was hired in 1938, and his hiring inaugurated an uninterrupted stretch during which ASU faculty members who were, or would be, explicitly connected to the field of rhetoric and composition proper were employed in the English department. English department chairs, including Myers, Wilfred A. Ferrell, and Nicholas A. Salerno, published composition textbooks (Myers published the widely adopted *Guide to American English*, and Ferrell and Salerno [1968] co-edited *Strategies in Prose*, a collection of readings for use in first-year composition that had at least five editions). Other former and current faculty members have published widely in disciplinary venues. Some were publishing in disciplinary journals, including *College Composition and Communication, College English*, and *WPA: Writing Program Administration*, as early as the 1950s (e.g., Myers 1954, 1961; Ferrell 1963). Others have published influential rhetoric and composition textbooks representing a wide variety of theoretical and disciplinary approaches (e.g., Archer and Schwartz 1971; Bullock and Goggin 2006; Crowley and Hawhee 2012; Crowley and Stancliff 2008; D'Angelo 1980, 1999a; Glau and Duttagupta 2012; Glau and Jacobsen 2001; Ramage, Bean, and Johnson 2010; Roen, Glau, and Maid 2008).

9. Although various names are given to the first-year writing requirement in different times and places, I use "first-year composition" throughout this book for the sake of consistency.

10. See also Berlin (1984, 85); Connors (1997b, 11, 187); Crowley (1998a, 87).

11. As I discuss in chapter 3, English 101 did not replace English 1, but the assumption that it did guided my research for a considerable amount of time.

12. It is not my goal in this book to theorize "the institution," but I do believe deeper theorization of institutions and institutional rhetorics looms as a necessity for rhetoric and composition scholars given the importance institutions play in our professional and intellectual lives. Some early attempts have been made to do so in the field (e.g., Porter et al. 2000), but there is significant room to develop the study of institutional rhetorics as something beyond the study of rhetoric in institutions.

13. See, for example, Brereton (1995, xv, 11); Connors (1991b, 55); Masters (2004, 5–7); Moon (2007, 2).

14. See, for example, Brodkey (1996); Butler (2008, 55–58); Crowley (1998a, 255–56); McQuade (1992, 484); Skinnell (2010).

15. See also Bullock and Trimbur (1991); Enos (1987, v–vii); Fleming (2011, 8–9); Goggin (1995); Russell (2002, especially chapter 1).

16. This concession is obviously not without complexities, but whether composition teachers have claimed that student writing was barbarously deficient (Hill 1878) or entering a new stage of development (Shaughnessy 1977) or whatever else, a common thread is the concession that composition instruction is beneficial for students.

17. My own sense is that first-year composition has contributed to teaching ASU students to be better writers. Even so, my sense (which was widely shared) was not always borne out at the institutional level. As just one example, in the mid-2000s members of the English department successfully lobbied upper administration to reduce course caps to nineteen in first-year composition classes (Lester and Glau 2008). However, following the 2008 economic downturn, caps were raised again to twenty-five to address economic exigencies. As a teaching associate, I was not privy to the conversations that concerned this decision, but it was clear to me that upper administrators felt compelled to make a decision that benefited the institution, even if it was not the most pedagogically sound option.

18. Even as I say that Archer was apparently a receptive audience for abandoning composition, it seems worth repeating that he had chaired the CCCC just a decade earlier and was organizing a conference focused on composition teaching in two-year colleges the same year Durham sent this letter.

19. See Fleming (2009) for a thoughtful examination of this commonplace.

20. On a local level, it could also conceivably be a *disruptive* form of underlife, "a form which tries to undermine the nature of the institution and posit a different one in its place" (Brooke 1987, 151).

21. In part, this realization was a result of my interactions as a TA and assistant writing program administrator with other composition teachers and administrators from distant institutions. I was routinely struck by the commonalities in, say, institutional assessment mandates among institutions.

22. See Alumni Association of the State Normal School Tempe (1925); Felmley (1923); Harper (1970, 129–50); Herbst (1980); Lucas (1999, 53–59); Ogren (2005).

23. The English department's history alone is rife with fascinating, idiosyncratic stories and personalities. Among the more dramatic ones, which unfortunately do not bear sustained attention in this book, are accounts of a part-time English instructor's involvement in a burglary and murder in 1975 (Fitzpatrick 1992) and apocryphal tales of a creative writing professor in the 1960s who welcomed new faculty members to the department by inviting them to clothing-optional pool parties at his home (Salerno 2005).

24. It seems to me that potentially interesting connections can be made here to ecological and network theories being developed in the field (see, e.g., Brooke 2012; Dobrin 2012; Edbauer 2005; Rice 2012; Rivers and Weber 2011).

25.   Hopkins and Thomas offer interesting glimpses into their historical situatedness with descriptions such as the following: "Arizona, an Indian-ridden desert frontier, was the last of America's successive frontiers to be settled and conquered by the Westward Movement" (1960, viii).

26.   The cynic in me reckons that if success was harder to demonstrate in composition classes than in math or history classes, that fact strengthened, rather than weakened, composition's malleability and therefore its institutional value.

Chapter 1

1.   I follow Kirsch and Sullivan's (1992, 2) distinction here between a methodology (the underlying theory and analysis of how research does or should proceed) and a method (a technique or way of proceeding in gathering evidence).

2.   I will not speculate in the body of the text, that is. In the notes, I am happy to speculate that Kenneth Burke's concept of "trained incapacity" fairly describes my problem (1984b, 7–10).

3.   For additional examples, see Connors (1997a); Crowley (1986); Russell (2002, 6). See Heilker (1996) for an even further-reaching literature review.

4.   See also Meadows (1928, 1–3).

5.   See Heilker (1996, 109); Miller (2011, 130–32); Soliday (2002, chapter 2). For a detailed argument that first-year composition was designed to protect universities from unfit students, see Crowley (1998a, especially chapter 11).

6.   See Lamos (2009); Lindblom, Banks, and Quay (2007).

7.   See Berlin (1987, 3); Enos (1987, v–vii); Shaughnessy (1977). In chapter 12 of *Composition in the University*, Crowley (1998a) discusses this "needs discourse" in relation to disciplinary goals and in the meantime offers a laundry list of citations that make or rely on such claims.

8.   See Fleming (2011, 4); Connors (1986); Halloran (1990); Lerner (1996); Varnum (1986).

9.   See Russell (2002); Strickland (2011).

10.   See Anson (2002); Goggin and Beatty (2000, 52); McQuade (1992, 484).

11.   I find this argument in particular both intensely compelling and tremendously unsatisfying. Certainly, "cash cow" claims are persuasive when one considers first-year composition in relation to department or college budgets. It is much harder, though not impossible, to make the case for direct economic benefits at the institution level. See, for example, Collins (1997).

12.   This is certainly not a comprehensive list of institutional perspectives in the field. Most, like Winterowd (1998), situate the discipline in an institutional context without much explicit attention to the complexities of being "institutional." Katherine Tirabassi (2007) takes a different tack, positing the theoretical lens of "institutional writing cultures." Tirabassi uses institutional writing cultures to consider "external pressures, curricular choices, theoretical perspectives, extracurricular initiatives, and regional influences" as forces that shaped writing at the University of New Hampshire in the mid-twentieth century (2007, xiv). Although Tirabassi's institutional perspective is more consistent with mine than Winterowd's, like Russell and T. Miller, she ultimately focuses on writing instruction in different spaces throughout the institution.

13.   Ritter (2012, 8–9) provides a useful breakdown of some directions disciplinary histories have taken.

14.   See Gannett, Brereton, and Tirabassi (2010, 426); Gold (2008, 7); Hawhee and Olson (2013, 90–91); McComiskey (2016).

15. These histories include canonical works by historians such as Kitzhaber (1990), Berlin (1984, 1987), Connors (1997b), and Crowley (1998a), as well as more recent histories, such as Miller (2011) and Strickland (2011).

16. For some examples, see Bordelon (2011); Donahue and Moon (2007); Enoch (2008); Fleming (2011); Gold (2005, 2008); Henze, Selzer, and Sharer (2008); Lamos (2011); Masters (2004); Monroe (2007); Ritter (2009, 2012); Rothermel (2003); Shepley (2010); Soliday (2002); Stanley (2010); Tirabassi (2007).

17. This claim is not entirely in conflict with certain versions of micro-history. Eminent micro-historian Jill Lepore (2001, 141) argues, "However singular a [research subject] may be, the value of examining it lies in how it serves as an allegory for the culture as a whole"; likewise, Giovanni Levi (2001, 97–98) claims, "The unifying principle of all microhistorical research is the belief that microscopic observation will reveal factors previously unobserved" to draw "far wider generalizations"; and Carlo Ginzburg (2012, 207), perhaps the best-known micro-historian, asserts that "a close-up look permits us to grasp what eludes a comprehensive viewing, and vice versa." I return to these issues later in the chapter.

18. This extends similar claims by historians including Connors (1997b) and Stewart (1992).

19. Ginzburg (2012) offers a useful genealogy of micro-history and demonstrates there is significant complexity in the term across divergent intellectual traditions. See also Magnússon and Szijártó (2013). I use the term to refer to intensive local histories that characterize much recent work in rhetoric and composition.

20. Gretchen Flesher Moon (2007, 4–5) establishes at some length the working definition of "local" (i.e., micro-historical) comprised by the book's contributors by contrasting it to "composition's dominant historical narratives" (i.e., macro-historical).

21. I am certainly not the first historian to encounter this challenge. In 1964, historian Marc Bloch advocated shifting back and forth between macro- and micro-historical scopes—what some historians have since labeled "multiscopic history" (Ginzburg 2012, 207; Magnússon and Szijártó 2013, 27). More recently, in rhetorical studies, Debra Hawhee and Christa J. Olson theorize "pan-historiography" to allow for tacking back and forth between wide-ranging, expansive histories and more localized, tightly bound histories (2013, 90–91).

22. As Vandenberg (1996) demonstrates, disciplinarity is a highly contested concept in rhetoric and composition. It nevertheless remains an important organizing model for academic specialists.

23. To offer some examples, histories as apparently dissimilar as Schultz (1999), Royster (2000), Harris (1997), and Jarratt (1991) employ different circumferential scopes. Nevertheless they remain focused on drawing or redrawing the intellectual contours of disciplinary borders.

24. Ross Winterowd writes, "When we begin to define composition as a discipline, then, we ask, 'What questions constitute the field (if it is a field)?' I would answer, and I presume many compositionists would agree, that the master questions regard invention (ethos, pathos, logos), arrangement, style, and pedagogy. If that is the case, then composition is closely related to, if not a part of, rhetoric. Of course, some questions are unique to composition—for instance, those involving basic writing, literacy in relation to society, writing as thinking, writing and ideology, the relationships of writing and reading, the technical details of coherence in an array in space as opposed to an array in time, the relationships of composition and creative writing . . ." (1998, 221).

25. Variations of this point are made by a number of historians, including Connors (1997b, 18); Glenn and Enoch (2009, 11–13); Moon (2007, 2–3).

26. For discussions of the productively defamiliarizing possibilities of historical work, see Ballif (2013a); Berlin (1994, 122); Ercolini and Gehrke (2013); Fitzgerald (2001); Glenn (2000); Vitanza (1987, 1997).

27. See Connors (1986); Goggin (2000, 12–30); Strickland (2011).

28. The North Central Association of Colleges and Schools, the largest accreditation association and the one to which ASU currently belongs, reports having nearly 10,000 members.

29. Jacques Derrida (2007, 39) explores the genitive as a philosophical concern and ruminates on the subjective/objective ambiguity inherent in the concept:

> The invention of the other, the incoming of the other, is certainly not *constructed* as a subjective genitive, and just as assuredly not as an objective genitive either, even if the invention comes from the other—for this other is thenceforth neither subject nor object, neither a self nor a consciousness nor an unconscious. To get ready for this coming of the other is what can be called deconstruction. It deconstructs precisely this double genitive and, as deconstructive invention, itself comes back in the step [*pas*]—and also as the step—of the other. To invent would then be to "know" how to say "come" and to answer the "come" of the other. Does that ever come about? Of this event one is never sure.

Derrida's "double genitive"—simultaneously subjective and objective—is apparent in the linguistic version of the genitive, but the linguistic concept is less tied to the philosophical ethics Derrida explores.

30. Matthew Heard pointed out to me that the Latin root of genitive (*gen-*) comprises notions of heredity and parentage. There is certainly an "ancestral" resonance in the genitive, especially in the case of someone owning their face, for example. But the genitive is a rather loose ancestral connection, given that it also covers such usages as "Mendel's pea shoots," which obviously bears no direct genetic connection.

31. Connors makes much the same case throughout *Composition-Rhetoric* (1997b). Halloran (1990, 175) makes a similar argument, asserting that composition evolved as "an attempt to adapt rhetoric to dramatically changed conditions both inside and outside the academy, conditions produced by the industrial revolution and the new middle-class and professional mores." See also Crowley (1986); Fleming (2011); Lindblom, Banks, and Quay (2007); Miller (1997, 2011); Russell (2002); Strickland (2011).

32. By appropriate, I mean that a school would have had to be in the right "associational grouping" at the time under consideration. For instance, California State University, Long Beach was founded in 1949, so it would not be an appropriate site to seek evidence of accreditation of the sort that predominated in the 1920s.

Chapter 2

1. For many years, education historians all but ignored normal schools. For instance, in his landmark, 600+-page, Pulitzer Prize–winning history, Lawrence A. Cremin (1982) relegates normal schools to no more than a few casual mentions (146–47, 364; see also Cremin 1961, 1990). Even when education historians have examined normal schools, they have tended to view them as substandard institutions (Ogren 2005, 1–2). For good examples, see Lucas (1999, 22–37, 2006, 139–44). Recently, normals have begun to receive more critical attention. For some important historical and contemporary sources that take normal schools seriously, see *American Normal Schools* (1860); Barnard (1851); Barnhardt (2001);

Freed (2008); Harper (1970); Hawkins (1912); Herbst (1980, 1989); Ogren (2003, 2005); Rettger (1923).

2. See Bordelon (2011); Fitzgerald (2001, 2002, 2007); Gold (2005, 2008); Gray (2007); Jarratt (2009); Lindblom, Banks, and Quay (2007); Ritter (2012); Rothermel (2003, 2007); Salvatori (1996); Skinnell (2013).

3. According to David Felmley (1923, 47), president of the State Normal University in Normal, Illinois, "We use the term teacher training [as opposed to 'teacher education'] because we recognize that teaching is an art in which skill is to be acquired rather than a science of which knowledge is to be gained." See Lucas (2006, 22–37); Minnich (1923, 32–33); Morgan (1923, 56–57); Ogren (2005, 57–59, 213–35) for discussions of normal schools' expansion in the late nineteenth and early twentieth centuries. See Burke (1982, 216) and Harris (1904, xiv–xix) for discussions of normal school enrollments.

4. Tempe Normal School was initially named Territorial Normal School in Tempe. In 1889, it became Arizona Territorial Normal School; in 1896, it became Normal School of Arizona; and in 1903, it finally became Tempe Normal School of Arizona. I have chosen to stick with the last of the four monikers for three reasons—first, it is the simplest. Second, the name lasted the longest (see Hronek 1985, 113n1). And third, it is more precise than some of the other options given the founding of a second normal school in Flagstaff, Arizona, in 1899. In light of my central argument, however, the name changes were no small affair. They had to be proposed to and authorized by the state legislature, and there were deeply held convictions about names and name changes that signaled any number of educational, political, and regional/local commitments.

5. Universities were designed to advance research (Lucas 2006, 194–95), and colleges offered students a liberal education (Cohen 1998, 145–47).

6. Debra Hawhee (2004) traces the connection between physical and rhetorical exercises back to Ancient Greece.

7. I realize "current-traditional" has been critiqued as a concept (e.g., Connors 1997b), but it still serves as convenient shorthand for the elements of early composition/rhetoric theory I aim to discuss.

8. See, for example, Connors (1981, 1983); Crowley (1990, especially chapter 6); Kitzhaber (1990, 191–96). EDNA refers to exposition, definition, narrative, and argument.

9. Most of these texts are discussed in Carr, Carr, and Schultz (2005) as predecessors to present-day composition textbooks.

10. Interestingly, membership in one of the two literary societies, Zetetic or Hisperion, excused TNS students from taking a rhetoric course (Hopkins and Thomas 1960, 111). For discussions about college and university literary societies, see Applebee (1974, 12–13); Connors (1997b, 47–48); Gere (1987, chapter 1); Westbrook (2002); Wozniak (1978, 45–47).

11. For discussion of student journals, magazines, and newspapers, see Gold (2008, especially chapter 2); Jarratt (2009); Ritter (2012, chapter 2); Schultz (1999, 135–43).

12. See, for example, Gold (2008); Russell (2002, 44–45). See Keenan (2009) for a brief history of early intercollegiate debate.

13. I contend in "Harvard, Again" (Skinnell 2014) that English A actually came into being for institutional reasons, not because of faculty dismay about student writing.

14. Hopkins and Thomas (1960) begin with the school's founding as Tempe Normal. Their history is clearly epideictic. They paint Tempe Normal's founder, Hayden, as a benevolent patriarch, shepherding Tempe through its early days as a small settlement by advancing an educational mission. Nevertheless, Hopkins and Thomas

offer extensive descriptions of the school's history based on primary evidence that are useful for considering how the institution came into existence and subsequently developed. The epideictic nature of *The Arizona State University Story* is also notable because fawning institutional histories exist for hundreds, if not thousands, of post-secondary institutions. They are often remarkably similar despite real differences between institutions. A comparative analysis of these histories might yield interesting insights into the prominent institutional factors that shaped the implementation of curriculum generally and composition/literacy curriculum specifically.

15. Although it was established during the same legislative session as Tempe Normal in 1885, the university did not open until 1891.

16. Only Long, as superintendent of public instruction, served on both the board of education and the university's board of regents. It is unclear what Long's feelings about the university were, but Hopkins and Thomas (1960, 73) claim that Long "fortunately, favored the Normal School." In 1888, Principal Farmer was dismissed for undisclosed reasons (Arizona Board of Regents 1888), and Long took over as TNS's principal for two years (Arizona Board of Regents 1889). After stepping down as principal, Long remained superintendent of public instruction and was involved with the normal in varying capacities for many years.

17. Likewise, the University of Arizona was supposed to have a normal department, but university officials "pointed out that the Normal Department was being adequately served by the Territorial Normal School" (Mitchell 1985, 26).

18. Initially, there were two tracks at TNS: elementary and advanced. Both tracks prepared students to teach in Arizona's schools, but the advanced course was longer and included classical subjects such as Latin, Virgil, rhetoric, and German history. In recognition of the lack of high schools in Arizona, the advanced course was designed to prepare students for college instead of, or in addition to, teaching in primary schools. The curriculum was arranged so students who did not want to become teachers could still get an education meant to rival what other high schools offered (Thomas 1960b, 131). After Hiram Farmer left TNS in 1888, Robert Long redesigned the curriculum into a single track, though many students left before completing the whole course of study.

19. This line is repeated in a number of speeches Everett gave on multiple occasions throughout the mid-century in his capacity as a normal school advocate and elected official.

20. See also Barnard (1851); Lyte (1904); National Education Association (1899). Mariolina Salvatori (1996, xiv) claims that the professional focus of normal schools became a political problem in the 1880s when some people "began to argue for the inadequacy of normal schools 'to educate' teachers . . . because of their exclusive and limiting reliance on 'methods.'" Education historian Christopher J. Lucas (2006, 144) likewise claims that normal schools' professional focus eventually contributed to their disappearance (see also Herbst 1989, 172). However, normal school proponents continued to argue for the value of focusing on methods well into the twentieth century (e.g., Rettger 1923). In chapter 4, I argue that normal schools' downfall was as much a result of inter-institutional animosity, operationalized vis-à-vis accreditation associations, as of normal schools' pedagogical focus.

21. See also Lucas (2006, 29–30); Ogren (2005, 125–26).

22. I suggested at the beginning of this chapter that there is a dearth of contemporary scholarship on normal schools, which is true, but the historical literature is vast. Several national organizations, including the American Normal School Association and the Peabody Education Fund, held annual conferences and published proceedings. The National Education Association had a normal school division with regularly published reports and proceedings into the twentieth century. The US

Commissioner of Education compiled yearly reports about normal schools for decades, as did most state commissioners of education. And countless books, articles, reports, masters theses, and doctoral dissertations extensively detail normal schools' theories and practices. I cite some of the available scholarship in this and other chapters, but there is a treasure trove that is virtually untouched by most historians, both in rhetoric and composition and in education more generally. Frankly, given the abundant materials available, it is somewhat shocking that more work is not being done to understand normal schools on their own terms.

23. As with Tempe Normal, North Texas Normal College had numerous names. It started as Texas Normal College and Teacher Training Institute (1890–94), then became North Texas Normal College (1894–1901), and eventually became North Texas State Normal College (1901–23). At the risk of obscuring important events signified by these name changes, I use North Texas Normal College throughout this chapter for reasons of economy and consistency.

24. Incidentally, grammar and rhetoric were two "studies that require full time."

25. Arizona's legislature passed a similar law in 1909, the Uniform Courses of Study Act, which mandated that "the courses of study leading to graduation from the Territorial Normal Schools of Arizona shall be uniform and shall be approved by the Territorial Board of Education" (Uniform Courses of Study Act 1909).

26. In response to an earlier draft, Rebecca Hohn asked me what not conceding would look like. It was an incisive and ultimately generative question, and for that I am grateful.

Chapter 3

1. The six are Middle States Association of Colleges and Schools, New England Association of Schools and Colleges, North Central Association of Colleges and Schools, Northwest Commission on Colleges and Universities, Southern Association of Colleges and Schools, and Western Association of Schools and Colleges.

2. Because of its ubiquity, any perceived threat to conventional forms of accreditation can generate serious concern in higher education (see, e.g., Adler-Kassner and O'Neill 2010, esp. chapter 2; Jaschik 2005; Lederman 2007). For a recent accreditation controversy, see Eric Kelderman's (2013) essay about San Francisco City College.

3. Adler-Kassner and O'Neill represent an exception inasmuch as they explicate accreditation issues to a significant degree. However, their stated goal is to make writing scholars and teachers "knowledgeable about writing assessment so we can harness the power associated both with the process of undertaking this research and with the idea about assessment itself to improve teaching and learning" (Adler-Kassner and O'Neill 2010, 41). In brief, their explication invokes "the topos of improvement = appreciation" I discussed in my introduction. This is particularly interesting in light of their opening anecdote about upper administrators making decisions about the writing program without consulting anyone in the writing program—what I would consider an instance of conceding composition that directly contradicts any possibility that "improvement = appreciation."

4. ASU's copy of the 1927–28 "Bulletin" is missing the page describing "English 101/102: First Year English." However, the 1927–28 catalog has that page and is otherwise identical to the 1928–29 catalog. I've referred to the 1928–29 catalog, confident that it replicates the previous year's language.

5. Research challenging the stagnation narrative from other perspectives has been done, notably by Katherine Tirabassi (2007) and Robin Varnum (1992).

6. Qualifying examinations were the primary instrument for determining a teacher's employment qualifications at the turn of the twentieth century.

7. California's entire postsecondary system was reformed in the 1920s. One potential point of interest is that UC Berkeley introduced a first-year composition requirement in 1922, at precisely the same time California's normal schools became teachers' colleges (Merlino 1962).

8. Friction among national, regional, state, and local agencies regarding teacher education standards was intense (Ducharme and Ducharme 1998, 3–15; Harper 1970; Judd 1920; Maxwell 1923; Mayor 1965; Rettger 1923; Roames 1987; Selden 1960; Tansil 1929). Although the relationships between organizations vying for control of teacher education were often strained, the upshot was a steady push to make teacher education more rigorous.

9. Normal schools and teachers' colleges were stripped of their eligibility for regular membership in the NCA in 1913 on the grounds that "most of them were so far inferior on the [higher] standards" adopted for colleges and universities (Ludeman 1931, 364–65).

10. Matthews may have been involved in defining standards in American education. He'd been a member of the National Education Association (NEA), the most powerful education interest group in the country, since 1899. He was secretary of the NEA's executive council and served in other capacities from 1904 until at least 1925 (Hopkins and Thomas 1960, 211; Richardson 1964, 15). The NEA took responsibility for overseeing the American Association of Teachers' Colleges in 1925, and it is conceivable that Matthews was involved. Whether he was directly involved or not, however, there can be no doubt he was aware of the circumstances, especially considering the NEA's role in shaping normal school standards and teachers' college standards beginning as early as 1858 (Roames 1987, 82–101).

11. Regional accreditation was a pressing concern for Texas's teachers' colleges, too. In 1924 they applied en bloc to the Southern Association of Colleges and Schools, but SACS did not have a teachers' college policy and therefore rejected the application ("Schedule of Classes" 1924). Texas's teachers' college administrators threatened to join the NCA to leverage admission in SACS (see, e.g., Bruce 1923).

12. Although the accreditation agreement with California is no longer mentioned after 1923, presumably the change from normal school to teachers' college restored Tempe graduates' opportunities to teach in California and other states.

13. The faculty members dismissed were those without advanced degrees (Thomas 1960b, 436).

14. As of 1931, "rank" denoted associate or full professor status: "We are using the ruling that to be eligible to academic rank a faculty member must possess the master's degree. Faculty members who do not possess master's degrees are now classified as assistants. They will be ranked as soon as the master's degrees are earned" (North Central Association of Colleges and Schools 1931–32, 5). James Lee Felton, chair of Tempe's English department for twenty years, was ranked as an associate because he held a masters degree. However, he was later removed as chair because he did not hold a PhD.

15. According to NCA regulations, classes (exclusive of lectures) should be capped at thirty students. Classes larger than thirty "should be interpreted as endangering educational efficiency" (North Central Association of Colleges and Schools 1930–31, 2).

16. The term *writing program* is one I'm applying to the agglomeration of writing courses at TSTC for my purposes. There is no indication that faculty or administrators considered it a unified "writing program" in the way we use the term now.

17. Until the 1940s, there was no official general education program—every major had its own requirements. Faculty and administrators for a given major could technically decline to require first-year composition, which some did in the 1930s. Such refusals were generally short-lived, however.

18. In fall 1929, there were 523 students enrolled; by spring 1932, approximately 864 students were enrolled, an increase of more than 65 percent in less than three years. Even before ASU boasted staggering enrollments, the school maintained fairly steady growth from year to year, with enrollment increasing in fifty-seven of the first seventy-five years (Thomas 1960e, 9). Nine of the eighteen years in which enrollment shrank were war years. Of the remaining nine, eight followed institutional redesigns that disestablished curricular offerings for entire grades of students—in 1921, for example, the ninth grade curriculum was abandoned, so there wasn't an incoming ninth grade class. Since 1960, enrollments have maintained a similar pattern, occasionally dropping minimally or remaining flat for a couple of years, but generally increasing steadily. Between 1970 and 2010, fall enrollment decreased only five times (ASU Office of Institutional Analysis 2010).

19. In his 1936 report to the president, English department chair Lionel Stevenson notes that in the five sections of English 101 offered in fall 1935, enrollments were between fifty and seventy students (ASU Department of English 1936). By 1937, enrollments were apparently down to more manageable levels.

20. Interestingly, David Fleming describes what seems to be a very similar process of hierarchicalizing composition at the same at the University of Wisconsin, Madison (2011, 40–44). Notably, Wisconsin was also accredited by the NCA.

21. As I argue in chapter 4, concessions related to federal funding were being implemented at TSTC in 1934. Whether accreditation and federal funding were explicitly linked at that point is unclear to me, but the timing is suggestive.

22. English A lasted only one year. In 1935, Lionel Stevenson returned as chair after a sabbatical. Stevenson's feelings about the course are not apparent, but for whatever reason, English A ceased after his return. Students who did not meet the entrance requirements were simply prevented from entering English 101/102 until they could demonstrate proficiency. Depending on their scores, some students were refused entrance to the school altogether, while others were allowed to take other courses while they worked on their English proficiency in anticipation of a retest.

23. The Western Association of Schools and Colleges was founded in 1923. Until then, NCA oversaw accreditation almost everywhere west of the Mississippi River.

24. Composition historians have repeatedly cited Harvard's Reports of the Board of Overseers (Adams, Godkin, and Quincy 1995 [1892]; Adams, Godkin, and Nutter 1895, 1995 [1897]) as evidence of the faculty's open hostility to composition in higher education. VanOverbeke (2008b), however, reads these reports as interventions in national arguments about standardizing and hierarchalizing American education. Read in that context, the Harvard Reports take on a completely different cast than the sinister ones historians in rhetoric and composition have often accorded them (e.g., Kitzhaber 1990, 43–49).

25. Eliot describes some of these pressures in talks and essays from his forty years as Harvard's president (see, e.g., Eliot 1885, 1893, 1894, 1896a, 1896b). See also Butts and Cremin (1953); Cremin (1969, 1982, 1990); Selden (1960, 1962); VanOverbeke (2008b) regarding attempts to streamline American education.

26. When the US Department of Education was founded in 1867, its sole purpose was to assemble education statistics (Snyder 1993, 1). In the 1876–77 *Report of the Commissioner of Education*, it was necessary to clarify that purpose (US Commissioner of Education 1879). In his preliminary report, Commissioner John Eaton wrote, "As has been well said, 'the Office may be termed a clearing house of educational

information.' But, however comprehensive its duty in regard to collecting and disseminating information, it provides for no exercise of authority and none should be expected from it" (US Commissioner of Education 1879, x). See Blauch (1959, 10–14); Butts (1895); Parsons (2003, 31–32); Reichel (1969 [1901], 288–89); Selden (1960); VanOverbeke (2008b).

27. Yale was the most famous holdout, in large part because its administrators openly opposed Eliot's elective curriculum. The "Yale Report of 1828" is the locus classicus for defending the traditional curriculum to which Eliot's modern curriculum responded (Yale University 1828).

28. The preparatory requirements were essentially the "common branches" I described in chapter 2, including English grammar, composition, and elocution.

29. It was not first-year composition in the conventional sense because the university's postsecondary curricula were still organized on the classical college model, albeit a modernized version whereby students could choose a Classical, Scientific, or Modern Languages course of study. Nevertheless, "In each course the requirements were the same for all students" (Griffin 1974, 126).

30. I have reduced the considerable complexity of accreditation's history in the late nineteenth century because of space limitations. For instance, the development and expansion of entrance exams and accreditation were far more complex than I have made them out to be (see Blauch 1959; Parsons 2003; Scott 1901; Selden 1960; Trachsel 1992; VanOverbeke 2008b; Zook and Haggerty 1936). Nevertheless, it should be clear even from this simplified narrative that articulation, standardization, and accreditation were pervasive in deliberations about education around the turn of the twentieth century.

31. To facilitate this hierarchalization process, accreditation incorporated wide-ranging attempts at institutional standardization. At a basic level, there needed to be standard definitions for high schools, colleges, and universities if the processes by which students moved among them were to be formalized. But there were also attempts, with varying degrees of success, to standardize curricula, instructors' credentials, program length, matriculants' ages, assessment measures, and more. Accreditation associations, led by prominent secondary and postsecondary educators, were centrally involved in efforts to develop these standards and definitions. The process of using accreditation to achieve articulation and standardization was fundamentally political and bitterly divisive (Kirtland 1905; Selden 1960, 1962; Stinnett 1951; Zook 1939).

32. Rereading rhetoric and composition histories vis-à-vis accreditation is bracing. Common historical signposts, including the founding of the MLA, the founding of NCTE, the Committee of Ten Reports, and the Harvard Reports, to name a few, take on very different resonances in the context of accreditation than they do in most histories of composition.

Chapter 4

1. Although I am primarily interested in federal funds, there were also massive influxes of money into higher education from private entities such as the Ford Foundation and the Carnegie Corporation during roughly the same period I examine here.

2. The NDEA was inaugurated in 1958 in response to Russia's launch of Sputnik, and it was one of the most prominent federal research programs of the twentieth century. The program provided federal funds for expanding and improving math, science, and engineering education with the idea that American students needed to

be better trained for the kinds of jobs and careers that could contribute to national defense. In 1961, representatives from NCTE, MLA, and other English organizations testified before the US Congress that improving English teaching would also contribute to national defense (Squire et al. 1961). Eventually, Congress authorized Project English—the English counterpart to the STEM programs already in effect. Beginning in 1962, hundreds of thousands—and eventually millions—of federal dollars were poured into expanding and improving English teaching. With these funds, research centers were established, research agendas were formulated and funded, and English programs in elementary and high schools were redesigned, as was teacher education. It is not surprising that Project English has received a significant amount of rhetoric and composition historians' attention, though I think that attention generally overlooks larger postsecondary reorientations to federal funding. For a good discussion of composition's relationship to the NDEA, see Strain (2005). For discussions of the NDEA's broader effects on higher education, see Geiger (2008); Thelin (2004, 272); Whitman and Weiss (1982, 4).

3.   In 1941, the North Central Association of Colleges and Schools distributed a revised manual of accrediting that outlined general education requirements. At that point, general education appears to have been primarily a college entrance requirement. According to the manual, "Each institution will be expected to show that it offers a program of general education or that it requires the completion of an adequate program of general education of collegiate quality for entrance" (North Central Association of Colleges and Schools 1941, 1). However, there is also some suggestion that general education was, or was becoming, a college requirement as well. The manual continues, "For the purposes of accreditment the term 'general education' signifies acquaintance with the major areas of knowledge; it implies the possession of the facts in such areas and some proficiency in the modes of thought involved in understanding such facts. In its purposes and in its content is a continuation of the kind of education offered in secondary schools" (ibid.).

4.   There are varying dates attributed to this survey, between 1936 and 1938. I am persuaded the 1936 date is correct because a number of other decisions were predicated on the results, including hiring, which began in early 1937.

5.   Finnegan and Wallace (2014) are primarily concerned with connections between English rhetoricians and communications rhetoricians, but composition histories also largely neglect the period. Crowley (1998a, 103) sums up the basic consensus about the period well: "During the thirties, instruction in the required course settled into a comfortable pattern that combined current-traditional formalism with more or less literary study, depending upon the history and mission of a given college or university and the intellectual bent of faculty who designed the course." In other words, the decade was all but intellectually stagnant—there is therefore nothing worth discussing. Berlin (1987), Mulderig (1987), Russell (2002), and Fleming (2011) offer slightly more complicated views of the decade, but almost entirely in either cultural or intellectual terms. Notwithstanding these few exceptions, the absence of the Great Depression in our disciplinary histories is frankly troubling.

6.   The committee was also chaired, incidentally, by TSTC's president Gammage.

7.   Myers's contributions to rhetoric and composition over the span of his thirty-five-year career are impressive. He was influential in the early development of CCCC as a perennial conference attendee and then executive board member; he wrote and published textbooks that were adopted in writing classes across the country (e.g., Myers 1959); and he published articles in disciplinary journals, including *College Composition and Communication* and *College English*, that combined cutting-edge linguistics research with rhetoric and composition teaching (e.g., Myers 1954). Much of his work, including his 1940 *Arizona Teacher* article, "A Step toward Correlation in

English Teaching," evidence a progressive attitude toward linguistic standards that presaged in attitude CCCC's 1974 *Students' Right to Their Own Language* (see also Myers 1948).

8. In the 1957–58 annual report, acting chair Collice Portnoff writes tellingly that the abolition of remedial English would result in "a general tightening and added richness of instruction, in deference both to the increasing academic rigor of the college and to the national sentiment that higher education standards should prevail" (ASU Department of English 1958).

9. This process of changing the school's organizational structure to pressure legislators to change its mission closely mirrors the process in the decade leading up to World War II.

10. It is not clear exactly how long DEd students taught composition courses, but there are references to DEd students into the late 1950s, even after the English MA was established in 1956.

11. English MA coursework began in 1956, but the Arizona Board of Regents did not officially sanction the degree program until the following year. The 1956 students were technically earning credits toward a DEd or an MA in education with the expectation that the MA in English would be authorized. To minimize confusion, I mark 1956 as the beginning of the MA in English because that's when teaching assistantships in the English department began.

12. Obviously, this report raises the specter of contingent faculty and the consequences of the move toward contingent labor that remain among the most pressing concerns in higher education.

13. The first six PhD programs were in chemistry, education, engineering, English, physics, and psychology.

14. Extensive discussions about the connections of higher education and the war had been taking place on an official, national level since at least 1940 (American Council on Education 1946)—more than a year before Pearl Harbor. The negotiations that took place between federal officials and higher education officials are fascinating and bear far more attention from rhetoric and composition scholars.

15. Incidentally, arguments about redundancy are pervasive in the histories of other "aspiring" institutions, including ASU and UNT.

16. Stanley (2010) discusses the complicated relationship of the universities to the community colleges, especially where composition transfer credits were concerned (see esp. chapter 6).

Conclusion

1. The same generalization cannot necessarily be made about composition on an international scale (see, e.g., Bazerman et al. 2012; Thaiss et al. 2012).

2. For one, Professor Schwalm directed me to several other people who graciously agreed to interview requests (some of them multiple times). They were Frank D'Angelo, Marvin Fisher, Delmar Kehl, Helen Nebeker, Nicholas A. Salerno, and Mary Clare Sweeney. *Conceding Composition* has moved almost entirely away from the specific issues I spoke with them about, but I am profoundly grateful for their support and guidance. Plus, they were phenomenally kind and wonderful to talk with.

3. A number of fascinating documents detailing the so-called Basic Writing Wars and English 071 deliberations are collected in Schwalm's materials in the National Archives of Composition and Rhetoric at the University of Rhode Island.

4. Stretch composition has been adopted by institutions throughout the country as a model for developmental writing. In short, Stretch takes a single semester of

English 101 and stretches it over two semesters for students who need additional practice as college writers. When Stretch was first developed, there were negotiations over what to call the first semester because Arizona law prohibits "remedial" work from counting for college credit. Stretch is not "remedial," but at ASU, any course number lower than 101 is considered "remedial." Therefore, the first semester of Stretch could not be named "English 100." To sidestep this problem, the first semester of ASU's Stretch program is "Writing across the Curriculum 101." The second semester is "English 101: Stretch." Both earn college credit, and upon completion of both, students are eligible (and generally well-prepared) to enter English 102.

5.   A fascinating example that bears more consideration than I can give it here is ASU's "Rainbow Sections." The Rainbow Sections, later "English 101 and 102: Indigenous Rhetoric," were originally designed in 1984 by English education professor G. Lynn Nelson to support the retention of ASU's significant Native American student population (Wilson 2009). In fact, the Rainbow Sections were one of several efforts on the part of composition specialists to develop curricula responsive to the varying needs of Arizona State University's increasingly diverse student population.

6.   I do not mean to let myself off the hook here. I have made assertions in my own work based on assumptions of the field's invisibility. It does not escape me (in retrospect) that I did so even as I argued that composition is very visible outside of academia and is therefore the subject of much public debate (Skinnell 2010, 160).

REFERENCES

"An Act Changing Tempe Normal School to Tempe State Teachers College." 1925. University Archives, Arizona State University, Tempe.

"An Act to Locate, Establish, and Endow, and Provide for the Maintenance of a Territorial Normal School." 1885. University Manuscripts, University Archives, Arizona State University, Tempe.

Adams, Charles Francis, Edwin Lawrence Godkin, and George R. Nutter. 1895. "Report of the Committee on Composition and Rhetoric." In *Reports of Visiting Committees of the Board of Overseers*, 275–87. Cambridge, MA: Harvard University.

Adams, Charles Francis, Edwin Lawrence Godkin, and George R. Nutter. 1995 [1897]. "Report of the Committee on Composition and Rhetoric." In *The Origins of Composition Studies in the American College, 1875–1925: A Documentary History*, ed. John C. Brereton, 101–26. Pittsburgh: University of Pittsburgh Press.

Adams, Charles Francis, Edwin Lawrence Godkin, and Josiah Quincy. 1995 [1892]. "Report of the Committee on Composition and Rhetoric (1892)." In *The Origins of Composition Studies in the American College, 1875–1925: A Documentary History*, ed. John C. Brereton, 73–100. Pittsburgh: University of Pittsburgh Press.

Adler-Kassner, Linda, and Peggy O'Neill. 2010. *Reframing Writing Assessment to Improve Teaching and Learning*. Logan: Utah State University Press.

Agamben, Giorgio. 2009. *The Signature of All Things: On Method*. New York: Zone Books.

Alumni Association of the State Normal School Tempe. 1925. "Arguments for the State Teachers' College, 1925." Arthur John Matthews Papers, University Archives, Arizona State University, Tempe.

American Council on Education. 1946. *Higher Education and National Defense*. Washington, DC: American Council on Education.

American Normal Schools: Their Theory, Their Workings, and Their Results, as Embodied in the Proceedings of the First Annual Convention of the American Normal School Association, Held at Trenton, New Jersey, August 19 and 20, 1859. 1860. New York: A. S. Barnes and Burr.

"Annual Catalogs/Reports, 1888–1889." 1889. University Archives, University of Kansas, Lawrence.

"Annual Catalogs/Reports, 1892–1893." 1893. University Archives, University of Kansas, Lawrence.

"Annual Catalogue, 1886–1887." 1887. State Normal School, Los Angeles. UCLA Libraries Special Collections, University Archives, University of California, Los Angeles.

Anson, Chris M. 2002. "Who Wants Composition? Reflections on the Rise and Fall of an Independent Program." In *Field of Dreams: Independent Writing Programs and the Future of Composition*, ed. Peggy O'Neill, Angelo Crow, and Larry W. Burton, 153–69. Logan: Utah State University Press.

Applebee, Arthur N. 1974. *Tradition and Reform in the Teaching of English: A History*. Urbana, IL: National Council of Teachers of English.

Archer, Jerome W., and Wilfred A. Ferrell. 1965. *Research and the Development of English Programs in the Junior College: Proceedings of the Tempe Conference, 1965*. Champaign, IL: National Council of Teachers of English.

Archer, Jerome W., and Joseph Schwartz. 1971. *Exposition*, 2nd ed. New York: McGraw-Hill.

Aristotle. 2007. *On Rhetoric: A Theory of Civic Discourse*, 2nd ed. Trans. George A. Kennedy. New York: Oxford University Press.

DOI: 10.7330/9781607325055.c007

Arizona Board of Regents. 1888. Meeting Minutes, June 11, 1888. University Archives, Arizona State University, Tempe.

Arizona Board of Regents. 1889. Meeting Minutes, Aug. 17, 1889. University Archives, Arizona State University, Tempe.

Arizona Board of Regents. 1925. Meeting Minutes, May 25, 1925. University Archives, Arizona State University, Tempe.

Arizona Board of Regents. 1980. "Arizona University System Mission and Scope Statements, Arizona Board of Regents, July 1980." University Archives, Arizona State University, Tempe.

Arizona State Committee. 1938. "Report of the Arizona Appraisal Committee." United States Community Improvement Appraisal. Phoenix: US Work Projects Administration.

ASU Department of English. 1936. "Annual Report of the English Department, 1935–1936." *Annual Reports to President by Department, September 1934–May 1940, ASC, Tempe*, vol. 1. University Archives, Arizona State University, Tempe.

ASU Department of English. 1938. "Annual Report of the English Department, 1937–1938." *Annual Reports to President by Department, September 1934–May 1940, ASC, Tempe*, vol. 1. University Archives, Arizona State University, Tempe.

ASU Department of English. 1953. "Annual Report of the English Department, 1952–1953." *Annual Reports to President by Department, September 1952–May 1953, ASC, Tempe*, vol. 7. University Archives, Arizona State University, Tempe.

ASU Department of English. 1954. "Annual Report of the English Department, 1953–1954." *Annual Reports to President by Department, September 1953–May 1954, ASC, Tempe*, vol. 8. University Archives, Arizona State University, Tempe.

ASU Department of English. 1956. "Annual Report of the English Department, 1955–1956." *Annual Reports to President by Department, September 1955–May 1956, ASC, Tempe*, vol. 10. University Archives, Arizona State University, Tempe.

ASU Department of English. 1958. "Annual Report of the English Department, 1957–1958." *Annual Reports to President by Department, September 1957–May 1958, ASC, Tempe*, vol. 12. University Archives, Arizona State University, Tempe.

ASU Department of English. 1984. "Decennial Review of Academic Program Department of English, 1974–1984: Volume 1." University Archives, Arizona State University, Tempe.

ASU Office of Institutional Analysis. 2010. "ASU Student Enrollment History." Tempe: Arizona State University. Accessed December 16, 2014. http://uoia.asu.edu/archive-asu-enrollment-data.

Axt, Richard G. 1952. *The Federal Government and Financing Higher Education.* New York: Columbia University Press.

Ballif, Michelle. 2013a. "Historiography as Hauntology: Paranormal Investigations into the History of Rhetoric." In *Theorizing Histories of Rhetoric*, ed. Michelle Ballif, 139–53. Carbondale: Southern Illinois University Press.

Ballif, Michelle. 2013b. "Introduction." In *Theorizing Histories of Rhetoric*, ed. Michelle Ballif, 1–7. Carbondale: Southern Illinois University Press.

Barnard, Henry. 1851. *Normal Schools, and Other Institutions, Agencies, and Means Designed for the Professional Education of Teachers.* Hartford, CT: Case.

Barnhardt, Terry A. 2001. "Educating the Masses: The Normal-School Movement and the Origins of Eastern Illinois University, 1895–1899." *Journal of Illinois History* 4: 193–218.

Bartholomae, David. 2000. "Composition, 1900–2000." *PMLA* 115 (7): 1950–54. http://dx.doi.org/10.2307/463613.

Bazerman, Charles. 1988. *Shaping Written Knowledge: The Genre and Activity of the Experimental Article in Science.* Madison: University of Wisconsin Press.

Bazerman, Charles, Chris Dean, Jessica Early, Karen Lunsford, Suzie Null, Paul Rogers, and Amanda Stansell, eds. 2012. *International Advances in Writing Research: Cultures, Places, Measures.* Anderson, SC: Parlor.

Berlin, James A. 1984. *Writing Instruction in Nineteenth-Century American Colleges.* Carbondale: Southern Illinois University Press.

Berlin, James A. 1987. *Rhetoric and Reality: Writing Instruction in American Colleges, 1900–1985.* Carbondale: Southern Illinois University Press.

Berlin, James A. 1994. "Revisionary Histories of Rhetoric: Politics, Power, and Plurality." In *Writing Histories of Rhetoric*, ed. Victor J. Vitanza, 112–27. Carbondale: Southern Illinois University Press.

Blauch, Lloyd E. 1959. *Accreditation in Higher Education.* New York: Greenwood.

Bloland, Harland G. 1969. *Higher Education Associations in a Decentralized Education System.* Washington, DC: US Department of Health, Education and Welfare, Office of Education, Bureau of Research.

Bordelon, Suzanne. 2011. "Participating on an 'Equal Footing': The Rhetorical Significance of California State Normal School in the Late Nineteenth Century." *Rhetoric Society Quarterly* 41 (2): 168–90. http://dx.doi.org/10.1080/02773945.2011.553767.

Brereton, John C. 1988. "Composition and English Departments: 1900–1925." In *Audits of Meaning: A Festschrift in Honor of Ann E. Berthoff*, ed. Louise Z. Smith, 41–54. Portsmouth, NH: Heinemann.

Brereton, John C., ed. 1985. *Traditions of Inquiry.* New York: Oxford University Press.

Brereton, John C., ed. 1995. *The Origins of Composition Studies in the American College, 1875–1925: A Documentary History.* Pittsburgh: University of Pittsburgh Press.

Brodkey, Linda. 1996. *Writing Permitted in Designated Areas Only.* Minneapolis: University of Minnesota Press.

Brooke, Colin Gifford. 2012. "Discipline and Publish: Reading and Writing the Scholarly Network." In *Ecology, Writing Theory, and New Media*, ed. Sydney I. Dobrin, 92–105. New York: Routledge.

Brooke, Robert. 1987. "Underlife and Writing Instruction." *College Composition and Communication* 38 (2): 141–53. http://dx.doi.org/10.2307/357715.

Broome, Edwin Cornelius. 1902. *A Historical and Critical Discussion of College Admission Requirements.* New York: Columbia University Press.

Brown, Elmer Ellsworth. 1903. "Secondary Education." In *Report of the Commissioner of Education, 1903,* vol. 1, 553–83. Washington, DC: Government Printing Office.

Brown, Henry E., ed. 1918. *Proceedings of the Annual Meeting of the North Central Association of Colleges and Schools*, vol. 23. Chicago: North Central Association of Colleges and Schools.

Bruce, William H. 1921. "Bulletin Giving Data Concerning the Work of the North Texas State Normal College for the First Twenty Years of Its History." President William H. Bruce Records, University Archives, University of North Texas, Denton.

Bruce, William H. 1923. Letter to C. E. Evans, December 17. President William H. Bruce Records, University Archives, University of North Texas, Denton.

Bullock, Richard, and Maureen Daly Goggin. 2006. *The Norton Field Guide to Writing with Readings.* New York: Norton.

Bullock, Richard, and John Trimbur, eds. 1991. *The Politics of Writing Instruction: Postsecondary.* Portsmouth, NH: Boynton/Cook.

Burke, Colin B. 1982. *American Collegiate Populations: A Test of the Traditional View.* New York: New York University Press.

Burke, Kenneth. 1969. *A Grammar of Motives.* Berkeley: University of California Press.

Burke, Kenneth. 1984a. *Attitudes toward History*, 3rd ed. Berkeley: University of California Press.

Burke, Kenneth. 1984b. *Permanence and Change: An Anatomy of Purpose*, 3rd ed. Berkeley: University of California Press.

Burton, Larry D. 2010. "Common School Curriculum." In *Encyclopedia of Curriculum Studies*, vol. 1, ed. Craig Kridel, 128–29. Thousand Oaks, CA: Sage. http://dx.doi.org /10.4135/9781412958806.n74.

Butler, Paul. 2008. "Style and the Public Intellectual: Rethinking Composition in the Public Sphere." *JAC: A Journal of Rhetoric, Culture, and Politics* 28 (1–2): 55–84.

Butts, R. Freeman, and Lawrence A. Cremin. 1953. *A History of Education in American Culture.* New York: Holt, Rinehart, and Winston.

Butts, William H. 1895. "National Uniformity in Secondary Instruction." *School Review* 3 (2): 65–86. http://dx.doi.org/10.1086/433532.

California State Department of Education. 1960. *A Master Plan for Higher Education in California, 1960–1975.* Sacramento: California State Department of Education.

Carr, Jean Ferguson, Stephen L. Carr, and Lucille Schultz. 2005. *Archives of Instruction: Nineteenth-Century Rhetorics, Readers, and Composition Books in the United States.* Carbondale: Southern Illinois University Press.

Charters, Werrett Wallace. 1924. *Teaching the Common Branches.* Boston: Hough.

Clark, Thomas Arkle, ed. 1912. *Proceedings of the Seventeenth Annual Meeting of the North Central Association of Colleges and Schools.* Chicago: North Central Association of Colleges and Schools.

Cohen, Arthur M. 1998. *The Shaping of American Higher Education: Emergence and Growth of the Contemporary System.* San Francisco: Jossey-Bass.

Cohen, Arthur M., and Carrie B. Kisker. 2010. *The Shaping of American Higher Education: Emergence and Growth of the Contemporary System,* 2nd ed. San Francisco: Jossey-Bass.

Collins, Terence G. 1997. "A Response to Ira Shor's 'Our Apartheid: Writing Instruction and Inequality.'" *Journal of Basic Writing* 16: 95–100.

Commission of Colleges. 1887. *First Annual Report of the Commission of Colleges in New England on Admission Examinations, 1886–1887.* Providence: Providence Press.

Committee on the Liberal Arts Curriculum. 1944. "Report of the Committee on the Liberal Arts Curriculum, 1944." In *General Education Committee Minutes, 1944–1963.* Arizona Collection, University Archives, Arizona State University, Tempe.

Connors, Robert J. 1981. "The Rise and Fall of the Modes of Discourse." *College Composition and Communication* 32 (4): 444–55. http://dx.doi.org/10.2307/356607.

Connors, Robert J. 1983. "Static Abstractions and Composition." *Freshman English News* 12: 1–4, 9–12.

Connors, Robert J. 1984. "Historical Inquiry in Composition Studies." *Writing Instructor* 3: 157–67.

Connors, Robert J. 1986. "The Rhetoric of Mechanical Correctness." In *Only Connect: Uniting Reading and Writing,* ed. Thomas Newkirk, 27–58. Upper Montclair, NJ: Boynton/Cook.

Connors, Robert J. 1987. "Personal Writing Assignments." *College Composition and Communication* 38 (2): 166–83. http://dx.doi.org/10.2307/357717.

Connors, Robert J. 1991a. "Rhetoric in the Modern University: The Creation of an Underclass." In *The Politics of Writing Instruction: Postsecondary,* ed. Richard Bullock and John Trimbur, 55–84. Portsmouth, NH: Boynton/Cook.

Connors, Robert J. 1991b. "Writing the History of Our Discipline." In *An Introduction to Composition Studies,* ed. Gary Tate and Erika C. Lindemann, 49–71. New York: Oxford University Press.

Connors, Robert J. 1997a. "The Abolition Debate in Composition: A Short History." In *Composition in the Twenty-First Century: Crisis and Change,* ed. Lynn Z. Bloom, Donald A. Daiker, and Edward M. White, 47–63. Carbondale: Southern Illinois University Press.

Connors, Robert J. 1997b. *Composition-Rhetoric: Backgrounds, Theory, and Pedagogy.* Pittsburgh: University of Pittsburgh Press.

Connors, Robert J. 1999. "Composition History and Disciplinarity." In *History, Reflection, and Narrative: The Professionalization of Composition 1963–1983,* ed. Mary Rosner, Beth Boehm, and Debra Journet, 3–21. Greenwich, CT: Ablex.

Corbett, Edward P.J. 1984. Letter to Nicholas Salerno, November 6. Nicholas Salerno Papers, University Archives, Arizona State University, Tempe.

Corbett, Edward P.J. 1993. "A History of Writing Program Administration." In *Learning from the Histories of Rhetoric: Essays in Honor of Winifred Bryan Horner*, ed. Theresa Enos, 60–71. Carbondale: Southern Illinois University Press.

"Course of Study." 1907. Western Illinois State Normal School. Macomb: Western Illinois State Normal School.

Cremin, Lawrence A. 1961. *The Transformation of the School: Progressivism in American Education, 1876–1957*. New York: Knopf.

Cremin, Lawrence A. 1982. *American Education: The National Experience, 1783–1876*. New York: Harper Colophon.

Cremin, Lawrence A. 1990. *American Education: The Metropolitan Experience, 1876–1980*. New York: HarperCollins.

Cremin, Lawrence A., ed. 1969. *Reports of the Mosely Educational Commission to the United States*. New York: Arno.

Crowley, Sharon. 1986. "The Perilous Life and Times of Freshman English." *Freshman English News* 14: 11–16.

Crowley, Sharon. 1990. *The Methodical Memory: Invention in Current-Traditional Rhetoric*. Carbondale: Southern Illinois University Press.

Crowley, Sharon. 1998a. *Composition in the University: Historical and Polemical Essays*. Pittsburgh: University of Pittsburgh Press.

Crowley, Sharon. 1998b. "Review: Histories of Pedagogy, English Studies, and Composition." *College Composition and Communication* 49 (1): 109–14. http://dx.doi.org/10.2307/358565.

Crowley, Sharon. 2002. "How the Professional Lives of WPAs Would Change if FYC Were Elective." In *The Writing Program Administrator's Handbook: A Guide to Reflective Institutional Change and Practice*, ed. Stuart C. Brown, Theresa Enos, and Catherine Chaput, 219–32. Mahwah, NJ: Lawrence Erlbaum.

Crowley, Sharon. 2006. *Toward a Civil Discourse: Rhetoric and Fundamentalism*. Pittsburgh: University of Pittsburgh Press.

Crowley, Sharon, and Debra Hawhee. 2012. *Ancient Rhetorics for Contemporary Students*, 5th ed. New York: Pearson.

Crowley, Sharon, and Michael Stancliff. 2008. *Critical Situations: A Rhetoric and Workshops*. New York: Longman/Pearson.

Crumley, J. J. 1935. Letter to W. N. Masters, February 27. President John J. Crumley Records, University Archives, University of North Texas, Denton.

Curriculum Committee. 1917. "Report of the Committee on Course of Study, June 13, 1917." Arthur John Matthews Papers, University Archives, Arizona State University, Tempe.

D'Angelo, Frank J. 1980. *Process and Thought in Composition*, 2nd ed. Cambridge, MA: Little, Brown.

D'Angelo, Frank J. 1999a. *Composition in the Classical Tradition*. New York: Longman.

D'Angelo, Frank J. 1999b. "In Search of the American Dream." In *Living Rhetoric and Composition: Stories of the Discipline*, ed. Duane H. Roen, Stuart C. Brown, and Theresa Enos, 55–64. Mahwah, NJ: Lawrence Erlbaum.

D'Angelo, Frank J. 1999c. "Professing Rhetoric and Composition: A Personal Odyssey." In *History, Reflection, and Narrative: The Professionalization of Composition 1963–1983*, ed. Mary Rosner, Beth Boehm, and Debra Journet, 269–81. Greenwich, CT: Ablex.

Darnton, Robert. 1999. *The Great Cat Massacre and Other Episodes in French Cultural History*. New York: Basic.

Davis, Calvin O. 1926. "Quantitative Work in English." *North Central Association Quarterly* 1: 221–42.

Davis, Calvin O. 1945. *A History of the North Central Association of Colleges and Schools, 1895–1945*. Ann Arbor: North Central Association.

DeGarmo, Charles. 1893. "Co-ordination of the Normal School and the University in the Training of Teachers." *Journal of Addresses and Proceedings of the National Education Association* 1892: 411–14.

Derrida, Jacques. 2007. *Psyche: Invention of the Other*, vol. 1. Stanford: Stanford University Press.

Dobrin, Sidney I., ed. 2012. *Ecology, Writing Theory, and New Media*. New York: Routledge.

Donahue, Patricia, and Gretchen Flesher Moon, eds. 2007. *Local Histories: Reading the Archives of Composition*. Pittsburgh: University of Pittsburgh Press.

Doughty, W. F., and R. B. Binnion. n.d. "Classification of Public High Schools by the State Department of Education and Complete List of High Schools Showing the Class to Which Each Belongs." President William H. Bruce Records, University Archives, University of North Texas, Denton.

Ducharme, Edward R., and Mary K. Ducharme. 1998. *The American Association of Colleges for Teacher Education: A History*. Washington, DC: American Association of Colleges for Teacher Education.

Durham, G. Homer. 1965. Letter to Jerome Archer, November 23. G. Homer Durham Papers, University Archives, Arizona State University, Tempe.

Durrill, Wayne K. 1997. "New Schooling for a New South: A Community Study of Education and Social Change, 1875–1885." *Journal of Social History* 31 (1): 155–81. http://dx.doi.org/10.1353/jsh/31.1.155.

Eaton, Judith S. 2001. *Distance Learning: Academic and Political Challenges for Higher Education Accreditation*. Washington, DC: Council for Higher Education Accreditation.

Edbauer, Jenny. 2005. "Unframing Models of Public Distribution: From Rhetorical Situation to Rhetorical Ecologies." *Rhetoric Society Quarterly* 35 (4): 5–24. http://dx.doi.org/10.1080/02773940509391320.

"Editorial." 1892. In *School and College: Devoted to Secondary and Higher Education*, ed. Ray Greene Huiling, 548–51. Boston: Ginn.

Eliot, Charles W. 1876. "Address at Classical and High School Teachers Association." Records of President Charles W. Eliot, Harvard University Archives, Cambridge, MA.

Eliot, Charles W. 1885. "Present Relations of Mass. High Schools to Mass. Colleges." *Journal of Education* 2: 19–20.

Eliot, Charles W. 1892. "Shortening and Enriching the Grammar School Course." Speech Proceedings, 1892. Records of President Charles W. Eliot, Harvard University Archives, Cambridge, MA.

Eliot, Charles W. 1893. "Secondary School Programmes and the Conferences of the Committee of Ten." Records of President Charles W. Eliot, Harvard University Archives, Cambridge, MA.

Eliot, Charles W. 1894. "The Elementary Schools, the High Schools, and the Colleges." Records of President Charles W. Eliot, Harvard University Archives, Cambridge, MA.

Eliot, Charles W. 1896a. "Address at the Tenth Annual Convention of the Association of Colleges and Preparatory Schools." Records of President Charles W. Eliot, Harvard University Archives, Cambridge, MA.

Eliot, Charles W. 1896b. "High School Programmes." Records of President Charles W. Eliot, Harvard University Archives, Cambridge, MA.

Eliot, Charles W. 1903. "Address at the Harvard Teachers Association Regarding Secondary Education." Records of President Charles W. Eliot, Harvard University Archives, Cambridge, MA.

Eliot, Charles W. 1904. "What Has Been Gained in Uniformity of College Admission Requirements in the Past Twenty Years?" Records of President Charles W. Eliot, Harvard University Archives, Cambridge, MA.

Enoch, Jessica. 2008. *Refiguring Rhetorical Education: Women Teaching African American, Native American, and Chicano/a Students, 1865–1911*. Carbondale: Southern Illinois University Press.

Enos, Theresa, ed. 1987. *A Sourcebook for Basic Writing Teachers*. New York: Random House.

Ercolini, G. L., and J. Pat Gehrke. 2013. "Writing Future Rhetoric." In *Theorizing Histories of Rhetoric*, ed. Michelle Ballif, 154–71. Carbondale: Southern Illinois University Press.

Erwin, Andrew, and Marjorie Wood. 2014. *The One Percent at State U: How Public University Presidents Profit from Rising Student Debt and Low-Wage Faculty Labor.* Washington, DC: Institute for Policy Studies.

"Faculty Personnel Policy." 1956. Grady Gammage Papers, University Archives, Arizona State University, Tempe.

Faigley, Lester. 1998. "Veterans' Stories on the Porch." In *History, Reflection, and Narrative: The Professionalization of Composition 1963–1983,* ed. Mary Rosner, Beth Boehm, and Debra Journet, 23–38. Greenwich, CT: Ablex.

Farmer, Hiram Bradford. 1886. "Course of Study, 1886–1887." University Archives, Arizona State University, Tempe.

Fass, Paula S. 1982. "Without Design: Education Policy in the New Deal." *American Journal of Education* 91 (1): 36–64. http://dx.doi.org/10.1086/443664.

Felmley, David. 1923. "The Collegiate Rank of the Normal School." In *Proceedings of the Centennial Conference on Teacher Training, Terre Haute, 1923,* ed. L. J. Rettger, 41–52. Spec. issue of *Indiana State Normal School Bulletin* 17.

Felton, James Lee. 1911. "Difficulties in English Composition." *Arizona Journal of Education* 2: 139–44.

Ferrell, Wilfred A. 1963. "At Arizona State University." *College Composition and Communication* 14 (2): 78–80. http://dx.doi.org/10.2307/355003.

Ferrell, Wilfred A., and Nicholas A. Salerno. 1968. *Strategies in Prose.* New York: Holt.

Finnegan, Cara A., and Marissa Lowe Wallace. 2014. "Origin Stories and Dreams of Collaboration: Rethinking Histories of the Communication Course and the Relationships between English and Speech." *Rhetoric Society Quarterly* 44 (5): 401–26. http://dx.doi.org/10.1080/02773945.2014.957412.

Fitzgerald, Kathryn. 2001. "A Rediscovered Tradition: European Pedagogy and Composition in Nineteenth-Century Midwestern Normal Schools." *College Composition and Communication* 53 (2): 224–50. http://dx.doi.org/10.2307/359077.

Fitzgerald, Kathryn. 2002. "The Platteville Papers: Inscribing Frontier Ideology and Culture in a Nineteenth-Century Writing Assignment." *College English* 64 (3): 273–301. http://dx.doi.org/10.2307/3250735.

Fitzgerald, Kathryn. 2007. "The Platteville Papers Revisited: Gender and Genre in a Normal School Writing Assignment." In *Local Histories: Reading the Archives of Composition,* ed. Patricia Donahue and Gretchen Flesher Moon, 115–33. Pittsburgh: University of Pittsburgh Press.

Fitzpatrick, Tom. 1992. "Hime [*sic*] for Christmas." *Phoenix New Times.* Accessed December 16, 2014. http://www.phoenixnewtimes.com/1992-01-08/news/hime-for-christmas/.

Flaherty, Colleen. 2014. "One Course without Pay." *Inside Higher Ed.* Accessed August 4, 2015. https://www.insidehighered.com/news/2014/12/16/arizona-state-tells-non-tenure-track-writing-instructors-teach-extra-course-each.

Flanagan, Thomas. 1967. Letter to Chancellor Roger W. Heyns, May 31. Chancellor Records, University Archives, University of California, Berkeley.

Fleming, David. 2009. "Rhetoric Revival or Process Revolution? Revisiting the Emergence of Composition-Rhetoric as a Discipline." In *Renewing Rhetoric's Relation to Composition: Essays in Honor of Theresa Jarnagin Enos,* ed. Shane Borrowman, Stuart C. Brown, and Thomas P. Miller, 25–52. New York: Routledge.

Fleming, David. 2011. *From Form to Meaning: Freshman Composition and the Long Sixties, 1957–1974.* Pittsburgh: University of Pittsburgh Press.

Foucault, Michel. 1977. "Nietzsche, Genealogy, History." In *Language, Counter-Memory, Practice: Selected Essays and Interviews,* ed. Donald F. Bouchard, 139–64. Ithaca, NY: Cornell University Press.

Freed, John B. 2008. "The Founding of Illinois State Normal University: Normal School or State University?" *Journal of the Illinois State Historical Society* 101: 106–26.

Gammage, Grady. 1958. Letter to Dr. Richardson, Mr. Cady, Dr. Wager, and Dr. Bateman, May 13. Grady Gammage Papers, University Archives, Arizona State University, Tempe.

Gammel, Hans Peter Mareus Neilsen. 1902. *The Laws of Texas, 1897–1902*, vol. 11, 74–75. Austin: Gammel.

Gannett, Cinthia, John C. Brereton, and Katherine E. Tirabassi. 2010. "'We All Got History': Process and Product in the History of Composition." *Pedagogy* 10 (2): 425–50. http://dx.doi .org/10.1215/15314200-2009-046.

Geiger, Louis G. 1970. *Voluntary Accreditation: A History of the North Central Association, 1945–1970*. Menasha, WI: Banta.

Geiger, Roger L. 1986. *To Advance Knowledge: The Growth of American Research Universities, 1900–1940*. New York: Oxford University Press.

Geiger, Roger L. 2008. *Research and Relevant Knowledge: American Research Universities since World War II*. New Brunswick, NJ: Transaction.

"General Catalogue, 1888–1889." 1888. Arizona State University. University Archives, Arizona State University, Tempe.

"General Catalogue, 1896–1897." 1896. Arizona State University. University Archives, Arizona State University, Tempe.

"General Catalogue, 1901–1902." 1901. Arizona State University. University Archives, Arizona State University, Tempe.

"General Catalogue, 1902–1903." 1902. Arizona State University. University Archives, Arizona State University, Tempe.

"General Catalogue, 1904–1905." 1904. Arizona State University. University Archives, Arizona State University, Tempe.

"General Catalogue, 1909–1910." 1909. Arizona State University. University Archives, Arizona State University, Tempe.

"General Catalogue, 1918–1919." 1918. Arizona State University. University Archives, Arizona State University, Tempe.

"General Catalogue, 1928–1929." 1928. Arizona State University. University Archives, Arizona State University, Tempe.

"General Catalogue, 1931–1932." 1931. Arizona State University. University Archives, Arizona State University, Tempe.

"General Catalogue, 1933–1934." 1933. Arizona State University. University Archives, Arizona State University, Tempe.

"General Catalogue, 1950–1951." 1950. Arizona State University. University Archives, Arizona State University, Tempe.

General Education Committee. 1954. "Report of the Committee on General Education, Faculty Planning Conference, September 18, 1954." General Education Committee Minutes, 1944–63. Arizona Collection, University Archives, Arizona State University, Tempe.

George, Diana, and John Trimbur. 1999. "The 'Communication Battle,' or Whatever Happened to the 4th C?" *College Composition and Communication* 50 (4): 682–98. http://dx.doi .org/10.2307/358487.

Gere, Anne Ruggles. 1987. *Writing Groups: History, Theory, and Implications*. Carbondale: Southern Illinois University Press.

Giberson, Greg A., and Thomas A. Moriarty. 2010. *What We Are Becoming: Developments in Undergraduate Writing Majors*. Logan: Utah State University Press.

Ginzburg, Carlo. 2012. "Microhistory: Two or Three Things I Know about It." In *Threads and Traces*, ed. Carlo Ginzburg, 193–214. Berkeley: University of California Press.

Glau, Gregory R. 1996. "The 'Stretch Program': Arizona State University's New Model of University-Level Basic Writing Instruction." *WPA: Writing Program Administration* 20: 79–91.

Glau, Gregory R., and Chitralekha De Duttagupta. 2012. *Everyday Writing*. Boston: Pearson.

Glau, Gregory R., and Craig Jacobsen. 2001. *Scenarios for Writing: Issues, Analysis, and Response.* New York: McGraw-Hill.

Glenn, Cheryl. 2000. "Truth, Lies, and Method: Revisiting Feminist Historiography." *College English* 62 (3): 387–89. http://dx.doi.org/10.2307/378937.

Glenn, Cheryl, and Jessica Enoch. 2009. "Invigorating Historiographic Practices in Rhetoric and Composition." In *Working in the Archives: Practical Research Methods for Rhetoric and Composition,* ed. Alexis E. Ramsey, Wendy B. Sharer, Barbara L'Eplattenier, and Lisa S. Mastrangelo, 11–27. Carbondale: Southern Illinois University Press.

Goggin, Maureen Daly. 1995. "The Disciplinary Instability of Composition." In *Reconceiving Writing, Rethinking Writing Instruction,* ed. Joseph Petraglia, 27–48. Mahwah, NJ: Lawrence Erlbaum.

Goggin, Maureen Daly. 2000. *Authorizing a Discipline: Scholarly Journals and the Post–World War II Emergence of Rhetoric and Composition.* Mahwah, NJ: Lawrence Erlbaum.

Goggin, Maureen Daly, and Steve Beatty. 2000. "Accounting for 'Well-Worn Grooves': Composition as a Self-Reinforcing Mechanism." In *Inventing a Discipline: Rhetoric Scholarship in Honor of Richard E. Young,* ed. Maureen Daly Goggin, 29–66. Urbana, IL: National Council of Teachers of English.

Gold, David. 2005. "'Where Brains Had a Chance': William Mayo and Rhetorical Instruction at East Texas Normal College, 1889–1917." *College English* 67 (3): 311–30. http://dx.doi.org/10.2307/30044639.

Gold, David. 2008. *Rhetoric at the Margins: Revisiting the History of Writing Instruction in American Colleges, 1873–1947.* Carbondale: Southern Illinois University Press.

Good, Irby J. 1921. "President's Report to the Board of Trustees, March 16, 1921." Irby J. Good Papers, 1915–44, University Archives, University of Indianapolis, Indianapolis, IN.

Good, Irby J. 1926. "President's Report to the Board of Trustees, December 17, 1926." Irby J. Good Papers, 1915–44, University Archives, University of Indianapolis, Indianapolis, IN.

Gove, Aaron. 1904. "Chapter VII: The Public Schools Systems of the United States." In *Report of the Commissioner of Education, 1903,* vol. 1, ed. US Commissioner of Education, 351–88. Washington, DC: Government Printing Office.

Graff, Gerald. 1989. *Professing Literature: An Institutional History.* Chicago: University of Chicago Press.

Graham, Hugh Davis, and Nancy Diamond. 1997. *American Research Universities: Elites and Challengers in the Postwar Era.* Baltimore: Johns Hopkins University Press.

Gray, Patrice K. 2007. "Life in the Margins: Student Writing and Curricular Change at Fitchburg Normal, 1895–1910." In *Local Histories: Reading the Archives of Composition,* ed. Patricia Donahue and Gretchen Flesher Moon, 159–80. Pittsburgh: University of Pittsburgh Press.

Greenbaum, Leonard. 1969. "The Tradition of Complaint." *College English* 31 (2): 174–87. http://dx.doi.org/10.2307/374119.

Grieder, Calvin. 1945. "Principal Emergency Federal Education Projects, 1933–1944." *Educational Forum* 9 (4): 435–42. http://dx.doi.org/10.1080/00131724509339811.

Griffin, Clifford S. 1966. "The University of Kansas and the Years of Frustration, 1854–1864." *Kansas Historical Quarterly* 32: 1–32.

Griffin, Clifford S. 1974. *The University of Kansas: A History.* Lawrence: University Press of Kansas.

Hairston, Maxine. 1982. "The Winds of Change: Thomas Kuhn and the Revolution in the Teaching of Writing." *College Composition and Communication* 33 (1): 76–88. http://dx.doi.org/10.2307/357846.

Halloran, S. Michael. 1990. "From Rhetoric to Composition: The Teaching of Writing in America to 1900." In *A Short History of Writing Instruction from Ancient Greece to Twentieth-Century America,* ed. James J. Murphy, 151–83. Davis, CA: Hermagoras.

Harper, Charles Athiel. 1970. *A Century of Public Teacher Education: The Story of the State Teachers Colleges as They Evolved from the Normal Schools.* New York: Greenwood.

Harris, Joseph. 1997. *A Teaching Subject: Composition since 1966.* Upper Saddle River, NJ: Prentice-Hall.

Harris, William T. 1904. "The Commissioner's Introduction." In *Report of the Commissioner of Education, 1903,* vol. 1, ed. US Commissioner of Education, ix–lxxvi. Washington, DC: Government Printing Office.

Harvard University. 1884. *Harvard University Catalogue, 1884–1885.* Cambridge, MA: College Press.

Hawhee, Debra. 2004. *Bodily Arts: Rhetoric and Athletics in Ancient Greece.* Austin: University of Texas Press.

Hawhee, Debra, and Christa J. Olson. 2013. "Pan-historiography: The Challenges of Writing History across Time and Space." In *Theorizing Histories of Rhetoric,* ed. Michelle Ballif, 90–105. Carbondale: Southern Illinois University Press.

Hawkins, W. J. 1912. "The Attitude of the Normal Schools toward Education." In *Journal of Proceedings Addresses, National Education Association,* 810–16. Chicago: University of Chicago Press.

Heckathorn, Amy. 1999. "The Struggle toward Professionalization: The Historical Evolution of Writing Program Administrators." PhD dissertation, Texas Christian University, Fort Worth.

Heckathorn, Amy. 2004. "Moving toward a Group Identity: WPA Professionalization from the 1940s to the 1970s." In *Historical Studies of Writing Program Administration: Individuals, Communities, and the Formation of a Discipline,* ed. Barbara L'Eplattenier and Lisa Mastrangelo, 191–219. West Lafayette, IN: Parlor.

Heilker, Paul. 1996. "Freshman English." In *Keywords in Composition Studies,* ed. Paul Heilker and Peter Vandenberg, 107–10. Portsmouth, NH: Boynton/Cook.

Henze, Brent, Jack Selzer, and Wendy Sharer. 2008. *1977: A Cultural Moment in Composition.* West Lafayette, IN: Parlor.

Herbst, Jürgen. 1980. "Nineteenth-Century Normal Schools in the United States: A Fresh Look." *History of Education* 9 (3):219–27. http://dx.doi.org/10.1080/0046760800090303.

Herbst, Jürgen. 1989. *And Sadly Teach: Teacher Education and Professionalization in American Culture.* Madison: University of Wisconsin Press.

Hesse, Doug. 2005. "Who Owns Writing?" *College Composition and Communication* 57 (2): 335–57.

Heyda, John. 1999. "Fighting over Freshman English: CCCC's Early Years and the Turf Wars of the 1950s." *College Composition and Communication* 50 (4): 663–81. http://dx.doi.org/10.2307/358486.

Higher Learning Commission. 2014. *The Criteria for Accreditation and Core Components.* Chicago: North Central Association Higher Learning Commission.

Hill, Adams Sherman. 1878. *The Principles of Rhetoric.* New York: Harper Bros.

Hill, Frederick D. 2003. *"Downright Devotion to the Cause": A History of the University of Indianapolis and Its Legacy of Service.* Indianapolis: University of Indianapolis Press.

Holbrook, Alfred. 1859. *The Normal: or, Methods of Teaching the Common Branches, Orthoepy, Orthography, Grammar, Geography, Arithmetic and Elocution.* New York: Barnes and Burr.

Hopkins, Edwin. 1912. "Can Good Composition Teaching Be Done under Present Conditions?" *English Journal* 1 (1): 1–8. http://dx.doi.org/10.2307/800827.

Hopkins, Edwin. 1923. *The Labor and Cost of the Teaching of English in Colleges and Secondary Schools with Especial Reference to English Composition.* Chicago: National Council of Teachers of English.

Hopkins, Ernest J., and Alfred Thomas Jr. 1960. *The Arizona State University Story.* Phoenix: Southwest.

Hronek, Pamela Claire. 1985. "Women and Normal Schools: Tempe Normal, a Case Study, 1885–1925." PhD dissertation, Arizona State University, Tempe.

Hurst, Homer. 1948. *Illinois State Normal University and the Public Normal School Movement.* Nashville, TN: Cullom and Ghertner.

Indiana Central University. 1906. *First Annual Catalog of Indiana Central University, 1905–1906.* Indianapolis: American Printing Company.

Indiana Central University. 1914. "Bulletin, October 1914." University Heights: Indiana Central University.

"Inspection Report, Arizona State Teachers College, Tempe, Arizona." 1933. Ralph W. Swetman Papers, University Archives, Arizona State University, Tempe.

Jarratt, Susan C. 1991. *Rereading the Sophists.* Carbondale: Southern Illinois University Press.

Jarratt, Susan C. 2009. "Classics and Counterpublics in Nineteenth-Century Historically Black Colleges." *College English* 72 (2): 134–59.

Jaschik, Scott. 2005. "Demanding Credit." *Inside Higher Ed.* Accessed December 16, 2014. https://www.insidehighered.com/news/2005/10/19/transfer.

Jaschik, Scott. 2010. "Disappearing Languages at Albany." *Inside Higher Ed.* Accessed August 4, 2015. https://www.insidehighered.com/news/2010/10/04/Albany.

Judd, Charles H. 1920. "The Carnegie Survey of Normal Schools." *Elementary School Journal* 21 (1): 47–51. http://dx.doi.org/10.1086/454875.

Keeler, Sharon. 2014. "Record 82,000 Students Choose ASU." *ASU News,* Arizona State University. Accessed July 29, 2015. https://asunews.asu.edu/20140821-asu-fall-enrollment.

Keenan, Claudia J. 2009. "Intercollegiate Debate: Reflecting American Culture, 1900–1930." *Argumentation and Advocacy* 46: 79–97.

Keith, John A.H. 1926. "Plans for Studying, Modifying, and Enforcing These Standards." In *Year Book 1926,* 107–12. Oneonta, NY: American Association of Teachers' Colleges.

Kelderman, Eric. 2013. "Department of Education Warns Accreditor That Sanctioned City College of San Francisco." *Chronicle of Higher Education.* Accessed December 16, 2014. http://chronicle.com/article/Department-of-Education-Warns/141109/.

Kellner, Hans. 1989. *Language and Historical Representation: Getting the Story Crooked.* Madison: University of Wisconsin Press.

Kellner, Hans. 1994. "After the Fall: Reflections on Histories of Rhetoric." In *Writing Histories of Rhetoric,* ed. Victor J. Vitanza, 20–37. Carbondale: Southern Illinois University Press.

Kerr, Clark. 1957. "An Academic Plan for the Berkeley Campus, University of California, Report Draft, Jun. 15, 1957." Clark Kerr Personal and Professional Papers, University Archives, University of California, Berkeley.

Kerr, Clark. 1961. "A Proposed Academic Plan for the University of California, Report Draft, Jul. 21, 1961." Clark Kerr Personal and Professional Papers, University Archives, University of California, Berkeley.

Kerr, Clark. 1964. "Academic Plan, 1964–1975, of the University of California, November 1964." Clark Kerr Personal and Professional Papers, University Archives, University of California, Berkeley.

Kerr, Clark. 1966. "The Academic Plan of the University of California, 1966–1976, November 1966." Clark Kerr Personal and Professional Papers, University Archives, University of California, Berkeley.

Kerr, Clark. 2001a. *The Gold and the Blue: A Personal Memoir of the University of California, 1949–1967,* vol. 1. Berkeley: University of California Press.

Kerr, Clark. 2001b. *The Uses of the University,* 5th ed. Cambridge, MA: Harvard University Press.

Kirsch, Gesa, and Patricia A. Sullivan. 1992. *Methods and Methodology in Composition Research.* Carbondale: Southern Illinois University Press.

Kirtland, John C., Jr. 1905. "The College Requirements and the Secondary-School Work." *School Review* 13 (10): 818–27. http://dx.doi.org/10.1086/434772.

Kitzhaber, Albert R. 1990. *Rhetoric in American Colleges.* Dallas: Southern Methodist University Press.

L'Eplattenier, Barbara, and Lisa Mastrangelo, eds. 2004. *Historical Studies of Writing Program Administration: Individuals, Communities, and the Formation of a Discipline*. West Lafayette, IN: Parlor.

Lamos, Steve. 2009. "Literacy Crisis and Color-Blindness: The Problematic Racial Dynamics of Mid-1970s Language and Literacy Instruction for 'High-Risk' Minority Students." *College Composition and Communication* 61 (2): W125–48.

Lamos, Steven J. 2011. *Interests and Opportunities: Race, Racism, and University Writing Instruction in the Post–Civil Rights Era*. Pittsburgh: University of Pittsburgh Press.

Lederman, Doug. 2007. "Explaining the Accreditation Debate." *Inside Higher Ed.* Accessed December 16, 2014. https://www.insidehighered.com/news/2007/03/29/accredit.

Lepore, Jill. 2001. "Historians Who Love Too Much: Reflections on Microhistory and Biography." *Journal of American History* 88 (1): 129–44. http://dx.doi.org/10.2307/2674921.

Lerner, Neal. 1996. "The Institutionalization of Required English." *Composition Studies* 24 (1–2): 44–60.

Lester, Neal A., and Greg Glau. 2008. "Crow's Class-Size Order Yields Better Writing Students." *AZ Republic Online.* Accessed December 16, 2014. http://archive.azcentral.com/specials/special48/articles/0118asumyturn-lester.html.

Levi, Giovanni. 2001. "On Microhistory." In *New Perspectives on Historical Writing*, ed. Peter Burke, 97–119. University Park: Pennsylvania State University Press.

Levinthal, Dave. 2014. "Koch Foundation Proposal to College: Teach Our Curriculum, Get Millions." In *Consider the Source*. Washington, DC: Center for Public Integrity. Accessed August 4, 2015. http://www.publicintegrity.org/2014/09/12/15495/koch-foundation-proposal-college-teach-our-curriculum-get-millions.

Lindblom, Kenneth, William Banks, and Risë Quay. 2007. "Mid-Nineteenth-Century Writing Instruction at Illinois State Normal University: Credentials, Correctness, and the Rise of a Teaching Class." In *Local Histories: Reading the Archives of Composition*, ed. Patricia Donahue and Gretchen Flesher Moon, 94–114. Pittsburgh: University of Pittsburgh Press.

Lloyd-Jones, Richard. 1992. "Who We Were, Who We Should Become." *College Composition and Communication* 43 (4): 486–96. http://dx.doi.org/10.2307/358641.

Lucas, Christopher J. 1999. *Teacher Education in America: Reform Agendas for the Twenty-First Century*. New York: Palgrave.

Lucas, Christopher J. 2006. *American Higher Education, A History*, 2nd ed. New York: Palgrave.

Ludeman, Walter W. 1931. "Certain Influences in Teachers College Standardization." *Peabody Journal of Education* 8 (6): 362–70. http://dx.doi.org/10.1080/01619563109535032.

Lyte, Eliphalet Oram. 1904. "The State Normal Schools of the United States." In *Report of the Commissioner of Education, 1903*, vol. 1, ed. US Commissioner of Education, 1103–36. Washington, DC: Government Printing Office.

Magnússon, Sigurður Gylfi, and István M. Szijártó. 2013. *What Is Microhistory? Theory and Practice*. New York: Routledge.

Manulat, Paulo. 1938. "What America Means to Me, January 1938." Irma Wilson Papers, University Archives, Arizona State University, Tempe.

Masters, Thomas. 2004. *Practicing Writing: Postwar Discourse of Freshman English*. Pittsburgh: University of Pittsburgh Press.

Maxwell, G. E. 1923. "Standards for Teachers Colleges." In *Proceedings of the Centennial Conference on Teacher Training, Terre Haute, 1923*, ed. L. J. Rettger, 100–113. Spec. issue of *Indiana State Normal School Bulletin* 17.

Mayor, John R. 1965. *Accreditation in Teacher Education: Its Influence on Higher Education*. Washington, DC: National Commission on Accrediting.

McClintock, James H. 1900. "Biennial Report of the Normal Schools of Arizona, 1900." University Archives, Arizona State University, Tempe.

McComiskey, Bruce, ed. 2016. *Microhistories of Composition*. Logan: Utah State University Press.

McConn, Max. 1935. "Academic Standards vs. Individual Differences: The Dilemma of Democratic Education." *American School Board Journal* 91: 44, 46, 73.

McConnell, Joseph. 1937. Letter to William Eilers, Senior, June 25. Joseph McConnell Papers, University Archives, University of North Texas, Denton.

McCrea, Samuel Pressly. 1908. "Establishment of the Arizona School System." In *The Biennial Report of the Superintendent of Public Instruction of the Territory of Arizona*, ed. Robert L. Long, 72–141. Phoenix: W. H. McNeil.

McLeod, Susan H. 2007. *Writing Program Administration*. West Lafayette, IN: Parlor.

McQuade, Donald. 1992. "Composition and Literary Studies." In *Redrawing the Boundaries: The Transformation of English and American Literary Studies*, ed. Stephen Greenblatt and Giles Gunn, 482–519. New York: Modern Language Association.

Meadows, Leon Renfroe. 1928. *A Study in the Teaching of English Composition in Teachers Colleges in the United States with a Suggested Course of Procedure*. New York: Teachers' College, Columbia University.

Merlino, Maxine Ollie. 1962. "A History of the California State Normal Schools: Their Origin, Growth, and Transformation into Teachers Colleges." PhD dissertation, University of Southern California, Los Angeles.

Mignolo, Walter D. 2012. *Local Histories/Global Designs: Coloniality, Subaltern Knowledges, and Border Thinking*. Princeton, NJ: Princeton University Press. http://dx.doi.org/10.1515 /9781400845064.

Miller, Richard E. 1998. *As if Learning Mattered: Reforming Higher Education*. Ithaca, NY: Cornell University Press.

Miller, Richard E. 2001. "From Intellectual Wasteland to Resource-Rich Colony: Capitalizing on the Role of Writing Instruction in Higher Education." *WPA: Writing Program Administration* 24 (3): 25–40.

Miller, Susan. 1991. *Textual Carnivals: The Politics of Composition*. Carbondale: Southern Illinois University Press.

Miller, Susan. 1994. "Composition as a Cultural Artifact: Rethinking History as Theory." In *Writing Theory and Critical Theory*, ed. John Clifford and John Schilb, 19–32. New York: Modern Language Association.

Miller, Thomas P. 1997. *The Formation of College English: Rhetoric and Belles Lettres in the British Cultural Provinces*. Pittsburgh: University of Pittsburgh Press.

Miller, Thomas P. 2011. *The Evolution of College English: Literacy Studies from the Puritans to the Postmoderns*. Pittsburgh: University of Pittsburgh Press.

Milstone, David. 2010. "Outsourcing Services in Higher Education: Consider the Campus Climate." *Bulletin* 78: 30–39.

Minnich, H. C. 1923. "The History of Normal Schools in America." In *Proceedings of the Centennial Conference on Teacher Training, Terre Haute, 1923*, ed. L. J. Rettger, 28–40. Spec. issue of *Indiana State Normal School Bulletin* 17.

Mitchell, Margaret. 1985. "The Founding of the University of Arizona, 1885–1894." *Arizona and the West* 27: 5–36.

Monroe, Jonathan. 2007. *Local Knowledges, Local Practices*. Pittsburgh: University of Pittsburgh Press.

Moon, Gretchen Flesher. 2007. "Locating Composition History." In *Local Histories: Reading the Archives of Composition*, ed. Patricia Donahue and Gretchen Flesher Moon, 1–13. Pittsburgh: University of Pittsburgh Press.

Morgan, W. P. 1923. "The Growth of the State Normal School." In *Proceedings of the Centennial Conference on Teacher Training, Terre Haute, 1923*, ed. L. J. Rettger, 54–74. Spec. issue of *Indiana State Normal School Bulletin* 17.

Mulderig, Gerald P. 1987. "Composition Teaching in America, 1930–1950: Reconsidering Our Recent Past." *Rhetoric Society Quarterly* 17 (3): 305–19. http://dx.doi.org/10.1080 /02773948709390789.

Myers, Louis M. 1940. "A Step toward Correlation in English Teaching." *Arizona Teacher* 28: 267, 278–79.

Myers, Louis M. 1948. *An American English Grammar*. Tempe: Arizona State College.

Myers, Louis M. 1954. "Linguistics and the Teaching of Rhetoric." *College Composition and Communication* 5 (4): 166–70. http://dx.doi.org/10.2307/355432.

Myers, Louis M. 1959. *Guide to American English*, 2nd ed. Englewood Cliffs, NJ: Prentice-Hall.

Myers, Louis M. 1961. "The English Language Program at Arizona State University." *College Composition and Communication* 12 (2): 66–69.

National Education Association. 1899. "Report of the Committee on Normal Schools." In *Addresses and Proceedings, National Education Association of the United States*, vol. 38, 836–54. Chicago: University of Chicago Press.

Nebeker, Helen E. 1985. "Out of the Dark." In *The Road Retaken: Women Reenter the Academy*, ed. Irene Thompson and Audrey Roberts, 38–45. New York: Modern Language Association.

"New ASU Story." 2001. Department of Archives and Manuscripts, Arizona State University Libraries, Tempe. Accessed January 15, 2015. http://www.asu.edu/lib/archives/asu story/.

Nicotra, Jodie. 2009. "'Folksonomy' and the Restructuring of Writing Space." *College Composition and Communication* 61 (1): W259–76.

Nikiforidou, Kiki. 1991. "The Meanings of the Genitive: A Case Study in Semantic Structure and Semantic Change." *Cognitive Linguistics* 2 (2): 149–205. http://dx.doi.org/10.1515/cogl.1991.2.2.149.

"North Central Approves State College at Tempe." 1932–33. Ralph W. Swetman Papers, University Archives, Arizona State University, Tempe.

North Central Association of Colleges and Schools. 1930–31. "Regulations of the Commission on Institutions of Higher Education, North Central Association of Colleges and Schools." Ralph W. Swetman Papers, University Archives, Arizona State University, Tempe.

North Central Association of Colleges and Schools. 1931–32. "General Report—Colleges and Universities, North Central Association of Colleges and Schools, 1930–1931." Ralph W. Swetman Papers, University Archives, Arizona State University, Tempe.

North Central Association of Colleges and Schools. 1941. *Revised Manual of Accrediting. University Archives.* Tempe: Arizona State University.

North, Stephen M. 1987. *The Making of Knowledge in Composition: Portrait of an Emerging Field.* Portsmouth, NH: Boynton/Cook.

"The Octalog: The Politics of Historiography." 1988. *Rhetoric Review* 7: 5–49.

Ogden, John. 1879. *The Art of Teaching.* New York: American.

Ogren, Christine A. 2003. "Rethinking the 'Nontraditional' Student from a Historical Perspective: State Normal Schools in the Late Nineteenth and Early Twentieth Centuries." *Journal of Higher Education* 74 (6): 640–64. http://dx.doi.org/10.1353/jhe.2003.0046.

Ogren, Christine A. 2005. *The American State Normal School: "An Instrument of Great Good."* New York: Palgrave. http://dx.doi.org/10.1057/9781403979100.

Orlans, Harold. 1962. *The Effects of Federal Programs on Higher Education: A Study of 36 Universities and Colleges.* Washington, DC: Brookings Institution.

Parker, William Riley. 1967. "Where Do English Departments Come From?" *College English* 28 (5): 339–51. http://dx.doi.org/10.2307/374593.

Parsons, Michael D. 2003. "Accreditation in the United States: Higher Education." In *Encyclopedia of Education*, 2nd ed., ed. James W. Guthrie, 31–35. New York: Thompson Gale.

Phelps, Louise Wetherbee, and John M. Ackerman. 2010. "Making the Case for Disciplinarity in Rhetoric, Composition, and Writing Studies: The Visibility Project." *College Composition and Communication* 62: 180–215.

Popken, Randall. 2004. "The WPA as Publishing Scholar: Edwin Hopkins and the Labor and Cost of the Teaching of English." In *Historical Studies of Writing Program Administration: Individuals, Communities, and the Formation of a Discipline*, ed. Barbara L'Eplattenier and Lisa Mastrangelo, 5–22. West Lafayette, IN: Parlor.

Porter, James E., Patricia Sullivan, Stuart Blythe, Jeffrey T. Grabill, and Libby Miles. 2000. "Institutional Critique: A Rhetorical Methodology for Change." *College Composition and Communication* 51 (4): 610–42. http://dx.doi.org/10.2307/358914.

President of Harvard University. 1885. *Annual Report of the President of Harvard University to the Overseers on the State of the University for the Academic Year 1883–1884*. Cambridge, MA: Harvard University Press.

President of Harvard University. 1887. *Annual Report of the President of Harvard University to the Overseers on the State of the University for the Academic Year 1885–1886*. Cambridge, MA: Harvard University Press.

Ramage, John D., John C. Bean, and June Johnson. 2010. *Writing Arguments: A Rhetoric with Readings*, 8th ed. New York: Longman.

Ravitch, Diane. 1978. "On the History of Minority Group Education in the United States." In *History, Education, and Public Policy*, ed. Donald R. Warren, 150–68. Berkeley, CA: McCutchan.

Reichel, H. R. 1969 [1901]. "Report of Professor H. R. Reichel." In *Reports of the Mosely Educational Commission to the United States*, ed. Lawrence A. Cremin, 274–309. New York: Arno.

Research Division. 1943. "Education and Manpower." National Education Association. Joseph McConnell Papers, University Archives, University of North Texas, Denton.

Rettger, L. J., ed. 1923. *Proceedings of the Centennial Conference on Teacher Training, Terre Haute, 1923*. Spec. issue of *Indiana State Normal School Bulletin* 17.

Richardson, Harold D. 1958. Letter to Grady Gammage, April 1. Grady Gammage Papers, University Archives, Arizona State University, Tempe.

Richardson, Harold D. 1964. *Arizona State University: Dynamic Educational Leadership in the Great Southwest*. New York: Princeton University Press.

Rice, Jeff. 2012. *Digital Detroit: Rhetoric and Space in the Age of the Network*. Carbondale: Southern Illinois University Press.

Ritter, Kelly. 2009. *Before Shaughnessy: Basic Writing at Yale and Harvard, 1920–1960*. Carbondale: Southern Illinois University Press.

Ritter, Kelly. 2012. *To Know Her Own History: Writing at the Woman's College, 1943–1963*. Pittsburgh: University of Pittsburgh Press.

Rivers, Nathaniel A., and Ryan P. Weber. 2011. "Ecological, Pedagogical, Public Rhetoric." *College Composition and Communication* 63 (2): 187–218.

Roames, Richard L. 1987. "Accreditation in Teacher Education: A History of the Development of Standards by the National Council for Accreditation of Teacher Education." PhD dissertation, University of Akron, Akron, OH.

Robinson, Will H. 1919. *The Story of Arizona*. Phoenix, AZ: Berryhill.

Rodrigue, Tanya K. 2013. "A Portrait of a Scholar . . . in Progress: An Interview with Louise Wetherbee Phelps." *Composition Forum* 27. Accessed September 9, 2015. http://compositionforum.com/issue/27/louise-wetherbee-phelps-interview.php.

Roen, Duane H., Gregory R. Glau, and Barry M. Maid. 2008. *The McGraw-Hill Guide: Writing for College, Writing for Life*. New York: McGraw-Hill.

Rogers, James L. 2002. *The Story of North Texas: From Texas Normal College, 1890, to the University of North Texas System, 2001*. Denton: University of North Texas Press.

Rose, Mike. 1985. "The Language of Exclusion: Writing Instruction at the University." *College English* 47 (4): 341–59. http://dx.doi.org/10.2307/376957.

Rose, Shirley K., and Thomas Skeen. 2010. "Self-Study: ASU Writing Programs." Unpublished report. Tempe: Arizona State University English Department.

Rothermel, Beth Ann. 2003. "A Sphere of Noble Action: Gender, Rhetoric, and Influence at a Nineteenth-Century Massachusetts State Normal School." *Rhetoric Society Quarterly* 33 (1): 35–64. http://dx.doi.org/10.1080/02773940309391245.

Rothermel, Beth Ann. 2007. "'Our Life's Work': Rhetorical Preparation and Teacher Training at a Massachusetts State Normal School, 1839–1929." In *Local Histories: Reading the Archives of Composition*, ed. Patricia Donahue and Gretchen Flesher Moon, 134–58. Pittsburgh: University of Pittsburgh Press.

Royster, Jacqueline Jones. 2000. *Traces of a Stream: Literacy and Social Change among African American Women*. Pittsburgh: University of Pittsburgh Press.

Russell, David R. 2002. *Writing in the Academic Disciplines, 1870–1990: A Curricular History*, 2nd ed. Carbondale: Southern Illinois University Press.

Sabine, Gordon A. 1992. *G. Homer: A Biography of the President of Arizona State University, 1960–69*. Tempe: Arizona State University Libraries.

Salerno, Nicholas A. 2005. "A Very Personal History of the English Department." Public lecture to the Arizona State University Department of English, Tempe, February 16.

Salvatori, Mariolina Rizzi, ed. 1996. *Pedagogy: Disturbing History, 1819–1929*. Pittsburgh: University of Pittsburgh Press.

"Schedule of Classes, 1890–1891." 1890. University of North Texas. University Archives, University of North Texas, Denton.

"Schedule of Classes, 1894–1895." 1894. University of North Texas. University Archives, University of North Texas, Denton.

"Schedule of Classes, 1901–1902." 1901. University of North Texas. University Archives, University of North Texas, Denton.

"Schedule of Classes, December 1903." 1903. University of North Texas. University Archives, University of North Texas, Denton.

"Schedule of Classes, July 1912." 1912. University of North Texas. University Archives, University of North Texas, Denton.

"Schedule of Classes, July 1913." 1913. University of North Texas. University Archives, University of North Texas, Denton.

"Schedule of Classes, April 1914." 1914. University of North Texas. University Archives, University of North Texas, Denton.

"Schedule of Classes, January 1917." 1917. University of North Texas. University Archives, University of North Texas, Denton.

"Schedule of Classes, July 1920." 1920. University of North Texas. University Archives, University of North Texas, Denton.

"Schedule of Classes, July 1922." 1922. University of North Texas. University Archives, University of North Texas, Denton.

"Schedule of Classes, June 1924." 1924. University of North Texas. University Archives, University of North Texas, Denton.

"Schedule of Classes, June 1932." 1932. University of North Texas. University Archives, University of North Texas, Denton.

"Schedule of Classes, June 1933." 1933. University of North Texas. University Archives, University of North Texas, Denton.

"Schedule of Classes, June 1934." 1934. University of North Texas. University Archives, University of North Texas, Denton.

"Schedule of Classes, July 1939." 1939. University of North Texas. University Archives, University of North Texas, Denton.

"Schedule of Classes, July 1942." 1942. University of North Texas. University Archives, University of North Texas, Denton.

"Schedule of Classes, March 1944." 1944. University of North Texas. University Archives, University of North Texas, Denton.

"Schedule of Classes, July 1946–1947." 1946. University of North Texas. University Archives, University of North Texas, Denton.

Schultz, Lucille M. 1999. *The Young Composers: Composition's Beginnings in Nineteenth-Century Schools.* Carbondale: Southern Illinois University Press.

Schwalm, David E. 1989. "Teaching Basic Writing: The Community College on the University Campus." *WPA: Writing Program Administration* 13 (1–2): 15–24.

Scott, Fred Newton. 1901. "College-Entrance Requirements in English." *School Review* 9 (6): 365–78. http://dx.doi.org/10.1086/434259.

Seaborg, Glenn T., and Ray Colvig. 1994. *Chancellor at Berkeley.* Berkeley: University of California Institute.

Selden, William K. 1960. *Accreditation: A Struggle over Standards in Higher Education.* New York: Harper.

Selden, William K. 1962. "The Relative Unimportance of Regional Accreditation." *Journal of Teacher Education* 13 (3): 319–25. http://dx.doi.org/10.1177/002248716201300315.

Shaughnessy, Mina P. 1977. *Errors and Expectations: A Guide for the Teacher of Basic Writing.* New York: Oxford University Press.

Shepley, Nathan E. 2010. "Composition at the 'Harvard on the Hocking': Rhetoricizing Place and History." PhD dissertation, Ohio University, Athens.

Shumway, David R., and Craig Dionne, eds. 2002. *Disciplining English: Alternative Histories, Critical Perspectives.* Albany: State University of New York Press.

Shumway, David R., and Ellen Messer-Davidow. 1991. "Disciplinarity: An Introduction." *Poetics Today* 12 (2): 201–25. http://dx.doi.org/10.2307/1772850.

Skinnell, Ryan. 2010. ""A Problem of Publics and the Curious Case at Texas." *JAC: A Journal of Rhetoric, Culture, and Politics* 30 (1–2): 143–73.

Skinnell, Ryan. 2013. "Institutionalizing Normal: Rethinking Composition's Precedence in Normal Schools." *Composition Studies* 41 (1): 10–26.

Skinnell, Ryan. 2014. "Harvard, Again: Considering Articulation and Accreditation in Rhetoric and Composition's History." *Rhetoric Review* 33 (2): 95–112. http://dx.doi.org/10.1080/07350198.2014.884406.

Slevin, James. 1991. "Depoliticizing and Politicizing English Studies." In *The Politics of Writing Instruction: Postsecondary,* ed. Richard H. Bullock and John Trimbur, 1–21. Portsmouth, NH: Boynton/Cook.

Snyder, Thomas D., ed. 1993. *120 Years of American Education: A Statistical Portrait.* Washington, DC: National Center for Education Statistics.

Snow, Francis Huntington. 1890. "Inaugural Address, Responding to the Board of Regents." In *The University of Kansas: Addresses Concerning the Chancellorship, the University, Higher Education,* 21–48. Topeka: Kansas Publishing House.

Soliday, Mary. 2002. *The Politics of Remediation: Institutional and Student Needs in Higher Education.* Pittsburgh: University of Pittsburgh Press.

Squire, James R., Harold B. Allen, George H. Henry, J. N. Hook, Albert H. Marckwardt, Richard A. Meade, Joseph Mersand, Eugene E. Slaughter, George Winchester Stone Jr., and Ruth G. Strickland. 1961. *The National Interest and the Teaching of English.* Champaign, IL: National Council of Teachers of English.

Stadtman, Verne A. 1970. *The University of California, 1868–1968.* New York: McGraw-Hill.

Stanley, Jane. 2010. *The Rhetoric of Remediation: Negotiating Entitlement and Access to Higher Education.* Pittsburgh: University of Pittsburgh Press.

"Statement of President Marvin Regarding Accrediting Teachers' College Degrees at University of Arizona." 1925. Arthur John Matthews Papers, University Archives, Arizona State University, Tempe.

Stewart, Donald C. 1979. "Rediscovering Fred Newton Scott." *College English* 40 (5): 539–47. http://dx.doi.org/10.2307/376326.

Stewart, Donald C. 1992. "Harvard's Influence on English Studies: Perceptions from Three Universities in the Early Twentieth Century." *College Composition and Communication* 43 (4): 455–71. http://dx.doi.org/10.2307/358637.

Stinnett, Tim Moore. 1951. "The Accreditation of Institutions for Teacher Preparation." PhD dissertation, University of Texas, Austin.

Strain, Margaret M. 2005. "In Defense of a Nation: The National Defense Education Act, Project English, and the Origins of Empirical Research in Composition Studies." *JAC: Rhetoric, Writing, Culture, Politics* 25 (3): 513–42.

Strickland, Donna. 2011. *The Managerial Unconscious in the History of Composition Studies.* Carbondale: Southern Illinois University Press.

Sub-Committee on English. 1927. "Report of the Sub-Committee on English." *North Central Association Quarterly* 1: 445–66.

Swetman, Ralph W. 1933. "The Arizona State Teachers College at Tempe, Report to the State Superintendent of Public Instruction, the Members of the Legislature and to the Governor of Arizona, January 1, 1933." UM Small Manuscripts, University Archives, Arizona State University, Tempe.

Tansil, Rebecca C. 1929. "Steps in the History of Standardization of Normal Schools and Teachers Colleges." *Peabody Journal of Education* 7 (3): 164–67. http://dx.doi.org/10.1080/01619562909534919.

Tate, Gary, Amy Rupiper Taggart, Kurt Schick, and H. Brooke Hessler. 2014. *A Guide to Composition Pedagogies*, 2nd ed. New York: Oxford University Press.

Tetlow, John. 1886. Letter to Charles W. Eliot, Apr. 12. Records of President Charles W. Eliot, Harvard University Archives, Cambridge, MA.

Thaiss, Chris, Gerd Bräuer, Paula Carlino, Lisa Ganobcsik-Williams, and Aparna Sinha, eds. 2012. *Writing Programs Worldwide: Profiles of Academic Writing in Many Places.* Anderson, SC: Parlor.

Thelin, John R. 2004. *A History of American Higher Education.* Baltimore: Johns Hopkins University Press.

Thomas, Alfred, Jr. 1960a. *Arizona State University: A Documentary History of the First Seventy-Five Years, 1885–1960:* vol. 1: *The Formative Years, 1885–1900.* Arizona Collection, University Archives, Arizona State University, Tempe.

Thomas, Alfred, Jr. 1960b. *Arizona State University: A Documentary History of the First Seventy-Five Years, 1885–1960:* vol. 2: *From Normal School to Teachers College, 1900–1933.* Arizona Collection, University Archives, Arizona State University, Tempe.

Thomas, Alfred, Jr. 1960c. *Arizona State University: A Documentary History of the First Seventy-Five Years, 1885–1960:* vol. 3, no. 1: *From Teachers College to University, 1933–1960.* Arizona Collection, University Archives, Arizona State University, Tempe.

Thomas, Alfred, Jr. 1960d. *Arizona State University: A Documentary History of the First Seventy-Five Years, 1885–1960:* vol. 3, no. 2: *From Teachers College to University, 1933–1960.* Arizona Collection, University Archives, Arizona State University, Tempe.

Thomas, Alfred, Jr. 1960e. *Arizona State University: A Documentary History of the First Seventy-Five Years, 1885–1960:* vol. 4: *Growth and Development Statistics and General Information, 1885–1960.* Arizona Collection, University Archives, Arizona State University, Tempe.

Tirabassi, Katherine E. 2007. "Revisiting the 'Current-Traditional Era': Innovations in Writing Instruction at the University of New Hampshire, 1940–1949." PhD dissertation, University of New Hampshire, Durham.

Trachsel, Mary. 1992. *Institutionalizing Literacy: The Historical Role of College Entrance Examinations in English.* Carbondale: Southern Illinois University Press.

Turner, Katherine C. 1979. "History of the English Department: Arizona State University." Unpublished manuscript, Department of English, Arizona State University, Tempe.

Tyack, David. 1978. "Ways of Seeing: An Essay on the History of Compulsory Schooling." In *History, Education, and Public Policy*, ed. Donald R. Warren, 56–89. Berkeley, CA: McCutchan.

Uniform Courses of Study Act. 1909. Legislative Assembly of the Territory of Arizona. University Small Manuscripts, University Archives, Arizona State University, Tempe.

US Commissioner of Education. 1879. *Report of the Commissioner of Education, 1876–1877,* vol. 1. Washington, DC: Office of Education.

US Commissioner of Education. 1903. *Report of the Commissioner of Education, 1902–1903,* vol. 1. Washington, DC: Office of Education.

US Commissioner of Education. 1904. *Report of the Commissioner of Education, 1903,* vol. 1. Department of the Interior. Washington, DC: Department of the Interior.

Vandenberg, Peter. 1996. "Discipline." In *Keywords in Composition Studies,* ed. Paul Heilker and Peter Vandenberg, 62–66. Portsmouth, NH: Boynton/Cook.

VanOverbeke, Marc A. 2008a. "Linking Secondary and Higher Education, through the University of Michigan's Accreditation Program, 1870–1890." In *Curriculum, Accreditation, and Coming of Age of Higher Education,* ed. Roger L. Geiger, 33–63. New Brunswick, NJ: Transaction.

VanOverbeke, Marc A. 2008b. *The Standardization of American Schooling: Linking Secondary and Higher Education, 1870–1910.* New York: Palgrave. http://dx.doi.org/10.1057/9780230612594.

Varnum, Robin. 1986. "From Crisis to Crisis: The Evolution toward Higher Standards of Literacy in the United States." *Rhetoric Society Quarterly* 16 (3): 145–65. http://dx.doi.org/10.1080/02773948609390746.

Varnum, Robin. 1992. "The History of Composition: Reclaiming Our Lost Generations." *JAC: A Journal of Rhetoric, Culture, and Politics* 12 (1): 39–55.

Varnum, Robin. 1996. *Fencing with Words: A History of Writing Instruction at Amherst College during the Era of Theodore Baird, 1938–1966.* Urbana, IL: National Council of Teachers of English.

Veysey, Laurence R. 1970. *The Emergence of the American University.* Chicago: University of Chicago Press.

Vitanza, Victor J. 1987. "Critical Sub/Versions of the History of Philosophical Rhetoric." *Rhetoric Review* 6 (1): 41–66. http://dx.doi.org/10.1080/07350198709359152.

Vitanza, Victor J. 1991. "Three Countertheses: or, a Critical In(ter)vention into Composition Theories and Pedagogies." In *Contending with Words: Composition and Rhetoric in a Postmodern Age,* ed. Patricia Harkin and John Schilb, 139–72. New York: Modern Language Association.

Vitanza, Victor J. 1997. *Negation, Subjectivity, and the History of Rhetoric.* Albany: SUNY Press.

Westbrook, B. Evelyn. 2002. "Debating Both Sides: What Nineteenth-Century College Literary Societies Can Teach Us about Critical Pedagogies." *Rhetoric Review* 21 (4): 339–56. http://dx.doi.org/10.1207/S15327981RR2104_2.

Whitman, Neal, and Elaine Weiss. 1982. *Faculty Evaluation: The Use of Explicit Criteria for Promotion, Retention, and Tenure.* Washington, DC: American Association of Higher Education.

Wilson, Kyle Grant. 2009. "Indigenous Rhetoric: A History." *Writing Notes: Newsletter of Writing Programs at Arizona State University* 10: 2, 7.

Winterowd, W. Ross. 1998. *The English Department: A Personal and Institutional History.* Carbondale: Southern Illinois University Press.

Wozniak, John Michael. 1978. *English Composition in Eastern Colleges, 1850–1940.* Washington, DC: University Press of America.

Yale University. 1828. *Reports on the Courses of Instruction in Yale College by a Committee of the Corporation and the Academical Faculty.* New Haven, CT: Hezekiah Howe.

Zook, George F. 1939. "Who Should Control Our Higher Institutions?" *Educational Record* 20: 28–43.

Zook, George F., and Melvin E. Haggerty. 1936. *The Evaluation of Higher Institutions: Principles of Accrediting Higher Institutions.* Chicago: University of Chicago Press.

ABOUT THE AUTHOR

Ryan Skinnell is assistant professor of rhetoric and composition and assistant writing program administrator in the Department of English and Comparative Literature at San José State University. He is a coeditor of *What We Wish We'd Known: Negotiating Graduate School* and his research has appeared in *Composition Studies, Enculturation, JAC, Rhetoric Review, WPA: Writing Program Administration,* and edited collections.

INDEX

(secondary) curriculum, 9, 59–64, 66–68, 70, 79, 82; as an economic investment, 57–58; and institutional mission, 49–50, 57, 60–61, 64, 66, 72; "professional" (postsecondary) curriculum, 61–63, 67–68, 70, 81, 152(n20); and split curriculum, 8–9, 59–62, 68, 70; and teacher-training methods, 8, 60–63, 66, 73, 84, 151(n3), 152(n20)
North Central Association of Colleges and Secondary Schools (NCA), 82–88, 90–91, 94, 100–101, 150(n28), 153(n1), 154(n9, n11, n15), 155(n20, n23), 157(n3)
North Texas Normal College. *See* University of North Texas
North Texas State Teachers' College. *See* University of North Texas
Northwest Commission on Colleges and Universities, 153(n1)

Office of Education. *See* US Office of Education
Ogren, Christine A., 57, 151(n3)
O'Neill, Peggy, 74–75, 153(n3)
open admissions, 25, 34

Parker, William Riley, 31
Peabody Education Fund, 152(n22)
pedagogy, 8, 10–11, 16–17, 19–24, 26, 31–32, 34–35, 37–39, 44–45, 53–56, 61–62, 70, 72, 73, 84, 112, 133, 136, 142–43, 147(n17), 149(n24), 152(n20)
Phelps, Louise Wetherbee, 141
postsecondary courses, 9, 12, 23, 25, 27, 29–30, 35, 46, 50–51, 56, 59, 61–65, 68, 79, 81–83, 85, 90–91, 93–94, 96–99, 102–6, 108, 118, 121–22, 128, 133, 152(n14), 154(n7), 156(n29, n31), 157(n2)
preparatory course (incl. "preparatory department"), 95–98, 156(n28)
Project English (US), 157(n2)
Public Works Administration, 116–17, 119, 128

Quackenbos, George, 53

rainbow sections, of first-year composition (ASU). *See* Indigenous rhetoric
Ramage, John, 145(n2, n3)
Reagan, Ronald, 135
Reconstruction Finance Corporation, 117
reduplication. *See* institutional reduplication

remedial education, 11, 18. *See also* basic subjects
remedial English, 11, 18, 44, 56, 61, 79, 87, 123–26, 139, 158(n8), 159(n4); bonehead English, 124. *See also* basic writing
Report of the Commissioner of Education, 59, 61, 155(n26)
Richardson, Harold D., 110, 124
Ritter, Kelly, 34–35, 148(n13)
Roen, Duane, 145(n2)
Rogers, James L. 65–66, 128
Rose, Mike, 15
Rose, Shirley K., 145(n2)
Russell, David R., 32, 75, 148(n12), 157(n5)

Safford, Anson P.K., 49
Salerno, Nicholas A., 126, 146(n6, n8), 158(n2)
Schwalm, David, 4, 5, 138–39, 141, 145(n2, n3), 158(n2, n3)
scope. *See* historiography
Scott, Fred Newton, 53, 78
secondary level (incl. "high school level"), x, 6, 8–9, 12, 49, 59–64, 66–71, 78–79, 81–83, 85, 90–104, 111, 121, 135, 152(n18), 156(n31), 157(n2, n3); in normal schools, 9, 59, 60, 61–64, 66, 68, 79, 82
Selden, William K., 98
Selzer, Jack, 33–34, 36, 40
service function, 4, 17, 22–23, 130, 136, 146(n5)
Sharer, Wendy, 33–34, 36, 40
Shumway, David R., 36, 37
Signature of All Things: On Method, The, 28
Snow, Francis H., 95, 97
Soliday, Mary, 11
South Mountain Community College (AZ), 139
Southern Association of Colleges and Schools (SACS), 90, 153(n1), 154(n11)
Southern Connecticut State University, 35
Spellings' Commission, 74
standardization. *See* coordination
Stanley, Jane, 11, 132, 134, 136, 158(n16)
State Normal School in Los Angeles, 63–64, 131
Stevenson, Lionel, 155(n19, n22)
StraighterLine, 35
stretch composition, 145(n3), 158(n4)
Sullivan, Patricia A., 148(n1)
Sweeney, M. Clare, 146(n6), 158(n4)
Swetman, Ralph, 116